Teaching English in Africa

Teaching English in Africa

A Guide to the Practice of
English Language Teaching for Teachers
and Trainee Teachers

Jason Anderson

**East African
Educational Publishers Ltd.**
Nairobi • Kampala • Dar es Salaam • Kigali • Lilongwe • Lusaka

Published by
East African Educational Publishers Ltd.
Brick Court, Mpaka Road/Woodvale Grove
Westlands, P.O. Box 45314
Nairobi – 00100
KENYA.

email: eaep@eastafricanpublishers.com
website: www.eastafricanpublishers.com

East African Educational Publishers Ltd.
C/o Gustro Ltd.
P.O. BOX 9997
Kampala
UGANDA.

Ujuzi Books Ltd.
P.O. Box 38260
Dar es Salaam
TANZANIA.

East African Publishers Rwanda Ltd.
Tabs Plaza, Kimironko Road,
Opposite Kigali Institute of Education
P.O. Box 5151, Kigali
RWANDA.

© Jason Anderson, 2015

First published 2015

All Rights Reserved.

ISBN 978-9966-56-005-6

Printed in Kenya by
Printwell Industries Ltd.
P. O. Box 5216-0506
Nairobi, Kenya

Contents

Acknowledgements xi
Abbreviations xii
Introduction xiii

Part A – Key Concepts 1

A1 – You, the Teacher 2
    What is the role of the teacher? 2
    Practical task: What are the qualities of a good teacher? 3
    Commentary to practical task: What are the qualities of a good
        teacher? 4
    Your continuing professional development (CPD) 6

A2 – Your Learners 9
    How do children learn languages? 9
    Practical task: The five needs of our learners 10
    Commentary to practical task: The five needs of our learners 11
    Different types of learning styles or intelligence 12
    Thinking skills and Bloom's taxonomy of learning 14
    Learner Independence 15

A3 – Child-centred Learning 18
    What is child-centred learning? 18
    How child-centred are your lessons? 19
    C H I L D 19
    Pairwork and groupwork 20
    How to make your classroom more child-centred 21
    An example of a child-centred lesson 24
    Practical task: Chantal's lesson 26
    Commentary to practical task: Chantal's lesson 26
    Changing to child-centred learning – slowly but surely 27

A4 – The Phases of a Lesson 29
    Why do lessons need structure? 29
    New language lessons 29
    Skills practice lessons with three phases 33
    Time for more practice? 34
    Practical task: Ordering the stages of a lesson 34
    Commentary to practical task: Ordering the stages of a lesson 35

A5 – Planning **37**
    Yearly planning: From the national curriculum to the lesson plan 37
    The scheme of work 38
    Weekly planning 40
    Practical task: Planning a week's lessons 41
    Commentary to practical task: Planning a week's lessons 41
    Planning lessons 43

A6 – Classroom Management and Behaviour Management **46**
    Two types of management 46
    Classroom management and the activity cycle 46
    Behaviour management 48
    Clear routines 49
    Clear rules 49
    Rewards for good behaviour 50
    Sanctions for bad behaviour 50
    Ineffective sanctions 52
    Practical task: Mgeni's class 52
    Commentary to practical task: Mgeni's class 53

A7 – Use of the Mother Tongue in English Language Learning **55**
    What do we mean by 'use of the mother tongue'? 55
    The current situation 56
    Practical task: Do the right thing 57
    Commentary to practical task: Do the right thing 59
    Guidelines for using the mother tongue 60
    The mother tongue as a learning resource 61

Part B – Literacy **65**

B1 – Introduction to Literacy **66**
    Three phases of literacy 66
    Two case studies 67
    Practical task: Obi and Beatrice 67
    Commentary to practical task: Obi and Beatrice 68

B2 – The Pre-alphabet Phase **70**
    What is the pre-alphabet phase? 70
    How old are children during this phase? 70
    What do they already know about language? 71
    The four areas of literacy awareness 72
    Your learners' names 73

The importance of the mother tongue at the pre-alphabet phase	73
How long will the pre-alphabet phase take?	74
Practical task: Exploring language	74
Commentary to practical task: Exploring language	74

B3 – The Alphabet Phase and Phonics ... 79

When does the alphabet phase start?	79
Using the mother tongue to help with English literacy	80
Phonics	81
The phonic alphabet	82
Teaching a new letter using phonics	84
Key skills in phonics	85
Digraphs, sight words and the magic 'e' rule	86
A suggested sequence for phonics teaching	88
Handwriting in the alphabet phase	90
Practical task: Our first story	91
Commentary to practical task: Our first story	92

B4 – The Sight Word Phase ... 94

What is the sight word phase and when does it begin?	94
Reading in the sight word phase	95
Writing in the sight word phase	97
Learning to spell	99
Practical task: Planning a topic-based lesson	100
Commentary to practical task: Planning a topic-based lesson	100

B5 – Children who Have Difficulty with Reading and Writing ... 102

Why do some children have difficulty with reading and writing?	102
Practical task: Six causes	102
Commentary to practical task: Six causes	103
Early assessment of reading and writing	104
How to help learners who have difficulty	104
How can learners help each other?	104
How can other family members help weak readers or writers?	105
Activities for assessing reading and writing skills	105

B6 – Parents and the Community in Literacy Learning ... 108

Why are parents important when learning to read and write?	108
How can parents help their children to read and write?	108
Advice for literate parents	109
Language assistants	109
Bringing English into the community	110

B7 – Resources and Activities for Developing Literacy 112
    Resources for developing literacy 112
    Activities for developing literacy 115

Part C – Teaching Practice 121

C1 – Teaching Grammar 122
    How should we teach grammar? 122
    An example grammar lesson 123
    Practical task: Introducing new grammar 125
    Commentary to practical task: Introducing new grammar 125
    Practising grammar 126
    Revisiting and revising grammar 128
    Ideas for grammar activities 128

C2 – Teaching Vocabulary 135
    How should we teach vocabulary? 135
    An example vocabulary lesson 136
    Practical task: Introducing new vocabulary 138
    Commentary to practical task: Introducing new vocabulary 138
    Practising new vocabulary 139
    Recycling and revising vocabulary 141
    Ideas for vocabulary activities 141

C3 – Teaching Pronunciation 147
    What accent should I teach my learners? 147
    What other aspects of pronunciation should I teach? 148
    Techniques for improving learners' pronunciation 149
    Practical task: Sound advice 150
    Commentary to practical task: Sound advice 150
    Ideas for pronunciation activities 151

C4 – Teaching Speaking 156
    Why teach speaking skills? 156
    An example speaking lesson 157
    Practical task: Help! 159
    Commentary to practical task: Help! 160
    Speaking skills and the curriculum 161
    Controlled speaking and free speaking 162
    Ideas for speaking activities 163

C5 – Teaching Listening 169

- What can we listen to? 169
- Listening practice at lower levels 171
- Preparing for listening lessons 172
- An example listening lesson 172
- The grasshopper and the frog 175
- Practical task: A listening lesson activity cycle 176
- Commentary to practical task: A listening lesson activity cycle 176
- Three key stages for listening activities 177
- Ideas for listening activities 177

C6 – Teaching Reading 182

- Why read? 182
- What can we read? 183
- We do not have anything to read! 184
- An example reading lesson 184
- An example reading text – Let's talk about teeth! 186
- Practical task: Comparing reading and listening lessons 188
- Commentary to practical task: Comparing reading and listening lessons 188
- Different reading tasks 188
- Ideas for reading activities 189

C7 – Teaching Writing 194

- Why is writing important? 194
- Two types of writing 195
- Who should our learners write for? 195
- Collaborative writing 196
- Practical task: An example writing lesson 197
- Commentary to practical task: An example writing lesson 199
- Correcting learners' writing 199
- Ideas for writing activities 201

C8 – Assessment 205

- What is assessment? 205
- Assessment for learning (formative) 206
- Assessment of learning (summative) 206
- How to assess for learning? 206
- Assessing achievement of objectives/lesson evaluation 207

What is the difference between correction and assessment? 208
Involving learners in their own assessment 208
Continuous assessment 209
Preparing learners for exams 209
Practical task: Assessment blues! 210
Commentary to practical task: Assessment blues! 211

C9 – CLIL: Content and Language Integrated Learning 212
What is CLIL? 212
Working together 213
An example CLIL lesson 214
Practical task: Analysing a CLIL lesson 216
Commentary to practical task: Analysing a CLIL lesson 216
Recommendations for teachers of content subjects 217

C10 – Games and Songs 220
Why are games and songs important in language learning? 220
Are games and songs only for small children? 221
Introducing and inventing games and songs 222
Games for vocabulary learning 222
Games for grammar practice 223
Games for skills practice 223
Songs for younger learners (lower primary school) 225
Songs for older learners (upper primary and secondary school) ... 228

C11 – Learning Resources 230
What are learning resources? 230
Why do we need learning resources? 230
Seven types of learning resources 231
Practical task: Any ideas? 237
Commentary to practical task: Any ideas? 238

C12 – 10 Essential Resources to Create 240
TALULAR 240
Three tips for resource creation 240

Bibliography 252
Useful Websites and Online Materials 255
Glossary 258
Index 267

Acknowledgements

Many thanks to all the inspirational and determined teachers and teacher trainers with whom I have worked in Africa and from whom I have learnt so much. This includes, but is not limited to, the following: In Eritrea; Tesfahannes Negash, Genet Ghebretensei, Yohannes Tekie, Abdullah Ibrahim, Lucia Angesom, Abdu Mahmud and the amazing Matiewas Ghebrechristus of Fitwi School. In Rwanda; Chantal Nyiranohimimana, Jeanette Kantarama, Jean Paul Gatete, Phoibe Nyirabugare, Angelique Muhorakeye, Solange Uwineza, Christine Usabinema, Samuel Bajeneza, Suzanne Mushimiyamana, Elie Gasuhuke and Christine Uwineza. In Kenya; Calvin Adwar, Joyce Agik, Faith Mbote, Grace Kanyiri and the inspirational Leah Asego. In Malawi; Misheck Munthali, Mathias January, Michael Lwanda, Liznet Mwadzaangati, Patrick Themu, Paul Chindamba, Patrick Kapito and last but definitely not least, the wonderful 'Professor TALULAR' – Gibson Zembeni.

I would also like to extend my thanks to AKM Kamaluddin for sharing the benefit of his extensive experience in improving the quality of education in schools worldwide. I would like to thank Louise Lambourne for her assistance with Part B of this book, and Paul Rogerson of the English Centre, Sassari for demonstrating the versatility and durability of the vocabulary box as a learning resource. I would like to thank the following organisations and all their staff for the opportunities they have provided me with to learn about teaching and learning in Africa; BNEP Rwanda, VSO Eritrea, VSO Rwanda, MINEDUC Rwanda, the Eritrean Ministry of Education, MOEST Malawi, MOE Kenya, UNICEF Kenya, UNICEF Malawi and UNICEF Rwanda.

Finally, I would like to thank the capable team at East African Educational Publishers Limited, including Jane Mathenge as Head of Department, Benson Shiholo as project manager, the artist Abdul Gugu and the designer Serah Muchai, and also my editor Dr. Lillian Kaviti for her rigorous scrutiny of the manuscript and thought-provoking comments.

While all the above have helped immeasurably to populate this book with knowledge, wisdom and learning, final responsibility for the content, all beliefs expressed and any failings herein rests solely with me as the author.

Jason Anderson
March 2015

Abbreviations

CHILD	A mnemonic to help readers remember the key features of child-centred learning
CLIL	Content and Language Integrated Learning
CPD	Continuing professional development
CV	Curriculum Vitae, also called 'résumé'
ELT	English language teaching
EMI	English as the medium of instruction
IPA	International phonetic alphabet
IQ	Intelligence quotient; a way of measuring intelligence
MOE	Ministry of Education
ODLP	Online distance learning programme
PTA	Parent teacher association
TALULAR	Teaching and learning using locally available resources
TESEP	Tertiary, Secondary and Primary; Adrian Holliday's terms (1994)
TPR	Total physical response
UNCRC	United Nations Convention on the Rights of the Child
UNICEF	United Nations International Children's Emergency Fund
USB	Universal serial bus; the most common type of connection plug for a computer

Introduction

Who is this book for?

Teaching English in Africa: A Guide to the Practice of English Language Teaching for Teachers and Trainee Teachers is a guide to the practice of English language teaching that has been written to meet the needs of teachers, trainee teachers and teacher educators working in primary or secondary schools in Africa. This includes:

- teachers working in government-funded (public) schools;
- teachers working in privately-funded schools;
- expatriate teachers from other countries working in schools in Africa, including 'native-speaker' teachers of English on short-term or volunteer placements;
- trainee teachers at university or college preparing to work in primary or secondary schools;
- teacher trainers, both pre-service and in-service.

It may also be useful to head teachers, school inspectors, materials writers and others working within the education sector in African countries.

There is, of course, a wide range of teaching contexts within every country in Africa, and often a wider difference between the countries themselves. A teacher of English working in a Francophone school in Côte d'Ivoire may face different challenges and issues compared to a teacher working in Nairobi or Accra where English is used in the wider community. Nonetheless, there are still a number of significant challenges shared by the majority of teachers working in sub-Saharan Africa. These include:

- large classes, from 40 to 100 learners or more;
- restricted access to **learning resources**, such as **textbooks**, visual aids, electrical equipment and computers;
- less pre-service training for new teachers than in other parts of the world;
- difficulties in accessing in-service training or other professional development opportunities;
- low **school readiness** of learners,[1] including difficulties with getting to school, paying for resources, focusing on learning and completing their education;
- the challenges of adopting and adapting methodology developed in other learning contexts;
- a frequently heavy workload, often including long hours, excessive marking and sometimes **double shifting**.

---

1   Britto and Limlingan, "School Readiness and Transitions."

This book relates the practice of English language teaching directly to these challenges and issues. As well as covering the underlying theory of how children learn languages and how teachers can best facilitate this learning, it also provides practical resources and ideas for activities and techniques that have proven to be successful in English classrooms in Africa, both at primary and secondary level. It is intended to be a practical guide, so references and citations are kept to a minimum and concepts are presented using examples that are likely to be familiar to most teachers working in Africa. If there is a bias in this book, it is towards the needs of teachers working in low-resource, isolated contexts in Africa, as these teachers are so often neglected by literature on teaching methodology.

How to use this book

This book can be used in the following ways:
- as a self-study or group-study guide for teachers of English interested in their own **continuing professional development** (CPD);
- as part of pre-service training for trainee teachers of English;
- as resource material for in-service teacher trainers.

Two types of tasks are included throughout the book to stimulate critical thinking and to aid learning: reflective tasks and practical tasks.

Reflective tasks, usually at the start of chapters, can be done alone or in groups through discussion. Reflective tasks help us to become reflective teachers; teachers who think about their own teaching practice and their beliefs about teaching and learning; teachers who can see clearly how their classroom practice relates to different ideas and theories about language learning and teaching.

Practical tasks require teachers to engage in specific problems and to find solutions to these problems, often asking teachers to apply the ideas in each chapter to specific case studies and their own classroom context. These also can be done individually or in groups. After each practical task, there is a **Commentary**, in which a possible solution to the task is given. Of course, practical tasks may have many different solutions, so a solution different to the one given may be appropriate or better, if it is relevant to the context in which you work.

While many of the chapters focus specifically on aspects of language teaching, there are several chapters on general methodology in *Part A* of the book that are relevant to teachers of other subjects, such as mathematics, social studies, science, etc. These chapters could be used in training programmes aimed at the professional development of mixed-subject groups of teachers or trainee teachers. Section B, on early **literacy** may also be useful to teachers who teach learners to read and write in other languages.

The English used in this book is intended to be clear and easy to understand for all readers, including those who have an intermediate level of English. Key features include:
- clear and detailed Contents, allowing readers to find what they need easily;
- all new concepts are explained clearly in simple English;

- specialist terms and technical vocabulary are made clear when they first appear in each chapter (using **bold** font) and explained in the **glossary** at the end of the book.

In addition to this, vocabulary and sentence grammar are both kept simple, avoiding long clauses and unnecessary subordination. Whenever possible, active rather than passive voice is chosen to help with comprehension.

Hope for the future

Despite the large number of guides and resource books written on the practice of English language teaching within the mainly private ELT industry, little has been written for the so-called **TESEP** language learning contexts (TESEP stands for 'Tertiary, Secondary and Primary').[2] Even less has been written for the teachers who work in the most challenging TESEP contexts, where learners are often so many and resources so few.

The drive for universal primary education of the United Nations Millennium Development Goals[3] has led to impressive increases in initial school enrolment across Africa. However, this has often come at the expense of quality of education and school completion rates. In some countries, the sight of over 100 learners sitting on the floor of a hot, dark classroom, sharing a few textbooks is still frequent. In front of them an overworked, underpaid teacher tries hard to get through an over-ambitious curriculum in a foreign language, leaving many of the learners behind in the process. It is, of course, everybody's hope that this sight should become a memory of the past, but while it remains even a rare occurrence, it is hoped that this book will provide some help to those teachers who need it most.

---

2   Holliday, "The House of TESEP and the Communicative Approach."
3   United Nations, "United Nations Millennium Declaration."

Part A – Key Concepts

What does Part A cover?

Part A of this book covers the theory behind good teaching practice. It has been written primarily for teachers of English, but could also be useful to teachers of other subjects (mathematics, science, social studies, etc.) working both in primary and secondary schools.

What can I expect to learn in Part A?

In *Part A* you can expect to learn about the teaching strategies used by effective teachers. This section focuses both on your role as a teacher and the needs of your learners. You will also learn about child-centred teaching methodology, lesson structure, lesson planning and **classroom management**. You will find detailed explanations of important ideas and techniques to help you improve your teaching. Practical examples and suggestions are also provided to relate the teaching theories explained to classroom practice.

A1 – You, the Teacher

In this chapter:

- What is the role of the teacher?
- Practical task: What are the qualities of a good teacher?
- Commentary to practical task: What are the qualities of a good teacher?
- Your continuing professional development

 **Reflective task**

"Without doctors, there are fewer healthy teachers in a community, but without teachers, there are no doctors in a community."

— **Lucia, Eritrean primary school teacher**

1. What do you think Lucia is saying about the role of teachers in a community?
2. What other problems occur in a community without teachers?

What is the role of the teacher?

In the past, education was often viewed from the teacher's point of view. We believed that good teachers were simply experts on their subject with loud voices and quiet classrooms. We thought that learners were like empty bottles that the teacher filled with knowledge. A good lesson was a lesson with lots of 'chalk and talk', where the learners kept silent, took notes and did not ask questions. We call this a **teacher-centred approach**.

Today we have a very different view of education. We see the teacher as a facilitator of learning, someone who guides the learners as they explore the world around them, building new understanding on what they already know, learning through communication and interaction. We call this a **child-centred approach** to learning and we will learn much more about it in *Chapter A3 – Child-centred Learning*.

Fig. A1.1: TEACHER-CENTRED AND CHILD-CENTRED APPROACHES

This role, as a **facilitator** of learning, has many advantages for the teacher and the learners:

- the teacher takes responsibility for helping all the learners in the class equally;
- learning is enjoyable for everyone;
- learners gain important social skills from studying together – skills they will need throughout their lives;
- all teachers, from pre-school to university are seen as having an equally important role to play in an education system;
- learners do not just gain knowledge, they learn how to learn so that they can continue learning for the rest of their lives.

Practical task: What are the qualities of a good teacher?

Read the statements 1 to 12 below and complete the boxes on the right. Write 'T' if you think it is true, 'F' if you think it is false or 'D' if you think it depends. In this context 'good' means 'effective at facilitating learning':

Statement	True or false?
1. A good teacher always writes detailed lesson plans.	
2. A good teacher always knows his/her objectives for each lesson.	
3. A good teacher's lessons are always quiet.	
4. A good teacher allows his/her learners to work together during lessons.	
5. A good teacher is an expert on his/her subject.	
6. A good teacher may adapt the planned lesson to suit the needs of the learners.	
7. A good teacher knows his/her learners very well (e.g. names, backgrounds, etc.).	
8. A good teacher gives responsibility to his/her learners.	
9. A good teacher corrects all the learners' work himself/herself.	
10. The learners of a good teacher ask lots of questions.	
11. A good teacher always follows the curriculum carefully.	
12. A good teacher's lessons are interesting and enjoyable for the learners.	

Compare and discuss your choices with colleagues, if possible.

Commentary to practical task: What are the qualities of a good teacher?

1. A good teacher always writes detailed lesson plans

Not necessarily. A good teacher always thinks about her lesson carefully. She knows what she is going to do, how and why. However, it is not necessary for experienced teachers to write detailed lesson plans for every lesson. Many good teachers write just short plans or a list of bullet points for each lesson.

2. A good teacher always knows his/her objectives for each lesson

True. A good teacher has a clear understanding of what he wants his learners to learn during the lesson and what they will be able to do at the end of the lesson (this is what we call the **learning outcomes** of the lesson). He also knows how this links to the curriculum and the needs of his learners.

3. A good teacher's lessons are always quiet

False. Noise in a classroom is a sign of communication. In a good teacher's classroom the learners often work together, discussing the activity, helping each other to learn and asking the teacher questions. Of course there are also quiet periods in a good teacher's lesson (e.g. when learners are reading silently), but good lessons are not always quiet.

4. A good teacher allows his/her learners to work together during lessons

True. Outside the school environment, children learn together naturally, for example by playing games, helping adults or sharing knowledge. This is because when learners interact, they help each other to learn (this is what we call **collaborative learning**). In class, a good teacher allows her learners to practise their speaking skills, compare their answers to exercises and work together on group projects.

5. A good teacher is an expert on his/her subject

Not always. Subject knowledge is important, but it is not enough. A good teacher must be an expert on the learning process and the needs of his learners. Many of us can think of teachers we know who have excellent subject knowledge, but do not always help their learners to understand it. We can probably also think of teachers who may not have very good subject knowledge, but are able to teach what they know well. So, while good subject knowledge is always useful to a teacher, there is, in fact, no direct relationship between subject knowledge and teaching ability.

6. A good teacher may adapt the planned lesson to suit the needs of the learners

True. We should always know our objectives at the start of the lesson. However, many interesting and unpredictable things can happen during the lesson. We might find that the learners cannot understand a new idea, or that they already know it! Or perhaps they do not have all the vocabulary they need to do an activity that we planned. In these situations, all good teachers adapt their objectives. Sometimes they add an extra activity, **revise** something the learners have forgotten, or move on to something they had planned to cover in a future lesson.

7. **A good teacher knows his/her learners very well (e.g. names, backgrounds, etc.)**

True. Many teachers working in Africa have hundreds of learners, and this can make it difficult to learn the names, backgrounds, strengths and weaknesses of each learner. However, good teachers try very hard to do this, and usually succeed. If we do not know them as individuals, it is much more difficult to provide the individual help and advice that each learner needs.

8. **A good teacher gives responsibility to his/her learners**

True. At school, learners do not just learn about their subject, they also learn about learning – how to do homework, how to study collaboratively in pairs or groups, how to give presentations in front of their classmates, etc. When they learn how to study effectively they can begin to learn independently of the teacher's direct control. Good teachers give responsibilities to their learners, for example by choosing different learners (called **class monitors**) to clean the chalkboard, hand out books or write the date on the chalkboard at the start of the lesson. See *Clear routines* in *Chapter A6 – Classroom Management and Behaviour Management* for more details.

9. **A good teacher corrects all the learners' work himself/herself**

False. Correction takes a long time, especially if you have many learners. This time is better spent learning, not assessing! You will need to mark some written texts or exam results yourself, but at other times, you can involve the learners in the correction process, using **self-correction** (they mark their own books) and **peer-correction** (they mark another learner's book). This reduces lesson time wasted on correction, and also helps the learners to take more responsibility for their own learning. See *Correction of learners' writing* in *Chapter C7 – Teaching Writing* for more details.

10. **The learners of a good teacher ask lots of questions**

True. In some classes learners are scared to ask questions. But good teachers encourage questions because questions are a sign of a creative mind and critical thinking at work. The questions also tell us what our learners do and do not understand, thereby helping us to assess what they have learnt. Of course, learners can sometimes ask questions that are very difficult to answer, but good teachers admit when they are not sure and say: *"Good question! I'll check and tell you tomorrow."*

11. **A good teacher always follows the curriculum carefully**

It depends. We should always use the curriculum as a 'guide' or a pathway, but our learners will dictate the speed at which we teach, not the curriculum. Different teachers in different parts of a country where the same curriculum is used can be teaching in very different situations, and some teachers will always need to go slower than others, even if they are teaching well and the learners are trying hard. See *The scheme of work* in *Chapter A5 – Planning* for more on this.

12. **A good teacher's lessons are interesting and enjoyable for the learners**

True. We all learn better when we are interested or enjoying ourselves, and this is especially true for children. Play is one of the most natural forms of learning, so whenever we choose interesting materials, teach with stimulating resources or use games and play activities to achieve our objectives, our learners learn more.

Your continuing professional development (CPD)

Continuing professional development (CPD) is the process through which we improve and develop as teachers. This includes attending workshops, undergoing observations and appraisals and studying for higher qualifications. It also includes learning to evaluate our own teaching, so that we become better teachers. Every school should have an active CPD programme. If your school does not, you can help your head teacher to start one. Here are five features of a CPD programme that you can organise for your school:

1. Regular teacher performance appraisals

This is when the head teacher or head of department evaluates your performance as a teacher. Appraisals are usually carried out once or twice a year both to help you to identify areas where you can improve, and to set goals for the next year. A typical teacher appraisal involves completing a teacher appraisal form, followed by an interview. It may also include a lesson observation and a discussion on the lesson. The teacher performance appraisal should not be a one-way process with your evaluator telling you how to improve. It should be a discussion, allowing you to evaluate your own performance and create your own goals for the next year.

2. Observations

An observation is when somebody watches a teacher's lesson, and is usually followed by a discussion of the lesson (this discussion is often called feedback). There are two main types of observation: peer observation and senior observation.

Peer observations involve two teachers observing each other as colleagues and then discussing both lessons afterwards. The discussion provides an opportunity to give both positive feedback and critical evaluation of their colleague's lesson. If the lessons are similar, they can even be compared. Peer observations are often most useful when the two teachers have a specific focus for the observation (e.g. **classroom management**, correction strategies, interaction between learners, etc.). They also provide an opportunity to share ideas for activities and solutions to shared problems. New teachers will often benefit from doing peer observation activities with a more experienced mentor who can provide guidance and advice at this challenging time.

Senior observations are more formal, and involve a more senior member of staff, such as a head of department, the school head teacher or an external school inspector observing your lesson and assessing how well you are teaching. You will normally be expected to produce a detailed lesson plan and give a copy to the observer before the lesson. For this reason, senior observations are usually arranged at least one day in advance. During the feedback discussion after the lesson, your observer should first give you an opportunity to evaluate your own lesson. You should be honest, even if the lesson did not go well, as this evaluation can help the observer to understand why a problem occurred and what advice to give. Your observer should comment on both your strengths and weaknesses, and provide practical suggestions for improvement whenever a criticism is made. You will often receive written feedback on your senior observation which will usually be included in your CPD folder and yearly appraisal.

3. Attending and presenting at workshops

Workshops are opportunities for teachers to learn about new methodology, new activities and useful resources for teaching. They can take place at national level, regional level or at school level. They can also be organised for **school clusters**, where three or four neighbouring schools meet together. They can vary in length from 30 minutes to several days. After teachers or head teachers have attended important national or regional workshops they should share what they have learnt or gained with their school colleagues. They could do this either by giving the same workshop to their colleagues, or by giving a short talk on the workshop, followed by a question and answer session.

If you would like to organise your own workshops, you can start by meeting for 30 minutes or an hour once a week with other teachers in your school. Each week a different teacher can present an idea, activity or even give a **demonstration lesson** while other teachers watch. You could also organise similar workshops once a term for your local school cluster. This allows for the sharing of good ideas, solutions to problems and useful resources between schools that often share similar challenges.

Fig. A1.2: TEACHERS AT A WORKSHOP

4. Studying for higher qualifications

Many teachers decide to continue their education by studying for higher qualifications as they work. This may involve evening classes, outreach classes (conducted during school vacations) or an internet-based learning programme (sometimes called ODLP, which stands for **Online Distance Learning Programme**). Most universities, polytechnics and institutes of education offer a range of useful qualifications for practicing teachers. In some countries, the Ministry of Education provides financial help for teachers on such courses. With a higher qualification (e.g. a Bachelor's or Master's degree) you may be able to gain promotion within your school (for example to head of department) or open up other career opportunities, such as becoming a head teacher or taking on a different role within the Ministry of Education.

5. Contributing to the development of your school

There are many ways that you can contribute to the development of your school. Here are some suggestions:

- Organise clubs and other social groups such as a culture club, a football or netball team or an English debating club.
- Get involved in your school's **parent-teacher association** (PTA). An active PTA improves bonds between the school and the local community. As a teacher, you could organise regular parents' evenings (when parents visit the school to discuss their children's progress with the teachers), or workshops for parents who want to help their children to learn.
- Organise evening classes for the local community such as **literacy** classes, computer lessons or English lessons for people who want to learn.
- Improve the resources in your English department. Arrange a meeting with other teachers of English in which you plan to create resources that can be shared, such as **flashcards**, reading posters or pocketboards (see *Chapter C12 – 10 Essential Resources to Create*).

Conclusion

In this chapter we have learnt the following:
- there are important differences in the role of the teacher between child-centred and teacher-centred approaches to learning;
- what good teachers are like and what they do;
- what CPD programmes are and why they are important;
- five things that we can do to enhance our professional development as teachers.

"I have come to believe that a great teacher is a great artist ... Teaching might even be the greatest of the arts since the medium is the human mind and spirit."

– John Steinbeck

A2 – Your Learners

In this chapter:

- How do children learn languages?
- Practical task: The five needs of our learners
- Commentary to practical task: The five needs of our learners
- Different types of learning style or intelligence
- Thinking skills and Bloom's taxonomy of learning
- Learner independence

 Reflective task

How much do you remember about your English lessons at school?

Answer these questions:

1. Which of your English teachers did you like most? Why?
2. Which activities helped you to learn the most? How did they help you?
3. Which activities did you dislike? Why?

How do children learn languages?

As teachers we can help our learners better if we understand more about how children learn foreign languages in the classroom. We know that the processes involved, even at a young age, are different to those of **first language acquisition** and that these differences increase as children get older.[4] Of course, there are many factors that influence individual language learning success, some of which the teacher cannot control. However, it is possible to identify five basic needs that our learners have and that we can provide for in the classroom:

1. Learners need meaningful, comprehensible input in English[5]

This means that learners need to listen to and read English that they can understand. This English should be as natural as possible. Here are some examples of meaningful, comprehensible input:

- when learners hear their English teacher greet them and ask real questions: *"Good morning students. How are you? How was the homework?"*
- when learners listen to a song in English that they can understand;
- when learners read a story in English;
- when learners read a street sign or an advertisement for a product written in English.

---

4   Haznedar and Gavruseva, "Childhood Second Language Acquisition."
5   Ellis, "Principles of Instructed Second Language Acquisition"; Barcroft and Wong, "Input, Input Processing and Focus on Form."

2. **Learners need to use English to communicate**[6]

In order to learn English, learners must have the opportunity to use it for real communication. Examples of using English communicatively include:

- when learners discuss an interesting topic in groups or pairs;
- when a learner writes a letter to a friend in English;
- when a learner asks a teacher or a classmate a real question in English: *"What does this word mean?", "Can I borrow some paper, please?"*.

3. **Learners need help to understand and remember vocabulary**[7]

Learners will learn faster if we help them to understand, write down and remember new vocabulary. We can show pictures, use mime and translate difficult words to explain new vocabulary. We can get them to use vocabulary notebooks and play vocabulary revision games to help them to remember it.

4. **Learners need to use grammar meaningfully to learn it**[8]

Although grammar exercises can be useful, they do not help children to use language meaningfully. In order for learners to learn grammar effectively, we should focus on the grammar they need to do the speaking or writing activities that we use in class. For example, if we want learners to discuss what they did at the weekend (which requires past simple tense), we can begin the lesson by reviewing the grammar of the past simple tense followed by the discussion.

5. **Learners will learn more if they enjoy their English lessons**

Scientific research has shown that motivation and enjoyment are important influences on success in language learning.[9] By playing games, singing songs and allowing social interaction during lessons, we can motivate children intrinsically in English. They are likely to learn more if they enjoy the experience. On the other hand, when children do not like a subject, they often do badly in it. Many of us can think of school subjects that we did not enjoy; these were often the subjects where we scored our lowest marks.

Practical task: The five needs of our learners

How sensitive are you to the needs of your learners? Underline one of the four words listed in the column on the right (regularly, sometimes, etc.), based on what happens in your lessons.

The five needs of our learners	This happens during my lessons ...	
1. Learners need meaningful, comprehensible input in English	regularly occasionally	sometimes never

---

6 Long, "The Role of the Linguistic Environment in Second Language Acquisition"; Ellis, "Principles of Instructed Second Language Acquisition."
7 Milton and Donzelli, "The Lexicon," 460.
8 Young, "The Negotiation of Meaning in Children's Foreign Language Acquisition"; Ellis, "Principles of Instructed Second Language Acquisition."
9 Dörnyei, *Motivation Strategies in the Language Classroom*.

The five needs of our learners	This happens during my lessons …	
2. Learners need to use English to communicate	regularly occasionally	sometimes never
3. Learners need help to understand and remember vocabulary	regularly occasionally	sometimes never
4. Learners need to use grammar meaningfully to learn it	regularly occasionally	sometimes never
5. Learners will learn more if they enjoy their English lessons	regularly occasionally	sometimes never

If you have underlined 'regularly' for each need, your learners are probably learning quickly and enjoyably. Well done! But if you have not, you can make improvements to your teaching. Make notes on how you can improve, and then discuss your notes with a colleague if possible. You will find some useful ideas to help you improve in *Chapter A3 – Child-centred Learning*.

Commentary to practical task: The five needs of our learners

The chapters in *Part C* of this book will provide many more ideas and suggestions to help you provide for your learners' needs. Here are some ideas to point you in the right direction:

1. **Provide meaningful, comprehensible input in English (*Chapters C4, C5* and *C6*)**
    - use English that your learners can understand; not too difficult, or too fast;
    - use English for everyday classroom communication (*"open your books …"*, *"raise your hand"*, etc.);
    - include regular reading activities in your lessons, using texts that are not too difficult for your learners;
    - use your voice as a listening resource, and share interesting information about your life and interests (for example, tell them about a problem you had yesterday or what you need to buy tomorrow);
    - provide opportunities for your learners to read stories for pleasure;
    - include songs in English that your learners know and like in your lessons; if you write the lyrics on the chalkboard, they can listen and read the lyrics at the same time.

2. **Provide opportunities for learners to use English to communicate (*Chapters C4* and *C7*)**
    - avoid doing too many *"repeat after me"* activities – this is not communication;
    - train your learners to do speaking activities in pairs;
    - teach your learners some common English expressions and useful phrases that they can use in class (e.g. *"Can I borrow …?"*, *"I found the homework difficult, because …"* etc.);

- practise a variety of speaking activities in class, involving **personalisation**, discussion and debate;
- provide learners with personalised writing tasks, where they write about their own world (their family, their house, their favourite animal, etc.).

3. **Provide help with understanding and remembering vocabulary** (*Chapter C2*)
   - teach vocabulary in **topic groups** (e.g. furniture, the weather, sports, etc.);
   - make sure learners write down any new vocabulary they learn (e.g. in vocabulary notebooks);
   - provide speaking practice for learners to use the vocabulary you have taught them;
   - do vocabulary revision games and activities every week.

4. **Provide opportunities for learners to use grammar meaningfully** (*Chapter C1*)
   - avoid spending too much time explaining grammar or doing grammar exercises;
   - always give your learners opportunities to use new grammar to talk and write about themselves;
   - after reading activities, help your learners to notice the grammar that was used in the text.

5. **Make English lessons enjoyable** (*Chapters C3 and C10*)
   - enjoy your lessons as much as possible – it is good to smile and laugh with your learners;
   - keep a list of your favourite games, songs and fun activities and add to it regularly;
   - share ideas for songs and games with other teachers from other schools;
   - use the internet to learn the melody to songs and use them regularly;
   - try to **reward** good behaviour with a quick game at the end of the lesson.

Different types of learning styles or intelligence

Traditional models of intelligence (such as IQ tests) often concentrated only on logical and linguistic intelligence, because these were easy to test and compare. They ignored other useful mental abilities that vary between individuals. For example, while some of us are good at mathematics, others are better at languages, and others at art or sports. Howard Gardner, an American psychologist, wanted to recognise the importance of all these abilities. He identified eight basic **learning intelligences**.[10] By this he meant that there are eight ways that we can learn:

1. **Interpersonal intelligence:** Some people prefer to do activities in groups, or pairs and learn through discussing and sharing ideas.
2. **Intrapersonal intelligence:** Other people prefer to do activities individually and need opportunities to work alone.

---

10   Gardner, *Frames of Mind*; Gardner, *Intelligence Reframed*.

3. **Linguistic intelligence:** Some people like to read and write novels and poetry. They usually have a large vocabulary and often enjoy doing crossword puzzles and word searches.
4. **Logical-mathematical intelligence:** Some people understand the logic of mathematics and science well. They can do calculations quickly and often like puzzles and abstract problems to solve.
5. **Spatial-visual intelligence:** Some people like to draw pictures and diagrams. They can learn by creating **mind-maps** and can take mental 'photographs' of pages to help them remember.
6. **Bodily-kinaesthetic intelligence:** Some people have good awareness of space. They are often good at sports or dance, and enjoy activities where they can move around the classroom or mime actions.
7. **Musical intelligence:** Some people enjoy songs and music more than others. They often learn the pronunciation of a language well, and can learn through singing songs and remembering **rhymes**.
8. **Naturalist intelligence:** Some people enjoy collecting things, analysing them and creating lists; they often observe natural things such as plants or birds well, and enjoy being able to identify things.

Gardner believed that we all have a combination of several of these intelligences and that our combination can change over time. Although Gardner's multiple intelligences theory has been criticised, many teachers find it useful because it helps them to develop children's ability in different areas. For example, we can include songs, movement and dance to help learners to develop their musical and bodily-kinaesthetic intelligences. We can get learners to draw pictures and to label them to help learners to make use of their spatial-visual intelligence. We can give them language puzzles, crosswords or word searches to help learners to develop logical-mathematical and linguistic intelligences. We can also include individual and **pair work** activities to help in both interpersonal and intrapersonal learning styles. Children still have very adaptable learning styles, so if we include a wide variety of activities in our lessons that appeal to all these intelligences, our learners are more likely to grow up well balanced and able to deal with the challenges that life throws at them.

 **Reflective task**

For each of the learning intelligences, think of one learner or person that you know who is strong in this intelligence.

1. Which of the learning intelligences described above are strongest in you as a learner?
2. Which learning intelligences are developed in the activity shown in the following photograph?

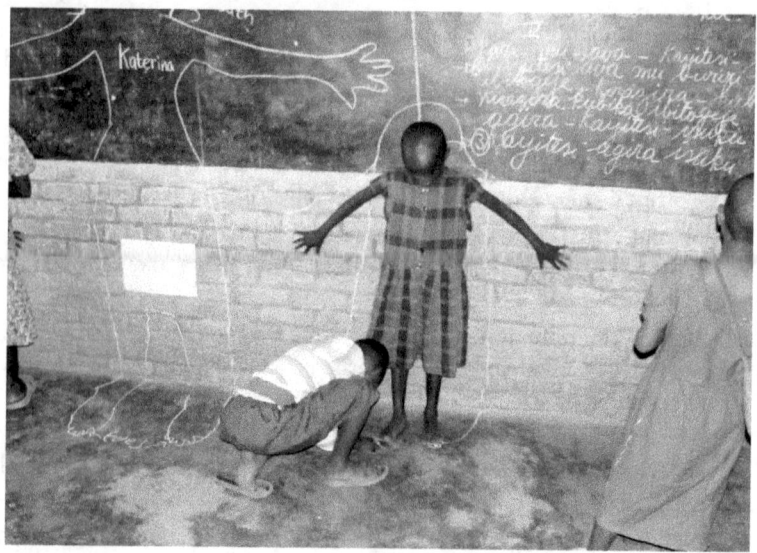

Fig. A2.1: CHILDREN TRACING CHALK LINES AROUND THEIR BODIES

Solution: *Your answers to questions 1 and 2 will be personalised. 3. The picture shows learners in Rwanda drawing chalk lines around each other and labelling their body parts. It may help to develop bodily-kinaesthetic, spatial-visual and interpersonal intelligences mainly. Linguistic intelligence would also be developed during the labelling activity.*

Thinking skills and Bloom's taxonomy of learning

In the past, education often placed a great deal of emphasis on memorising facts so that they could be repeated during lessons or in examinations. Today, we recognise that an important part of education involves helping children to develop a range of different thinking skills. Here are some of the most important ones, as described in Bloom's Taxonomy of Learning:

Creating:	When learners build something new (including new ideas and meanings) from different parts
Evaluating:	When learners give their opinions on a topic, text or idea and provide reasons for these opinions
Analysing:	When learners separate out the parts of a thing or an idea to help them to understand its structure
Applying:	When learners use a new idea in a different situation, applying what they have learnt
Understanding:	When learners show they understand an idea by explaining it to someone else or by drawing a diagram to illustrate it
Remembering:	When learners recall something they have learnt before.

Note for trainers: This is Anderson et. al.'s revised taxonomy;[11] it is more useful for teachers than the original taxonomy because it describes behaviour that we can observe in class.

Notice that the thinking skills at the top of Bloom's Taxonomy are more challenging, and require learners to think in new ways that will be useful when they have to solve problems and make decisions after they leave school.

 **Reflective task**

Answer these questions:

1. Which of the thinking skills are most important to you in your work as a teacher?
2. Think of a lesson you observed or taught recently. Which of the thinking skills did it help to develop? Which thinking skills were dominant? Provide specific examples if you can.

Learner Independence

From their first day at school, children begin learning about how to learn. As they progress through school and beyond, they move from complete dependence on the teacher at the start of year one, to being able to learn independently by the end of college or university. Good teachers encourage and support these changes, training their learners in new learning strategies and skills. Look at the five stages to Learner Independence below. You will notice that at each stage the learners gain new skills that the teacher had to help them with at earlier stages. You will also notice that they are adding more complex thinking skills from Bloom's Taxonomy as they progress through the stages:

Stage	Learners can ...
1. Teacher directs learners	<ul><li>listen to the teacher</li><li>obey commands</li><li>copy words or sentences from the chalkboard or a book</li><li>ask and answer questions</li></ul>

---

11   Anderson, Krathwohl, and Bloom, *A Taxonomy for Learning, Teaching, and Assessing*.

Stage		Learners can …
2.	Teacher guides learners	• work alone effectively • use stationery (e.g. ruler) and **textbooks** (e.g. finding pages and exercises) effectively • complete simple exercises • draw and label pictures • complete simple homework tasks
3.	Learners work together	• work effectively on exercises in pairs and groups of three • write their answers on the chalkboard or present their answers to the class • ask for clarification when they do not understand • complete longer homework tasks • choose books from the library
4.	Learners help each other to learn	• work effectively on activities in groups of four to six • take notes during teacher presentations and make simple presentations to the class • do speaking activities effectively in pairs or **threes** • do **peer-correction** (with teacher guidance) after exercises and homework • access the library independently and complete simple book reports
5.	Learners teach each other and evaluate their own learning	• work in groups on projects during the lesson, completing work to deadlines • carry out research for project work and presentations • participate in discussions and debates in small or large groups • consult their classmates when they need help • challenge classmates respectfully when they disagree • self-correct homework and exercises and peer-correct weekly progress tests • evaluate their own achievement of learning objectives

Think about one of your classes:
- Where are the learners on this table?
- How can you help them to progress to the next stage?

As your learners progress through the five stages, take time to introduce new learning skills, explaining what you would like them to do and why the skill is useful. If they find a skill too challenging, leave it for a while and introduce other skills from the same stage. Then try it again in a few weeks. By helping them to progress to the next stage, you are encouraging them to take more responsibility for their own learning. As they become better at learning, it becomes easier for you to teach them!

Conclusion

In this chapter we have learnt the following:

- how children learn additional languages;
- how we can provide for the five needs of our learners during our lessons;
- there are many types of learner intelligence, and everybody has a combination of these that changes regularly;
- we should include a variety of activity types in our lessons, both to cater for different learner intelligences and to strengthen weaker intelligences;
- we can help our learners to progress along the pathway to learner independence.

The philosophy of learning presented in this chapter can be summarised through an old Chinese proverb. Can you work out which of the three verbs goes into each gap?

understand   forget   remember

Tell me and I will _____.

Show me and I may _____.

Involve me and I will _____.

(the solution is given below)

Solution: 1. forget; 2. remember; 3. understand

A3 – Child-centred Learning

In this chapter:
- What is child-centred learning?
- How child-centred are your lessons?
- C H I L D
- Pairwork and groupwork
- How to make your classroom more child-centred
- An example of a child-centred lesson
- Practical task: Chantal's lesson
- Commentary to practical task: Chantal's lesson
- Changing to child-centred learning – slowly but surely

 Reflective task

Answer the following questions, working in pairs or small groups:
1. How much do you know about child-centred learning?
2. Have you ever tried it in your teaching?
3. How suitable is it to the context in which you teach?

What is child-centred learning?

Child-centred learning is an approach to teaching that places children at the centre of the learning process. We have already met it briefly in *Chapter A1 – You, the Teacher*. Here are six important ideas in child-centred learning:

1. learning is social; learners often do activities in pairs or groups and help each other to learn;
2. learners develop a wide range of **thinking skills**, such as analysing, creating and evaluating (see *Bloom's Taxonomy* in *Chapter A2 – Your Learners*);
3. the teacher is a facilitator of learning, not simply a source of knowledge;
4. the teacher plans lessons around the needs, interests and world of the learners;
5. each lesson starts from what the learners already know and builds on this;
6. the teacher adapts the curriculum or **scheme of work** to make sure that all the learners understand and can follow the lessons.

Many teachers agree that child-centred learning is good learning, and child-centred lessons are the best kind of lessons. However, it is often difficult for many teachers to change to this method, especially teachers who were trained in a more **teacher-centred approach** to learning.

 **Reflective task**

Look again at the six ideas in the previous paragraph. How many of them happen in your lessons? How often do they happen? Write each of the numbers 1 – 6 under one of the three headings:

A. This often happens in my lessons	B. This sometimes happens in my lessons	C. This never happens in my lessons

How child-centred are your lessons?

Some teachers think that child-centred learning is not possible in their school. Classes are too large, there are few **learning resources**, and there is no time because the curriculum is too demanding. For these reasons, they do not try to change. But we can all make our lessons more child-centred if we want to, and we can start with our next lesson. Let us not think of child-centred learning as a method of teaching – let us think of it as a quality. Do not ask *"Is child-centred learning possible in my lessons?"*, ask *"How child-centred are my lessons?"*

Look again at the answers you provided in the *Reflective task* above. How many answers do you have in each column? If you have written most of the numbers in column A, then your lessons are already child-centred. If you have more numbers in column C, your lessons are probably more teacher-centred. If so, there is no need to make sudden changes to your teaching. You can move gradually towards child-centred learning simply by doing more child-centred things in your lessons and noticing what happens.

CHILD

The acronym **CHILD** is a good place to start. It stands for five things that learners do in child-centred lessons. They can be done in any class, big or small, any subject, and without any special resources:

       C - Children **COMMUNICATE** with each other
       H - Children **HELP** each other to learn
       I - Children **IDENTIFY** with the lesson content
       L - Children **LEARN** at their own speed
       D - Children **DEMONSTRATE** what they have learnt

Let us look at each of these things in more detail:

'C' for COMMUNICATE

When children communicate with each other during lessons, they practise speaking skills and explain things to each other in their own way, like they do when they are learning at home or playing outside. Simply by doing more **pairwork** and **groupwork**, we can help this to happen in every lesson.

'H' for HELP

When children help each other to learn, the focus of the lessons moves from teacher-centred 'talk and chalk' to child-centred discovery. Learners stop competing with each other and start working together as a learning team.

'I' for IDENTIFY

When we adapt the lesson content from the curriculum to the world of our learners, we help them to identify with it. We use examples from their world to help them to understand how something works. We personalise what we are teaching, relating it to the home, family and interests of our learners.

'L' for LEARN at their own speed

While the curriculum can help us to choose what to teach our learners, only the learners themselves can dictate how quickly or how slowly we should teach it. By starting with what they know and building on this, we create strong foundations for learning. As we introduce new ideas and knowledge, we make sure they all understand it before we move on, so that no child is left behind.

'D' for DEMONSTRATE

When children demonstrate what they have learnt, we can easily assess their progress, and so can they. They can see how useful their learning is, and also how to apply it in the real world. Importantly, we can also decide what to teach next.

Pairwork and groupwork

Pairwork and groupwork are types of **collaborative learning**. They are important features of child-centred learning because they allow learners to communicate and help each other to learn. This is especially important in English lessons, where learners need to practise their speaking skills together.

Pairwork is when learners work in pairs (or sometimes groups of three) to do an activity, instead of doing it individually or with the teacher controlling everyone. The pairs are 'closed' (i.e. all the pairs are doing the activity at the same time), and the teacher is **monitoring** the learning by observing the pairwork carefully and offering help when needed.

Groupwork is when learners work together in groups of four to six to do an activity. As with pairwork, they communicate in order to discuss and evaluate ideas, and they may also produce shared answers or notes.

A3 – Child-centred Learning

Fig. A3.1: GROUPWORK IN A CLASS IN ERITREA

Pairwork and groupwork can be used in the following situations:
- to practise speaking skills;
- to do an exercise or to compare answers after doing an exercise individually;
- to work on a project or task;
- to create something, such as a diagram, a text or a picture;
- to give feedback to a classmate on something they have written.

Pairwork is usually best when you want every learner to participate in an activity, especially when you want them to practise speaking skills or compare answers to an exercise carefully. If your learners sit three to a desk, it is sometimes more practical to let them work in **threes** rather than pairs, but if you do this, make sure that they all participate. Groups are useful if an activity is more difficult, or if it requires lots of ideas or different roles. As a general rule, keep groups small (4 – 6 learners). Although large groups often seem to be easier to control, they have two disadvantages. Firstly, only one child can speak at a time, so each learner gets less speaking practice and spends more time listening. Secondly, during groupwork, one or two strong learners can sometimes dominate the activity. If you are not sure which one to use, try pairwork first.

During groupwork or pairwork, the teacher's role is to monitor the learners. Monitoring means moving around the class, watching and listening to the learners carefully and helping if needed. It is explained fully in *Chapter A6 – Classroom Management and Behaviour Management*.

How to make your classroom more child-centred

It is not difficult to make classes more child-centred. Let us look at three ways to do this:
1. change the seating arrangement;
2. make the classroom more stimulating and interesting;
3. allow the learners to personalise their own space.

A child-centred seating arrangement

For learners to do pairwork and groupwork, they need to face each other. However, many classes in public schools have desks attached to benches facing the teacher. Here are four solutions that we can use in these classes:

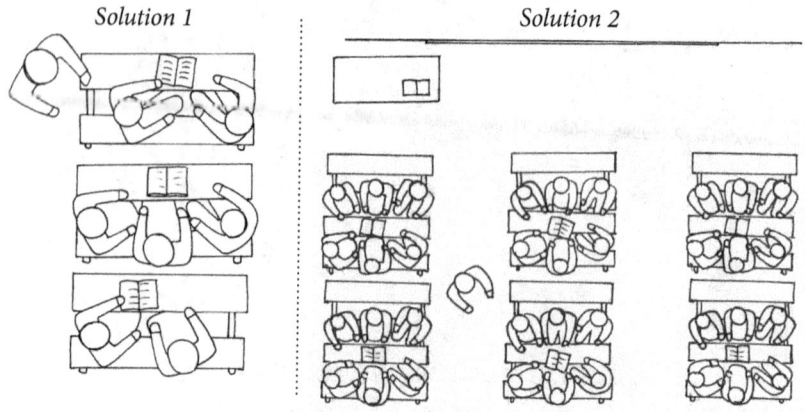

Fig. A3.2: SOLUTIONS 1 AND 2

Solution 1 shows how you can do pairwork without moving the desks. Learners turn to face their partner. If there are three learners sitting on a bench, the centre learner sits back a little and the outer two can face the centre. Solution 2 shows how you can do groupwork without moving the desks. Half the learners turn round to face the learners behind them. This solution provides a fast, easy way to change from facing the teacher and the chalkboard to facing their classmates for groupwork. In Solution 3, all the desks are turned sideways and pushed together, so that the learners are facing each other. The learners can see the chalkboard if necessary by looking to the side. Some teachers like to put the desks like this for the whole lesson. Finally, Solution 4 shows desks arranged in two rows in a 'C' shape. The learners on the inner circle turn around to do groupwork. It is usually only possible with classes of less than 50 learners.

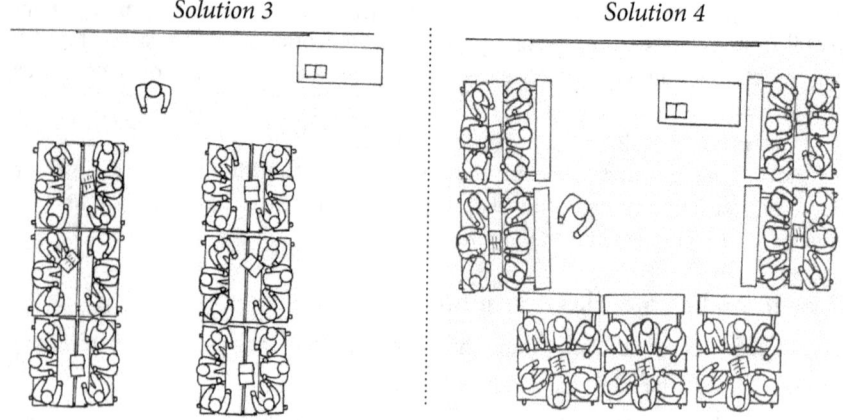

Fig. A3.3: SOLUTIONS 3 AND 4

Different solutions can be applied in different contexts. Try Solutions 1 and 2 first. As learners get used to working together, you can try Solution 3 for longer groupwork activities. Do not forget to discuss the different solutions with your head teacher, other teachers of the same class (who may also want to experiment with these solutions) and your learners, who will tell you which solution they prefer.

A more stimulating and interesting environment

Learners learn better when they are in a more stimulating environment. Just as with other aspects of child-centred learning, you can transform your classroom into a stimulating environment gradually. If the walls of your classroom are bare, you can begin by putting up some visual aids, such as posters, maps or alphabet **wall friezes**. You can make your own posters from card and rice sacks (see *Chapters C11 – Learning Resources* and *C12 – 10 Essential Resources to Create*), or find maps and posters in the staff room or school office. Many schools do not have visual aids on the walls because staff are worried that the learners will damage them. If so, you can put the posters high enough (over 1.5 m) so that the learners will not damage them by mistake. You can also put hanging displays in your classroom, which are small visual aids written on card and attached to strings that hang across the class. For more on how to make posters and hanging displays, see *Chapters C11* and *C12*.

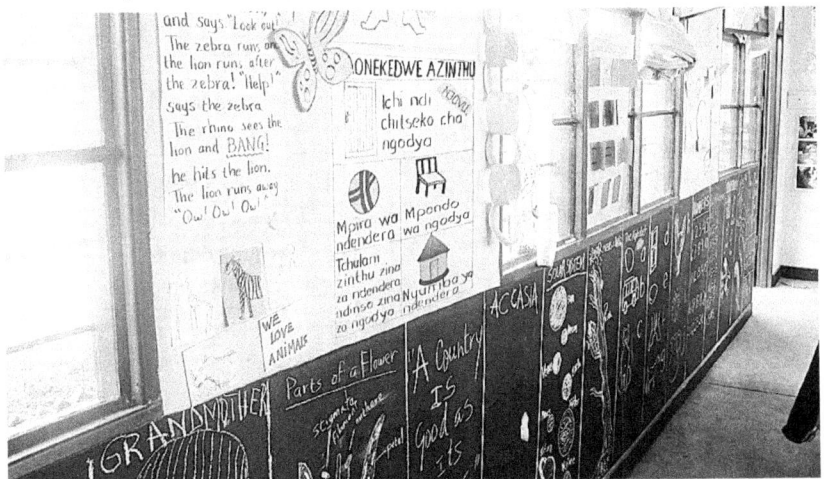

Fig. A3.4: A WALL IN A STIMULATING CLASSROOM

Space for learners to personalise their classroom

Another way to make our classrooms more child-centred is to get the learners to **personalise** it. This means making it personal to their interests and needs. The simplest way to do this is to create a class display board, where learners can display their work, such as pictures, poems and writing compositions. You can also make a **today chart** on which a learner changes the day, date and weather each day. Another way to promote personalisation is to add **wall boards** to your classroom. Wall boards are side walls of the classroom painted with chalkboard paint and divided to provide individual space for each learner. For more information on class display boards, today charts and wall boards see *Chapters C11* and *C12*.

An example of a child-centred lesson

Let us look at an example of a child-centred English lesson. This one was planned and taught by Chantal, a Rwandan primary school teacher.

Lesson title: Writing a shopping list for the market

Lesson objectives: The learners will be able to ask and answer questions about how much food they have at home, using the quantifiers 'a lot of', 'a few' and 'a little' in order to write a shopping list.

In the previous lesson: The learners learnt the names of different types of food, and how to ask and answer questions using 'How much?' and 'How many?'.

Time: 45 minutes

Number of learners: 56

Age of learners: 9 – 10

Level: Elementary

Stage	Time	Activities	Examples of language used*
1.	2 mins	The teacher greets the learners, introduces the lesson and asks them about the homework from yesterday.	T: "Today we are going to learn how to ask and answer questions and how to write shopping lists." T: "What did I ask you to do for homework?" Ls: "To bring in different food items from home."
2.	5 mins	Different learners put the food they have brought on the teacher's table.	L1: "These are tomatoes." T: "Thank you, Claudine." L2: "Here is some milk." T: "Well done, Theo."
3.	3 mins	The teacher shows different quantities of food and uses the quantifiers to name them. The learners watch and listen.	T: "We have a few tomatoes ... a lot of potatoes ... a little sugar ..."
4.	6 mins	The teacher clarifies the new grammar by using example sentences, questions and a little translation into the **mother tongue**. She allows learners to ask questions in both languages.	T: "So, which is correct: 'a few sugar', or 'a little sugar'?" L: "A little sugar." T: "Who can explain why?" etc. T: "What about tomatoes: 'a few tomatoes', or 'a little tomatoes'?"

Stage	Time	Activities	Examples of language used*
5.	6 mins	The teacher gets the learners to do an exercise working in groups of 3 or 4. The teacher monitors and encourages discussion.	Write a little, a few or a lot of in each gap: 1. We have _____ money. (0.05c) 2. They want to buy _____ flour. (20 kg) etc.
6.	5 mins	The teacher gets feedback from the learners. She asks one group and then asks for agreement before confirming the correct answer.	T: "Which group would like to try sentence number 1? The orange group, OK. What is your answer?" L: "We have a little money." T: "Raise your hand if you agree."
7.	4 mins	The teacher sets up a **role play** activity. She writes a list of food products on the chalkboard, and explains the activity. She gets two learners to demonstrate how to do it.	T: "You are planning to go shopping. Write a shopping list. Student A, ask questions and write the list. Student B, answer the questions using the information on the chalkboard."
8.	8 mins	Working in pairs, learners do the role play. One learner asks questions and writes the list. The other learner answers the questions based on what food they have (shown on the chalkboard). The teacher monitors.	L1: "Do we have any potatoes?" L2: "Yes, we do." L1: "How many do we have?" L2: "We only have a few." L1: "OK, so we need to buy some more." (writes it down)
9.	3 mins	Feedback: The teacher gets two pairs to the front of the class to perform their dialogue and then **praises** them.	T: "Who would like to perform their role play for the class?" "Everybody, clap your hands for them."
10.	2 mins	The teacher concludes the lesson by asking the learners what they learnt today, praises them all for their good work, and gives homework.	T: "What did we learn today?" Ls: "We learnt ..." (different learners contribute ideas) T: "Well done, everybody! Now, for homework ..." etc.

* This includes what the teacher and learners said and also examples from exercises and boardwork.
Note the following abbreviations are used above: T= teacher, L= learner, Ls= learners, L1= 1st learner, etc.

Practical task: Chantal's lesson

Let us analyse Chantal's lesson using the acronym CHILD that we learnt about earlier in this chapter. For each of the features below, decide how many times Chantal's learners did this in her lesson. Write the lesson stage in which they did it in the column on the right. Two examples have been completed for you. You can write several lesson stages in each box:

CHILD	When did Chantal's learners do this?
Children **Communicate** with each other	Stage 8
Children **Help** each other to learn	
Children **Identify** with the lesson content	Stage 2
Children **Learn** at their own speed	
Children **Demonstrate** what they have learnt	

Commentary to practical task: Chantal's lesson

Children Communicate with each other during lessons

This happened mainly in Stages 8 and 5 when they did the group and pairwork activities, but it also happened in Stage 2 when they showed their food to the class and during feedback Stages 6 and 9.

Children Help each other to learn

This happened mainly in Stage 5 while doing the exercise in pairs, but they also helped each other during the role play and demonstrations (7, 8 and 9).

Children Identify with the lesson content

This happened in Stage 2 when the learners presented real food from their own homes for the lesson. It also happened during the role play activity (7, 8 and 9), which involved them communicating to create a real shopping list for the market, something that their parents may also do.

Children Learn at their own speed

This is more difficult to say because we did not watch the lesson. However, in Stage 5 she invited questions in either language, in case any learners had not understood the explanation. In Stages 5 and 8 the learners worked in pairs, which they will naturally do at their own speed.

Children Demonstrate what they have learnt

This happened in Stage 9, when two pairs demonstrated the role play. It also happened in Stage 6 (feedback) and whenever the teacher was monitoring the pairwork in Stages 5 and 8. In Stage 2 the learners demonstrated what they had learnt in yesterday's lesson.

We can see that Chantal's learners did most of these things several times during her lesson, which makes it a good example of a child-centred lesson. Note that this was not a 'special' lesson. The main resources were the chalkboard, the **textbook** and some food that the learners had brought to class. It was taken from the curriculum and adapted to the needs and interests of her learners. She used a typical classroom, with benches and desks fixed together, and had a large class of 56 learners. It was child-centred because of what happened, not because of what they had.

Changing to child-centred learning – slowly but surely

In this chapter we have presented a model for child-centred learning that many teachers are finding effective. If child-centred learning is new to you, the challenges of changing from a teacher-centred approach may seem like a revolution in the classroom! Remember that you do not have to change suddenly – you can do it little by little. Do not be afraid to experiment with new activity types, or to make mistakes, as these often lead to the most important learning. Here is some advice to help you when you start using pairwork and groupwork:

Start with your favourite class

Do your first pairwork or groupwork activities with a class that you like, one that is well-behaved and enjoys your lessons. They will be happy to try something new.

Start with familiar, structured activities

Begin with activities that the learners have done before (e.g. grammar exercises, reading or writing tasks, etc.), but instead of doing them individually, they do them in pairs or small groups.

Explain what you are doing and why

Learners quickly understand the logic and the aim of pairwork or groupwork – they do them all the time at home, or when the teacher is not in the classroom! But the first time they do it during a lesson, you should explain to them that they will not be punished for talking to each other – this is not a sign of misbehaviour! You can use their mother tongue to explain this clearly.

Be patient

The first time you do a groupwork or pairwork activity with a class, give the instruction and wait. There may be a long period of silence but do not interrupt the silence yourself. When one group begins, smile and nod your head. Other groups will also begin.

Do not be scared of noise

In a big class, groupwork and pairwork can be noisy. Do not worry! Noise is part of communication, and in a child-centred class, communication is evidence of learning. Your learners might begin to worry as well! If they do, remind them that the noise is OK during pairwork and groupwork. If necessary, tell them to speak quietly.

Praise the learners for their successes

The learners will be nervous the first time you do groupwork or pairwork. Monitor the groups by walking round the class, and praise groups who are working well together. After the activity, give more praise and say why (e.g. *"This group here were speaking English very well and using the new vocabulary – well done!"*).

Get feedback from the learners

After the lesson, choose a few responsible learners and ask them what they thought of the pairwork/groupwork. You may be surprised about how well they can analyse what was happening and give opinions and useful suggestions.

Enjoy it

When learners learn to do groupwork and pairwork well, it can make your job easier. You will find that you are not always the centre of attention, and that you can even relax a little. They will enjoy it, so you should too!

Conclusion

In this chapter we have learnt the following:
- the important features of child-centred learning;
- how a child-centred approach can improve learning in any teaching context;
- the five features of the acronym CHILD;
- why pairwork and groupwork are important in child-centred learning;
- how you can make your classroom more child-centred;
- what an example child-centred lesson is like;
- how we can begin to implement child-centred learning in our lessons.

"I never teach my pupils, I only attempt to provide the conditions in which they can learn."

Albert Einstein

A4 – The Phases of a Lesson

In this chapter:

- Why do lessons need structure?
- New language lessons
- Skills practice lessons with three phases
- Time for more practice?
- Practical task: Ordering the stages of a lesson
- Commentary to practical task: Ordering the stages of a lesson

 Reflective task

Think about a lesson you have taught recently:
1. How many stages did it have?
2. What happened in each of these stages?

Why do lessons need structure?

In most countries a single lesson is typically from 30 – 45 minutes in length, usually with shorter lessons in primary schools and longer lessons in secondary schools. To ensure that this time is used productively, lessons need to have a clear structure, usually with three or four separate stages, which we will call **lesson phases**. This structure is important for several reasons:

- it helps the learners to understand what is happening;
- it helps to make sure that things happen in the right order;
- it helps the teacher to plan quickly and effectively.

Most teachers of English begin their lesson with an introduction and finish with a conclusion, but the phases in between will depend on what you are teaching. In this chapter we will look at two different lesson structures for two different types of English lessons:

- New Language Lessons (grammar and vocabulary lessons), with four phases
- Skills Practice Lessons (speaking, listening, reading and writing), with three phases

Let us look at these two types of lessons separately.

New language lessons

New language lessons are lessons where we want the learners to learn something new (or to **revisit** something they studied before). This might be a piece of grammar, such as the past simple tense (I went home, we played football, etc.) or prepositions of location (under, next to, etc.). Or it might be a vocabulary **topic group**, such as the names of animals, colours, or verbs to describe how we prepare food (peel potatoes, chop an onion, fry an egg, etc.). These lessons need two important phases between the introduction and the conclusion.

A new language lesson with four phases

1. Introduction *We start the lesson*	In this phase: • we **revise** previous lessons or vocabulary • we check or collect in any homework • we present our lesson objectives and write the lesson title on the chalkboard
2. New language *We present new grammar or vocabulary*	In this phase: • we provide examples of the new language in context • we help learners to understand the meaning of the new language • we show learners how to pronounce the new language when speaking • we show learners how to form the new language when writing
3. Practice activity *We give learners an opportunity to practise using the new language*	In this phase: • we prepare the learners for the practice activity • learners do the activity and we monitor • we check how the learners did in the activity (feedback)
4. Conclusion *We finish the lesson*	In this phase: • we check again for understanding of new language • we revise our lesson objectives • we praise the learners • we give homework to the learners

Let us look at each of these phases in more detail:

1. **Introduction**

After greeting the learners, it is a good idea to revise something that they have learnt before to make sure they do not forget it. You can play a vocabulary game (for example using the Vocabulary Box, explained in *Chapter C12 – 10 Essential Resources to Create*), ask questions to check if they remember what you taught in the last lesson, or provide two or three discussion questions on a previous lesson topic. This revision helps them to **warm up** their English.

During the introduction we can also check any homework that we gave them during the last lesson. Remember that you can start by giving the learners one or two minutes to check their answers together in pairs or groups of three. At this stage, you can monitor to see how they have done and to find out which questions were most difficult. After you have done this, elicit the answers from the learners and provide extra clarification or explanation if necessary.

During the introduction you should also introduce the lesson to the learners. Learners are more likely to achieve your objectives if they know what they are. At lower primary levels, you can do this simply:

"Today we are going to learn about 10 different types of food."

At higher levels, especially in secondary school, you can make this more formal:

"We are going to learn how to form the passive voice in the past simple tense and then we will practise using it."

If you do not think the learners will understand, you can repeat the objectives in the **mother tongue**. It is a good idea to write the lesson title on the chalkboard (e.g. "Different types of food" or "The Passive Voice of the Past Simple Tense"), and get the learners to copy it in their notebooks. Now the learners are ready for the new language.

2. New language

When you introduce new language (i.e. new grammar or new vocabulary), or revisit an area of language that they still have not fully learnt, you should do four things:

Provide **Examples** of the new language in context. You can provide examples in many ways; write a dialogue on the chalkboard, read a text in the **textbook** or tell the learners a story. The context is important, as it helps the learners to understand the new language and see how it can be used.

Help learners to **Understand** the meaning of the new language. There are many ways to do this. For example, you can use mime (e.g. learners could mime verbs in present continuous tense), you could use a visual example (e.g. compare learners to introduce comparative forms: *"David is taller than Saba."*), or translate it into the mother tongue or any shared language. Some teachers prefer not to use translation, but it is a simple and effective way to communicate the meaning of new language clearly, as long as the translation is correct and all your learners share the same language. Another advantage to translation is that it provides learners with a way to record the meaning by writing the translation in their notebooks. See *Chapter A7 – Use of the Mother Tongue in English Language Learning* for more ideas on using the mother tongue.

Show learners how to **Pronounce** the new language when speaking. Pronunciation is important because English sometimes has very difficult spellings, and sounds can be very different to the learners' mother tongues. Begin by saying the example sentences or words yourself while the learners just listen. After this, get them to repeat the new language after you, and finally check their pronunciation by choosing a few learners to repeat individually. You may also have time to get them to practise saying the new language in pairs while you monitor.

Show learners how to **Form** the new language when writing. The examples of the language in context should show the learners how to spell any new words they are learning, but if you are teaching grammar you can also check they know how to conjugate verb tenses, form questions and negatives and copy these down. Make sure you check any common irregular forms (e.g. past tenses or plurals such as 'women').

The order in which you do these four things may depend on your learners' needs, although the order given above is probably the most logical one. The examples of the new language will help you to show the meaning, provide a model for pronunciation work and also show the important aspects of the form of the new language. In *Chapters C1 – Teaching Grammar* and *C2 – Teaching Vocabulary*, we will look in more detail at how you can do these four things.

3. Practice activity

There are two types of practice activity; **controlled practice**, for example when we get learners to do a **gap-fill** exercise, and **free practice**, when we get learners to use the language in 'real' speaking or writing activities. Both of these are important, however there may not always be time to do both in one lesson. If not, you can do a controlled practice activity in the first lesson, and a free practice activity in the next lesson. A detailed explanation of the difference between these is given in *Chapter C1 – Teaching Grammar*, but here are a few examples:

Controlled practice: a gap-fill exercise (e.g. put the verb in the correct tense); a matching exercise (e.g. match each word to the correct definition or picture); a puzzle (e.g. a word search or a crossword); a 'spot the mistake' exercise (e.g. find the mistake in each sentence).

Free practice: a speaking practice activity that gets the learners using the new language (e.g. tell your partner what you did yesterday using the past simple tense); a writing practice activity that gets learners using the new language (e.g. write a letter to a pen friend describing your family).

In order for practice activities to be successful, learners need both a clear instruction and a clear demonstration or example. While learners are doing the activity you should monitor carefully, checking that they are all doing it correctly, providing individual help to weaker learners, and noticing any general problems that you can help them with during feedback. After the practice activity, feedback should be conducted. This is when you check the answers to a controlled practice activity or when you get a few 'samples' from the class of what they were doing after a free practice activity. See *Chapter A6 – Classroom Management and Behaviour Management* for more on how to do practice activities in the **activity cycle**.

4. Conclusion

No lesson is complete without a conclusion. It may only take a few minutes, but it is very important to check that the learners know what they have learnt (for example by asking them: What was the topic/objective of today's lesson?), and also to check their understanding of this (for example by asking them **concept check questions**: *"When do we use this grammar?" "Who can explain what this word means?" "Can anybody translate this sentence into our language?"* etc.). When you check understanding you will find out if they have learnt the new language well, or if they need more practice in the next lesson.

Two other things should be done during the Conclusion. Firstly, praise the learners for their hard work and achievement. For example by saying *"Well done!"*, *"Excellent!"*, *"Give your partner a high five!"*. Secondly, give out the homework, if needed. Always try to relate the homework to the lesson content. At secondary level you can sometimes give controlled practice or writing for homework, and do more speaking practice during the lesson.

Skills practice lessons with three phases

Skills practice lessons are similar in structure to new language lessons. But there are two important differences:

- **Difference 1:** the new language phase is absent or very short
- **Difference 2:** the aim is not for them to learn something new, but for them to practise one or more of the four skills (reading, writing, speaking or listening)

Skills practice lessons should happen as often as new language lessons. If you are doing more than 50% new language lessons, your learners will have less opportunity to practice the new language and may forget it as a result.

A skills lesson with three phases

1. **Introduction** *We start the lesson*	In this phase: • we do revision of previous lessons or vocabulary • we check or collect in any homework • we present our lesson objectives and write the lesson title on the chalkboard
2. **Practice Activity** *We give learners an opportunity to practise using the new language*	In this phase: • we prepare the learners for the practice activity • learners do the activity and we monitor • we check how the learners did in the activity (feedback)
3. **Conclusion** *We finish the lesson*	In this phase: • we revise our lesson objectives • we praise the learners • we give homework to the learners

The practice activity may be a reading, listening, speaking or writing activity, or a combination of two of these. You can read more about how to practise each of these skills effectively in *Chapters C4 to C7*. Here are some examples:

- **Reading activity:** learners read a text to answer five comprehension questions;

- **Listening activity:** learners listen to the teacher telling a story to answer three comprehension questions;
- **Speaking and listening activity:** learners describe the appearance of a family member to their partner;
- **Writing and reading activity:** learners write about a town or village that they have visited and then read what some of their classmates have written.

Time for more practice?

Learners in secondary school can often work more quickly than in primary school and lessons are often longer, so there may be time for two or three practice activities in a five phase lesson. In such lessons, we can order the practice activities so that the first one is more controlled, and the second one is a free practice activity. Here is an example of such a lesson:

Introduction	The teacher greets the learners, revises the last lesson, checks the homework and then introduces the new lesson: "Jobs in the City".
New language	Vocabulary: Eight jobs are introduced, using pictures, mime and explanation.
Practice activity 1	Learners complete a gap-fill exercise using the 'jobs vocabulary' from the textbook.
Practice activity 2	Learners play a **groupwork** game in which one of them describes a job, and the others have to guess which job it is.
Conclusion	The teacher checks for understanding, revises the lesson objectives, praises the learners and gives homework.

Practical task: Ordering the stages of a lesson

The table below shows ten stages from a new language lesson on the grammar of 'going to'. The lesson is designed for learners in upper primary school (age 9 – 11) with an intermediate level of English. It is 40 minutes long and has four phases and one practice activity.

However, there is a problem – the stages of the lesson are in the wrong order! You must put them in the right order and decide which lesson phase each stage belongs to. Write the lesson phase in the box on the left. There are several stages in each phase. The first stage is at the top. It has been done as an example:

Lesson phase: **Introduction**	The teacher greets the learners and asks them what they learnt in the last lesson.
Lesson phase:	The teacher praises the learners and gives them their homework.

Lesson phase:	The teacher writes a short dialogue on the chalkboard which includes the new language (going to). The teacher and one of the learners read the dialogue together.
Lesson phase:	The teacher asks five learners to feedback on what their partner said, praising them for their contributions.
Lesson phase:	The teacher underlines the sentences with the new language (going to), and checks that learners understand the meaning, the form and the pronunciation of the new language.
Lesson phase:	The learners compare homework from last night in pairs, then check with the teacher.
Lesson phase:	The teacher instructs the learners to tell their partner five things they are going to do this weekend and gives several examples herself. She tells them to take notes on their partners' answers.
Lesson phase:	The teacher introduces the new lesson: "Today you will learn a new way to talk about the future. It is called 'going to'." The teacher writes on the chalkboard: "Going to".
Lesson phase:	The teacher revises the lesson objectives and checks that learners understand the new language by asking questions.
Lesson phase:	The learners do the practice activity, talking and taking notes in pairs. The teacher monitors.

Commentary to practical task: Ordering the stages of a lesson

Here are the stages of the lesson in the most logical order.

Lesson phase: Introduction	The teacher greets the learners and asks them what they learnt in the last lesson.
Lesson phase: Introduction	The learners compare homework from last night in pairs, then check with the teacher.
Lesson phase: Introduction	The teacher introduces the new lesson: "Today you will learn a new way to talk about the future. It is called 'going to'." The teacher writes on the chalkboard: "Going to".
Lesson phase: New language	The teacher writes a short dialogue on the chalkboard which includes the new language (going to). The teacher and one of the learners read the dialogue together.

Lesson phase: New language	The teacher underlines the sentences with the new language (going to), and checks that learners understand the meaning, the form and the pronunciation of the new language.
Lesson phase: Practice activity	The teacher instructs the learners to tell their partner five things they are going to do this weekend and gives several examples herself. She tells them to take notes from their partners' answers.
Lesson phase: Practice activity	The learners do the practice activity, talking and taking notes in pairs. The teacher monitors.
Lesson phase: Practice activity	The teacher asks five learners to feedback on what their partner said, praising them for their contributions.
Lesson phase: Conclusion	The teacher revises the lesson objectives and checks that learners understand the new language by asking questions.
Lesson phase: Conclusion	The teacher praises the learners and gives them their homework.

Conclusion

In this chapter we have learnt the following:
- why lessons need structure;
- what a four phase new language lesson looks like;
- what we should do in each of these phases;
- what a three phase skills practice lesson looks like;
- how we can add more phases at higher levels.

A5 – Planning

In this chapter:

- Yearly planning: From the national curriculum to the lesson plan
- The scheme of work
- Weekly planning
- Practical task: Planning a week's lessons
- Commentary to practical task: Planning a week's lessons
- Planning lessons

 Reflective task

In your opinion, who should create the following for your learners?
1. *the curriculum that defines what my learners study*
2. *the scheme of work that organises this curriculum into terms and weeks*
3. *my weekly lesson plans*
4. *my individual lesson plans*

Choose from the four options below and give reasons for your choices.

    A. me   C. my school

    B. the **textbook** I use   D. the Ministry of Education

Yearly planning: From the national curriculum to the lesson plan

All countries have a **national curriculum** that tells teachers what needs to be taught in each academic year. All planning begins from this document. The content of the curriculum (i.e. the grammar, vocabulary, skills, etc. that the learners should learn) is then organised into a timetable for the year called a **scheme of work**. From this scheme of work, teachers can create **weekly plans**, and then write individual lesson plans.

National curricula for English should include vocabulary, specific skills and grammar that the learners should learn during the academic year. Some national curricula for English may have a strong grammar orientation, but the vocabulary and skills are just as important. Some national curricula also have methodological guidelines that advise you how you should teach. In some countries the word **syllabus** is used to describe the content of the curriculum and/or the order in which it is studied.

National curriculum	**Scheme of work**
The document that tells you what to teach. Usually produced by the Ministry of Education as a published document. It can often be downloaded from the Ministry of Education (MOE) website.	A document that organises the curriculum into the terms and weeks in your academic year. It is usually produced by the teacher, although in some countries it can be standardised by either the school or the Ministry of Education.
Lesson plan	**Weekly plan**
A document that describes the content of one lesson; the aims, structure and activities. Usually produced by the teacher.	A document that tells you what the learners should learn on each day of the week. Usually produced by the teacher.

The scheme of work

To begin planning your year, you should break the curriculum up into a scheme of work. This document guides you on what to teach each week throughout the year. Sometimes you can get examples or guidelines for schemes of work from the Ministry of Education or other teachers. If so, you should adapt these to the needs of your learners and your own personal preferences. Remember that you know your classes better than anybody else, and every class is different.

To create your scheme of work, it is a good idea to work with other teachers who have experience of teaching the same subject at the same level. Here are the basic stages to creating a scheme of work:

Stage 1

If you have a guideline scheme of work provided, check that it reflects the content of the curriculum accurately, including vocabulary and skills (not just grammar). If it does not, you will need to start again.

Stage 2

Decide how much time the learners need to learn each part of the curriculum, in weeks or half weeks. Do not try to fit too much into each week. Your learners also need to practise skills (speaking, listening, reading and writing) and do **revision**.

Plan for the speed and ability of your learners. Once you have finished, count the total number of weeks you have. This will probably be more weeks than you have in the academic year! Do not worry – this is a very common problem.

Stage 3

At this stage, you should think carefully about what is most important for your learners to learn. Put this first in your scheme of work. Check that the order you have chosen goes from easy to difficult (e.g. simple clothes vocabulary before uncommon clothes vocabulary, and past simple tense before past continuous tense).

Stage 4

You will probably find that some of the more difficult items on the curriculum do not fit into your scheme of work because there are not enough weeks in the year. You should put these areas at the end of your scheme of work, and label them 'optional'. This may sound like strange advice, especially if these areas are in the final exam, but remember the following piece of advice:

Learning a language is like building a house; if the foundations are not strong, the whole house will be weak!

If you rush at the start, the learners may forget everything. If you build strong foundations, they will learn faster, and you may find that you will have time for these optional areas at the end of your scheme of work.

Stage 5

Write up your scheme of work in a clear, easy-to-read document. Some teachers like to make a copy of this for their learners (mainly at secondary level) or other teachers in the same school. It may be possible to display the schemes of work for different subjects in the classrooms.

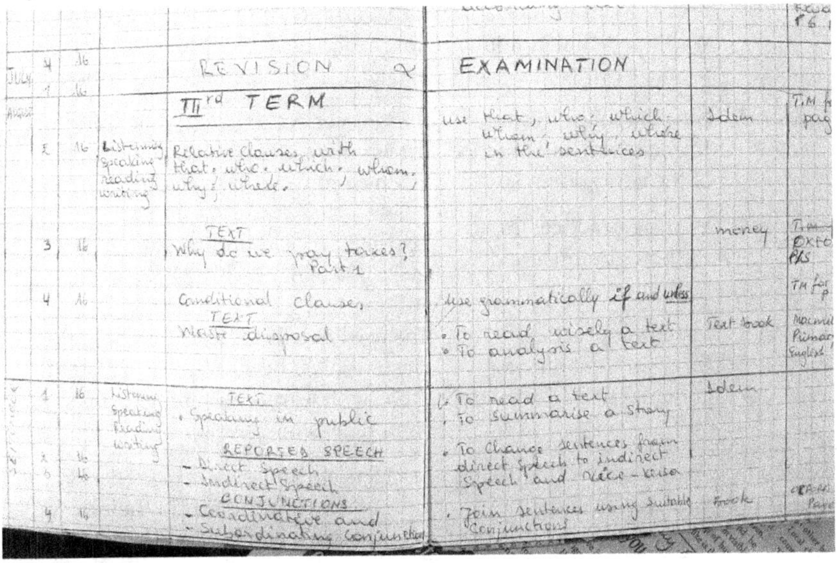

Fig. A5.1: PHOTO OF SAMPLE SCHEME OF WORK

Weekly planning

Most teachers of English working in public schools teach from three to eight subject lessons each week of 30 – 60 minutes each. If your learners have five lessons or more (excluding the early years – see *Part B – Literacy*), try to make sure they get the following each week:
- introduction and practice of new grammar (see *Chapter C1*);
- introduction and practice of new vocabulary (see *Chapter C2*);
- speaking practice (see *Chapter C4*);
- listening practice (see *Chapter C5*);
- reading practice (see *Chapter C6*);
- writing practice (see *Chapter C7*);
- revision of new language from this week and last week.

If you are able to **recycle** the new grammar and vocabulary for the week in the skills practice lessons, your learners will learn it more effectively. If your learners have fewer than five lessons of English per week, you can distribute this content over two weeks.

Let us look at an example of this from an upper primary class with seven English lessons each week. Notice how the topic for the week (transport and travel) is continued throughout the week, even during the skills practice lessons:

Lesson	Content	Example
Lesson 1	**New language lesson:** Introduction and practice of the new vocabulary	Types of transport, including related verbs and other vocabulary (bicycle, bus, drive, catch, reservation, etc.).
Lesson 2	**Reading practice:** The text includes the new vocabulary and grammar for the week	Text adapted from a newspaper about transportation problems in Lagos, and how things have changed. Learners read and answer comprehension questions.
Lesson 3	**New language lesson:** Introduction and practice of the new grammar	Present perfect simple (Public transport has improved.) Example sentences are taken from yesterday's reading text.
Lesson 4	**Writing practice:** Using the new grammar and vocabulary	Learners write a short text about one memorable journey they have made.
Lesson 5	**Listening practice:** Incorporating the new grammar and vocabulary	The teacher tells the learners about the places she has been, and why she went there, with learners listening to answer comprehension questions.
Lesson 6	**Speaking practice:** Using the new vocabulary	Learners ask and answer questions in pairs about the transport in their town, and how their family gets around.

Lesson	Content	Example
Lesson 7	Revision lesson	Revising the transportation vocabulary and present perfect simple grammar using games, speaking activities, etc.

The new language (both grammar and vocabulary) should usually come in the first half of the week, but it does not have to be in the first lessons. For example, you could start with a reading lesson on Monday in which the learners begin to notice the new language, or a listening lesson in which you use the new grammar when telling the learners a story.

Practical task: Planning a week's lessons

Using the vocabulary, grammar and reading texts given below, plan a week's lessons for a lower secondary teacher (learner age 12 – 13) who has six English lessons every week. Create a table like the one given above. Remember that you can change the order of the different lessons. Include example speaking and writing activities.

Vocabulary
Places and buildings in villages and towns, including related verbs: shop, mosque, church, school, administrative office, police station, library, bank, bus stop, visit, pray, withdraw money, report a crime, etc.

Grammar
Revision and practice of comparative and superlative adjectives and related structures (bigger than, as big as, the biggest of all, etc.)

Reading texts
1. Text about the capital city of your country (includes superlatives)
2. Text comparing two villages in different parts of Africa (includes comparatives)
3. Story about a girl who moved from a small village to her capital city (includes comparatives and superlatives)

Here is an example – the last lesson of the week:

Lesson 6	Revision lesson	Learners revise comparatives by talking about their village followed by a quiz game using superlatives.

Commentary to practical task: Planning a week's lessons

There are many ways to organise the week's lessons. Here is one possible solution:

Lesson	Content	Example
Lesson 1	Reading practice: Extensive reading for pleasure	Learners read a story about a girl who moved from a small village to her capital city and answer comprehension questions on the text.

Lesson	Content	Example
Lesson 2	**New language lesson:** Introduction and practice of the grammar to be revised (comparatives and superlatives)	Using yesterday's story to provide context, learners find and identify a range of comparative and superlative structures, followed by practice activities.
Lesson 3	**Listening and writing practice:** Listening to somebody expressing a personal opinion, then writing to express their own opinions	The teacher tells the learners about the advantages and disadvantages (in his opinion) of living in a small town. The learners then write their own opinions on the same topic.
Lesson 4	**New language lesson:** Including introduction and speaking practice	Learners learn vocabulary about places and facilities in villages and towns and describe their own village.
Lesson 5	**Speaking practice:** Discussion and debate	Learners discuss the relative advantages and disadvantages of living in villages, towns and cities in small groups, followed by debates in larger groups.
Lesson 6	**Revision lesson**	Learners revise comparatives by talking about their village followed by a quiz game using superlatives.

 Reflective task

Read the opinions of two teachers from Ghana and answer the two questions that follow:

Robert

"I teach two different levels in upper primary school. I usually take about one hour to plan each lesson. I do this at the end of the school day. I like to write a detailed lesson plan, and I try to follow it well in class. I hope to use these lesson plans again in the future."

Mary

"I teach three different English classes at secondary level. I only need about 10 – 20 minutes to plan each lesson, because I know the levels and the materials very well. I do not write a long lesson plan, just a few notes on a piece of paper. I spend more time preparing resources."

1. Which teacher are you most similar to?
2. Which teacher is more experienced? How do you know?

Planning lessons

Planning involves thinking carefully about what you will teach and how you will teach it. The written lesson plan helps you to remember this. If you are a trainee or a newly-qualified teacher, it is a good idea to write detailed lesson plans, but if you have plenty of experience, you can probably write quite short lesson plans in note form. Remember always to check with your head teacher about this, and always write detailed lesson plans if you are being observed. Here is an example of an experienced teacher's lesson plan:

Lesson 3, Tuesday 16/03/2015

Speaking Skills: Practising Asking and Answering Questions in Groups

1. Greet learners, play vocabulary game and check homework.
2. Introduce lesson.
3. Provide e.g. sentences, and elicit possible questions from learners:
   I went to a wedding at the weekend -> What did you do at the weekend?
4. Groupwork: Learners do question formation exercise from the coursebook in groups of 3 - 4. Monitor.
5. Groups compare answers.
6. Get feedback, elicit peer correction.
7. Groups practise speaking skills, asking & answering questions, providing real answers.
8. Feedback and praise.
9. Homework: Write three questions to ask your partner next lesson.

If you are a new teacher or a trainee teacher, you should plan your lessons in detail, like Robert. You will find it easier to teach, and it will help you to understand what went well and what did not. Each day, the process will become faster, and your written plans should become simpler.

Here are the key stages to writing a detailed lesson plan:
1. Write down your objectives. Remember to consult your scheme of work and write objectives that describe the **learning outcomes** of the lesson. For example, *"By the end of the lesson, the learners will be able to write a short text describing the members of their family."*
2. Decide what activities the learners will need to learn and do during the lesson to achieve your objectives.
3. Decide how many phases your lesson will need (see *Chapter A4 The Phases of a Lesson*). Work out how the activities from Stage 2 will fit into this lesson.
4. Write the detailed lesson plan. Remember to note down answers to any exercises you include and page numbers in the textbook. Add time estimates, which will always be approximate and flexible in order to cater for the needs of your learners and any unexpected occurrences.
5. Note down any resources that you will need for the lesson. This includes things that you need to make, such as **flashcards**, or resources that you need to bring to the lesson, such as books or real objects (**realia**) from home.

In most countries, the Ministry of Education has a recommended format for lesson plans. At the top, there are usually statistics and information about the lesson, the learners and the objectives. Below this there is usually a table that shows the different stages of the lesson. Here is an example lesson plan from Zambia, which also includes a lesson evaluation section at the end:

MINISTRY OF EDUCATION
BASIC SCHOOL LESSON PLAN
TEACHER'S NAME: DATE:
CLASS: DURATION:
SUBJECT: NO. OF PUPILS IN CLASS:
TOPIC:
SUB-TOPIC:
REFERENCE:
TEACHING/LEARNING RESOURCES:
RATIONALE:
OBJECTIVES: By the end of the lesson …
PRE-REQUISITE SKILLS AND KNOWLEDGE:

Time/Stage	Teaching/Learning activities	Learning points
Before (Introduction)		
During (Development)		
After (Conclusion)		
LESSON EVALUATION:		

If you find planning difficult, ask an experienced teacher or your head teacher to help you. If you have to prepare a detailed plan for every lesson, it is a good idea to build up a list of plans for the whole academic year. This way, you will have less work if you teach the same level the following year, and you can also share your plans with other teachers.

Conclusion

In this chapter we have learnt the following:
- how the process of planning begins with the curriculum and ends with the individual lesson plan;
- how to create a scheme of work from the national curriculum;
- how to plan a week's lessons;
- the different ways that experienced and new teachers plan lessons;
- what different types of lesson plan look like.

"Planning is essentially a thinking skill ... imagining the lesson before it happens."

Jim Scrivener[12]

---

12 Scrivener, *Learning Teaching*, 109.

A6 – Classroom Management and Behaviour Management

In this chapter:

- Two types of management
- Classroom management and the activity cycle
- Behaviour management
- Clear routines
- Clear rules
- Rewards for good behaviour
- Sanctions for bad behaviour
- Ineffective sanctions
- Practical task: Mgeni's class
- Commentary to practical task: Mgeni's class

 **Reflective task**

1. *What classroom rules do you have for your learners?*
2. *What punishment do you think is effective for bad behaviour?*
3. *Do you give rewards for good behaviour? Why?/Why not?*

Two types of management

This chapter focuses on the organisational skills that are important in our day-to-day teaching. These skills can be divided into two overlapping areas: classroom management and behaviour management. We will use the term **classroom management** to refer to our organisation and control of the *activities* that happen in class. This includes giving instructions, **monitoring** learners when they are doing an exercise, and organising feedback to activities. In contrast to this, we will use the term **behaviour management** to refer to our organisation and control of the *learners* to make sure that activities go well and we achieve our objectives for each lesson.

Classroom management and the activity cycle

Most of the activities that our learners do in English lessons have three stages. Together these stages happen in a regular order that we can call an **activity cycle**.

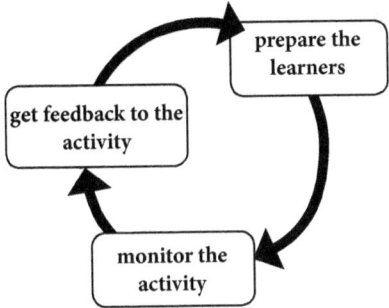

Fig. A6.1: THE ACTIVITY CYCLE

If each of the three stages in the activity cycle is done well, the activity usually goes well and our lesson is more likely to meet its objectives. Let us look at what should happen at each stage:

Prepare the learners

The most important part of the preparation stage is your instruction. However, before you give it, you should introduce the activity and, if necessary, teach any important language that the learners may need during the activity. This may be vocabulary in a reading or listening text or useful expressions for a speaking or writing activity. Your instruction should come next. If possible, give the instruction in English to provide listening practice for your learners. Here are three tips for giving instructions:

1. Get the attention of all the learners. Make sure everyone is listening.
2. Use imperatives to give the instruction. Explain what to do, how to do it and give a **time frame**. Speak loud and clear. For example, *"Tell your partner what you are going to do on Saturday. Work in pairs. You have five minutes."*
3. Do an example or a demonstration. For a **gap-fill** exercise, you can elicit the answer to the first question from the learners, or you can demonstrate how to answer a discussion question yourself.

In some situations it may be necessary to give the instruction in the **mother tongue**. For example, if the instruction is very complex, or if your learners are still at a very elementary level of English. As their English improves you can gradually increase the number of instructions you give in English. See *Chapter A7 – Use of the Mother Tongue in English Language Learning* for more on this.

Monitor the activity

When learners are doing an activity, the teacher should **monitor** them carefully. This is important both if they are working individually or in pairs and groups. There are five things we should do when we monitor an activity:

- make sure all learners are **on task** (i.e. they are doing the activity correctly) and working appropriately;
- provide help to any pairs or groups who are finding the activity difficult;
- make a note of any important or common mistakes for correction later;
- assess how well the learners are completing the activity;
- decide when to move on to feedback.

Do not interrupt pairs or groups who are working well when you monitor – just observe how they are doing. You will probably have both strong and weak learners in your class. If so, remember that you can challenge the stronger learners more by giving them a longer activity or even an extra activity to do if they finish early. This is called **differentiation**. Even if you do not have extra activities, you can differentiate by getting the strong learners to help the weak learners or to write their answers on the chalkboard once they have finished.

Get feedback to the activity

There are two common types of **feedback** in English lessons:

Feedback to check the answers

If an activity has right and wrong answers, we must check these answers for the learners to learn from the activity. This could be an exercise to practise grammar or vocabulary, or a reading comprehension activity. It is important to elicit answers (and sometimes reasons) from learners, then ask others if they agree before we give the correct answer.

Feedback after a speaking or writing practice activity

There are not always right or wrong answers to this type of activity, so we should get a few learners to tell the class what they discussed, what they wrote, or what conclusions they made. It is not necessary to get all the pairs/learners to provide feedback. We are looking for a 'sample' of what they did.

During feedback, we can provide correction of any common mistakes. For example, we can write a few errors on the chalkboard and ask the learners to correct them. Both during and after feedback, we should always praise learners for their answers.

There is an example activity cycle for a listening lesson in *Chapter C5 – Teaching Listening*.

Behaviour management

Effective behaviour management is an essential skill that all primary and secondary teachers must master, a skill that usually improves with experience. The way that you manage your learners' behaviour will always depend on your teaching context, including the age of the learners, the size of the classes and the type of school that you work in. However, it will also depend partly on how effectively you manage your classes and involve learners in the lesson. Behaviour management is not only about punishment. Good teachers also provide **rewards** for good behaviour to ensure that all their learners are engaged and motivated to learn. Probably the first step to effective behaviour management is to learn the names of all your learners. If your classes are small, this should not be difficult, but if they are large, it can be quite a challenge. However, it is a challenge that you should meet if you really want to understand what makes your learners behave the way they do.

Let us now look at four important areas of behaviour management: clear routines, clear rules, rewards for good behaviour and the sanctions we can use to deal with bad behaviour.

Clear routines

All good teachers have clear routines to their lessons every day. The learners know these routines, why they are done, and how to participate in them. We can give responsibility for different activities to different learners. Here are some examples of clear routines:

- Take the register (roll call) at the same time and in the same way every day.
- Have different **monitors** for different activities. For example a 'board monitor' (who cleans the chalkboard), a 'homework monitor' (who collects in homework) and a '**textbook** monitor' (who hands out or collects in textbooks).
- Organise **pairwork** and **groupwork** in the same way each lesson (See Chapter A3 – Child-centred Learning for more on how to do this).
- Give roles to different learners in groupwork activities. For example: team secretary, team leader or **language policeman** (see Practical Task: Do the right thing in Chapter A7 – Using the Mother Tongue in English Language Learning for more on language policemen).
- Establish a clear system for rewards and sanctions.

Whenever you want to change your routines, or to take a break from the routines for a lesson, do not forget to tell your learners and provide a reason if possible.

Clear rules

Rules on behaviour should be made clear to your learners at the beginning of each academic year. At higher levels, you can negotiate and agree your rules with the learners. For example, in the first week you can create a **classroom contract** and display it in the classroom all year. If somebody breaks a promise on the contract, you can point to it to remind them and get an apology. Remember that you must also apologise if you break your promises on the contract!

Classroom Contract
Class 3B

The Learners	The Teacher
We agree to:	I agree to:
1. speak only English during speaking practice activities	1. share my lesson aims at the start of each lesson
2. work together as a team	2. be punctual and well prepared for every lesson
3. do our homework on time	3. mark writing work within three days of receiving it
4. ask questions when we don't understand something	4. include at least one game or song in every lesson
5. learn 20 new words every week	

Fig. A6.2: SAMPLE CLASSROOM CONTRACT (SECONDARY SCHOOL)

Classroom rules, along with more general school rules help the learners to understand the difference between good and bad behaviour. As teachers, we should manage both of these consistently (i.e. we should apply the rules the same way at all times with all learners, like a good judge or football referee). The best way to do this is to give **rewards** for good behaviour, and to use (negative) **sanctions** (traditionally called 'punishments') to deal with bad behaviour.

Rewards for good behaviour

The most important reward that we can use with our learners is **praise**. You should praise them both for trying, and for succeeding. We can praise the learners in many ways:

- compliments from the teacher: *"Good!" "Well done!" "Good try!" "Excellent."*;
- actions such as giving the learner a high five, or shaking her hand;
- praise from other learners (called **peer-praise**): *"Everybody clap your hands for Simon."*;
- self-praise: *"Take a bow." "Give your team a point."*;
- encouragement: *"Nearly correct. Can you try again?" "Can anybody help her?"*;
- group praise at the end of the lesson: *"You all worked very hard today. Well done!"*.

Remember that there is a skill to praising learners. It is important to show that you mean what you say by smiling and sounding happy. If praise is not sincere, it is less effective.

If we want to give special rewards for very good behaviour we can use prizes and **privileges**. All parents use these. Prizes include food (a sweet) or presents (a flower or a book). Most of us cannot afford to give prizes every day, but we can use them on special occasions, for example after a **revision** test, an exam or a particularly challenging lesson.

Privileges are special opportunities to do things that the learners enjoy. We can give privileges to the whole class, to a group of learners, or to individuals, and use them to motivate learners to behave well. Examples of privileges are:

- **Whole class privilege:** *"If you do the reading activity well, we will play a game for the last five minutes of the lesson."*
- **Group privilege:** *"The team that speaks the most English during the groupwork activity will perform their conversation for the whole class."*
- **Individual privilege:** *"The student who improves the most in the revision test will be the textbook monitor for next week."*

Sanctions for bad behaviour

Sanctions (also called 'punishments' or, more correctly, 'negative sanctions') are given to learners who have behaved badly. Before we give a learner a sanction, there are two things we should do if possible:

- Make it clear that the behaviour is wrong. For example, when we say: *"Stop that!"*; *"Don't take her pen!"*; *"Walk, don't run, please!"*

- Give a clear warning. For example, *"David, if you do that again, you will not be able to play with the other children during the morning break."*

If a child does not heed the warning, you must give the sanction. If you do not, future warnings will not be effective. All learners and their parents should know the possible sanctions for bad behaviour. A learner must always understand the reason for the sanction. Here is a list of possible sanctions, from least serious to most serious:

1. **Verbal reprimand**

Do this after a lesson, not in front of other learners. Ask the learner what he did, why he did it, and either elicit or explain why it was wrong. Listen to any excuse he wants to make and give an honest response. Get him to apologise and to promise to improve in future.

2. **Giving work**

If a learner has not done some work (e.g. homework or project work), or has done it badly, ask them to repeat it and bring it to you for checking.

3. **Break time exclusion**

This is when a learner is not allowed to participate in a break (morning, afternoon or lunch break). At this time they go to a specific room, where they study under supervision. Always give them something useful to do.

4. **School or class community service**

This is when a learner does something useful for the school, such as picking up litter, fetching water or cleaning the classroom. It can be done during breaks, after school or even at weekends. Inform parents if it is outside of normal school hours.

5. **Detention and letter to parents**

Detention is when a learner stays at school for an extra period at the end of the day. A teacher supervises detention, which can be organised for the same day each week. Learners in detention do extra work. Usually the teacher who gives the sanction also gives the work. You should inform the parents by writing an official school letter that learners must take home for their parents to sign and return.

6. **Meeting with parents and the learner**

This should only take place after a repetition of bad behaviour. The teacher or head teacher asks the parents to come to school. The teacher explains about the learner's misbehaviour. This leads to a discussion and recommendations are made for improvement.

7. **Daily Report**

A serious sanction. The head teacher gives a learner a report card that each teacher must sign at the end of each lesson, and write a comment on the learner's behaviour. Once a week the head teacher meets the learner to discuss the report card. Parents may also sign the report card to say they have seen it. The learner stays on report until his/her behaviour improves.

8. Suspension

A very serious sanction. After meeting the parents and the learner, the head teacher decides that the learner is not allowed to attend school for a period of time. This may be anything between one day and two weeks.

Ineffective sanctions

Sanctions are only effective if the learners understand that their behaviour is not acceptable. If you behave in a similar way, they will think that their behaviour is acceptable. For example, if a learner hits another learner, you cannot hit them and tell them that it is wrong to hit somebody! The following two sanctions are not effective and violate the *United Nations Convention on the Rights of the Child*. [13]

Corporal punishment

When a teacher hits or hurts a learner physically, including using a stick, or an **endurance punishment**, such as making them squat in an uncomfortable position for a long time.

Humiliation

When we display a learner being punished in front of other learners. This encourages children to laugh at somebody else's misfortunes, which is also unacceptable behaviour.

Remember to consult your Ministry of Education about punishments. They will probably have an official policy on what you can and cannot do legally.

Practical task: Mgeni's class

Mgeni, a new teacher has a 'problem class.' Read what she said and then answer the questions that follow:

> "I'm having problems with one of my classes at the moment. Whenever I try to do groupwork or pairwork, it starts off well. Then after a few minutes they all get very loud and some of the students at the back of the class start speaking in their mother tongue. I always try to give a clear **time frame** for the activities, but some groups take much more time, and some groups even do the wrong exercise!
>
> I think there are three main troublemakers, who always sit together at the back of the class. I separate them for groupwork, but then they make the other students behave badly. Last Monday, these three did not do their homework. When they showed their empty exercise books, the other children just laughed. I made them all kneel in the playground for 30 minutes. But it didn't help because on Wednesday they did not do their homework again! So now I do less groupwork and give less homework. The other children are complaining, but I do not know what to do!"

---

13   United Nations, "United Nations Convention on the Rights of the Child (UNCRC)."

1. What problems does Mgeni have? Why does she have these problems?
2. Think of several recommendations that you would like to make to Mgeni to help her solve her problems.
3. Working in pairs, imagine that one of you is Mgeni and the other one is her friend, a more experienced teacher. **Role play** a conversation in which the experienced teacher gives Mgeni advice.

Commentary to practical task: Mgeni's class

1. Mgeni seems to be having a number of problems with both classroom management and behaviour management, which require separate solutions:
   - Her learners probably do not understand her instructions very well if some groups are doing the wrong exercise.
   - She is forgetting to check they are **on task** when she monitors. Some groups are finishing faster than others, which may also be caused by ineffective monitoring or perhaps by her choice of learners in each group.
   - She complains about volume levels and use of the mother tongue. This may be because the learners are enjoying the group activities, and forgetting to use English.
   - Her choice of punishment for the three troublemakers is probably not a good idea. Sometimes disruptive learners enjoy public punishment, and humiliation does not set a good example.

2. Four useful recommendations for Mgeni are:
   - After you give an instruction, do an example or a demonstration and then ask one of the stronger learners to repeat the instruction in the mother tongue so everyone can hear.
   - Monitor more carefully. First check if the learners are on task. If not, help them. Notice how each group is doing. If necessary, help the weaker groups more or give stronger groups an extra question to do.
   - Before group work, tell the class that they should speak quietly and use only English. Notice which learners are first to raise their voices or switch to the mother tongue. Speak to these learners after class. Remember to praise the class when group work goes well.
   - With your three troublemakers, begin with Sanctions 1 and 2 from the list above. After class one day, discuss their bad behaviour (in the mother tongue if you can) and ask why they are misbehaving. Ask them to do the work they have not done and give a clear date for them to show it to you. Then explain which sanction you will use if their bad behaviour continues, and why.

Conclusion

In this chapter we have learnt the following:
- there is a difference between classroom management and behaviour management;
- how the three key stages to the management of activities are linked together;
- how to give instructions, monitor activities and get feedback to activities effectively;
- how to establish clear routines and why these routines are important;
- how to establish clear rules for learners' behaviour;
- how to reward good behaviour and how to use sanctions for bad behaviour;
- why some punishments are not effective and should not be used.

"The greatest sign of success for a teacher ... is to be able to say, 'The children are now working as if I did not exist'."

Maria Montessori[14]

---

14 Montessori, *The Absorbent Mind*, 283.

A7 – Use of the Mother Tongue in English Language Learning

In this chapter:

- What do we mean by 'use of the mother tongue'?
- The current situation
- Practical task: Do the right thing
- Commentary to practical task: Do the right thing
- Guidelines for using mother tongue
- The mother tongue as a learning resource

What do we mean by 'use of the mother tongue'?

The **mother tongue** is the first language that a child learns at home. This is usually the language of the parents or another **caregiver**. Sometimes children learn two or more languages at home – these are all mother tongues. Often the language used at home is also the language used in the local community, but this can also be different, especially in towns and cities, meaning that many children in Africa grow up learning several languages naturally. In this chapter, we will use the term 'mother tongue' to refer both to languages learnt at home and to other **community languages** that are shared by learners in the classroom, such as Kiswahili in East Africa or Fula/Fulfulde in parts of West Africa.

In many countries, especially in primary school, the mother tongue is often used to teach other subjects, such as maths, science or social studies. Some teachers of English also make use of the mother tongue in the following ways:

- they communicate with their learners in the mother tongue, rather than in English (e.g. when giving instructions);
- they allow their learners to communicate with each other in the mother tongue during English lessons (e.g. when doing a grammar exercise in pairs);
- they use the mother tongue to help learners to understand English (e.g. when the teacher translates a word from English into the mother tongue);
- they allow their learners to use the mother tongue when taking notes (e.g. the learners write down new English vocabulary with translations in the mother tongue).

These examples are the most obvious ones. However, there are other ways that the mother tongue may be used by teachers of English. For example, some **textbooks** include explanations of grammar in the mother tongue, or sometimes teachers think about differences between their learners' mother tongue and English when planning lessons.

 **Reflective task**

In which of these situations do you use or allow your learners to use the mother tongue?

Tick one box in each row. If you tick 'sometimes' or 'occasionally', exactly what situations do you use it in? If you tick always or never, say why?

Statement	always	sometimes	occasionally	never
I use the mother tongue when I am giving instructions.				
I use the mother tongue for classroom language (e.g. "Good morning, pupils." "Sit down." etc.).				
I use the mother tongue to translate the meaning of new vocabulary to my learners.				
I allow my learners to use the mother tongue during English speaking practice activities.				
I use the mother tongue when I am presenting my lesson objectives to my learners.				
I use the mother tongue to explain grammar to my learners.				
I allow my learners to use the mother tongue when they are doing a grammar exercise in pairs.				
I think about differences between the mother tongue and English when I am preparing my lessons.				

We will return to this table later in the chapter.

The current situation

For many years there has been a lot of discussion and debate on the following question:

Should teachers use the mother tongue when teaching English?

Many factors influence our individual opinions as teachers, such as national policy documents, the languages in our country and community, advice from school inspectors or head teachers and our own experience in the classroom. Sometimes teachers have no choice. They are told to use only English. Sometimes they are allowed to decide for themselves.

Often teachers do not like to admit that they use the mother tongue when teaching English. Some think that it is old-fashioned to do so, although this is not true. An increasing number of respected and influential academics and teacher trainers are arguing for its use in foreign language learning,[15] with "some researchers and practitioners … claiming that strictly monolingual learning environments may actually be detrimental to language learning."[16] Many experienced teachers have learnt this from experience, and make appropriate use of the mother tongue as a resource for learning. So let us replace the question above with a more useful question:

How should we use the mother tongue when teaching English?

As teachers, we need to think about this question carefully, because there are helpful ways to use the mother tongue, and unhelpful ways to use it.

Practical task: Do the right thing

Read the opinions of eight different teachers below. They are all talking about using the mother tongue in their class. Do you think they are doing the right thing? Why? Why not?

"I sometimes use the mother tongue to explain vocabulary, but only difficult words. For easy words, such as objects or actions, I just draw or show them and say the English word."

Aster

"I use the mother tongue a lot so that all my students understand what I am explaining. As a result, they all do quite well in the exams, although they are not very good at speaking English."

Ogot

---

15 Cook, "Going beyond the Native Speaker in Language Teaching"; Deller and Rinvolucri, *Using the Mother Tongue*; Prodromou, "The Role of the Mother Tongue in the Classroom"; Widdowson, *Defining Issues in English Language Teaching*; Butzkamm and Caldwell, *The Bilingual Reform: A Paradigm Shift in Foreign Language Teaching*; Cook, *Translation in Language Teaching*.
16 Kerr, *Translation and Own-Language Activities*, 2.

Julie

"I never use the mother tongue. If you use the mother tongue, the students become lazy and just wait for the translation. My way forces the students to think in English."

"When my learners do English speaking practice in pairs I never allow them to use the mother tongue. I employ one or two of the learners as **language policemen**, and they **monitor** the other students to stop them using the mother tongue."

Abdullah

"I use the mother tongue sometimes, but I always use English for classroom language or everyday instructions. My students understand commands like: 'Open your books.' or 'Compare your answers.' They also ask questions in English, such as 'Can I go out, please?'"

Saran

"Sometimes, when I'm teaching science or social studies, I don't have time to let them read a text in English. I just translate it or explain it in the mother tongue. This way, it's fast and they all understand. Then I make them copy it into their notebooks in English."

Charles

"I teach year one in primary school. The pupils are very nervous when they start school, so I use the mother tongue to explain to the students what we are doing, why and how, and to check they understand what I am teaching."

Fatima

"Sometimes I get the students to translate sentences as an exercise. They notice the differences between English and their mother tongue which helps them to understand difficult grammar."

Marcell

Commentary to practical task: Do the right thing

Aster

This is a good idea. The mother tongue can be very useful for teaching difficult vocabulary. We can all teach 'cup' with a picture, or 'swim' with an action, but it is difficult to teach a word like 'assume' or 'even' to low level learners using these methods. You can use translation in these situations, but you can also give an example sentence in English, to show how to use the word.

Ogot

Many exams in Africa are written tests with lots of grammar exercises and reading comprehension. Ogot's method probably helps many of his learners to pass these exams. However, it sounds like he does not do much speaking practice in English. More communicative speaking practice can help them to learn faster (see *How do children learn languages?* in *Chapter A2 – Your Learners*). Furthermore, if he does not speak to them in English, they do not get much listening practice, so they probably have a poor understanding of spoken English. Ogot should try doing more speaking and listening activities. They will probably learn everything faster if he does.

Julie

Julie's learners will get a lot more listening practice than Ogot's learners, which is good. However, Julie should remember that her job is not to force them to think in English, but to train them to use English. This is a slow, gradual process which will take many years. Slower learners in her class may find her lessons too difficult, and give up. It is true that learners can become lazy if lessons are not challenging, but the activities we do influence this more than our choice of language.

Abdullah

Abdullah is doing the right thing. Learners should avoid using the mother tongue during English speaking practice activities. Abdullah's idea of using language police is useful in large classes. In smaller classes the teacher can make sure they all use English.

Saran

Saran is doing the right thing. Classroom language involves natural communication, just like language used at home. It is frequently repeated, so children can learn it easily. Saran's learners can learn important grammar (for example question forms), vocabulary, and also functional language (for example, making requests) from this classroom language.

Charles

This is not a good idea. By the end of the lesson, the learners will probably have notes in English that they do not understand, and they may forget Charles's explanation. They will also need him to translate future texts, so they are dependent on him. Charles should first teach difficult vocabulary from the text, and then give them comprehension questions to answer while they read in English. Although this method will take more time at first, the learners' reading skills will improve and their speed will increase as they learn more vocabulary. See *Chapter C9 – CLIL: Content and Language Integrated Learning* for ideas on teaching other subjects in English.

Fatima

This is a good idea. Many children find their first term at school stressful. It is important for them to understand why they are at school and what they are learning, which can only be explained using the mother tongue at this age. We can use it to train them, to encourage them and to **praise** them. To start with, we can use both mother tongue and English for classroom language and then reduce the mother tongue as soon as the children understand the English.

Marcell

This is a useful way to use the mother tongue. Although we should always use a variety of activity types, sentence translation is good for checking understanding, and helps them to notice grammatical differences between English and their first language.

Now look back at your choices in the *Reflective task* at the start of the chapter on page 56.

1. Can you see any similarities or differences between your opinion and the opinions of these eight teachers?
2. Do you agree with the advice given to these eight teachers?

Guidelines for using the mother tongue

Let us put together all the advice provided so far. Here is the table from the *Reflective task* above. It was completed by an upper primary teacher of English who works in a public school and uses a sensible balance of English and mother tongue. Teachers of lower levels may need to use more mother tongue, and teachers at higher levels can use more English.

Statement	always	sometimes	occasionally	never	comments
I use the mother tongue when I am giving instructions.			✓		Mainly at the start of the year or when I am giving difficult instructions.
I use the mother tongue for classroom language (e.g. "Good morning, pupils." "Sit down.", etc.).				✓	My learners and I use only English for classroom language.

A7 – Use of the Mother Tongue in English Language Learning

Statement	always	sometimes	occasionally	never	comments
I use the mother tongue to translate the meaning of new vocabulary to my learners.			✓		I use mother tongue for abstract or difficult vocabulary only. Otherwise I use English.
I allow my learners to use the mother tongue during English speaking practice activities.				✓	I stress 'English only' for these activities.
I use the mother tongue when I am presenting my lesson objectives to my learners.		✓			I use English if it's simple and mother tongue if I don't think they'll understand the English.
I use the mother tongue to explain grammar to my learners.			✓		Only for difficult grammar, or comparison of the two languages.
I allow my learners to use the mother tongue when they are doing a grammar exercise in pairs.		✓			I think quiet discussion helps them to analyse grammar effectively.
I think about differences between the mother tongue and English when I am preparing my lessons.	✓				I always think carefully about differences between languages. This helps me to anticipate difficulties and find links that can help learning.

The mother tongue as a learning resource

One of the reasons why the mother tongue is often excluded from the language classroom is because native-speaker teachers (e.g. British or American teachers), who often may not know their learners' mother tongues, cannot use it. As a result, teacher training methodology and teaching materials (especially textbooks) have avoided techniques and activities that relied on use of the mother tongue. It is sometimes also assumed that, because some native speaker teachers do not use the mother tongue, no teachers should use it. However, as a number of experts in the field of language teaching have shown, the mother tongue can be a useful resource to help us to teach more effectively.[17] If you are teaching in a context where you do not have many other resources, the mother tongue of your learners, if you know it, may be the most useful one you have.

When deciding which language to use, we should always remember two basic rules:

- **English first:** Always use English if possible. If you are not sure, try English first and give learners time to try to understand before using the mother tongue.
- **Reduce your use of mother tongue as the learners improve:** Use the mother tongue more when learners are beginning to learn English, and less as the learners improve.

Teachers who can speak the mother tongue of their learners can do many activities in class to help their learners to learn English more effectively. Here are some ideas:

1. Translation challenge

This is good for revision of grammar. Write several sentences on the chalkboard, either in English or in the mother tongue, put the learners in pairs or small groups and give them a few minutes to translate the sentences into the other language. Then check the answers. Remember that there can sometimes be more than one way to translate a sentence, so encourage discussion about different possible translations, which helps the learners to notice differences between languages and even different understandings of a sentence.

2. Bilingual vocabulary box

This is good for helping learners to learn new vocabulary. Each lesson, one learner (the 'vocabulary box monitor') writes any new English words on small pieces of paper and writes the translation on the other side. All the pieces of paper go into a box at the end of the lesson. At the beginning of the next lesson, a different vocabulary box monitor takes words from the box, and asks his/her classmates to translate them, either from English into mother tongue, or vice versa. The words are kept in the box for the whole term or academic year. See *Chapter C12 – 10 Essential Resources to Create* for details of how to make a Vocabulary Box, and more ideas for using it.

3. Checking for understanding

Teach a new area of grammar or an item of vocabulary without using the mother tongue. After you have finished, ask the learners: *"How do we say this sentence in our mother tongue?"* or *"How do we express this idea in our mother tongue?"* If they provide a good translation or explanation, it demonstrates they understand it. This method also helps weaker learners, who may not have understood the English explanation to understand the meaning and usage of the new language. You can also do this with instructions; give the instruction in English and then ask for a volunteer to repeat the instruction in the mother tongue. This is especially useful for complex instructions or when you are still training learners to understand instructions in English.

---

17 Deller and Rinvolucri, *Using the Mother Tongue*; Butzkamm and Caldwell, *The Bilingual Reform: A Paradigm Shift in Foreign Language Teaching*; Turnbull and Dailey-O'Cain, *First Language Use in Second and Foreign Language Learning*; Cook, *Translation in Language Teaching*; Kerr, *Translation and Own-Language Activities*.

4. **Keyword search**

When you are doing a reading lesson, choose several important or difficult words from the English text. Write translations of these words on the chalkboard in the mother tongue. Tell the learners to work in pairs or small groups to find these words in English in the text. This activity helps the learners to work out the meaning of vocabulary from context.

5. **Learning to think in English**

Give the learners a writing task to do in pairs (e.g. write an email to a friend and tell them about your village/town). Allow them to make notes (and if they want, to write a first draft) in the mother tongue. They should then check any words or expressions in their notes or first draft that they do not know in English, either using a dictionary or by asking you. After this, they write their final draft in English. This process helps learners to discover new vocabulary and expressions in English, and is often useful for slower learners.

There are many more ways that you can use the mother tongue when teaching English. For more ideas, see *Using the Mother Tongue. Making the Most of the Learner's Language* by Deller and Rinvolucri.

Conclusion

In this chapter we have learnt the following:
- many teachers around the world use the learners' mother tongue to help them to teach English;
- the mother tongue can help us to translate difficult vocabulary, teach difficult grammar, give difficult instructions and to make our lesson objectives clear to our pupils;
- the mother tongue should not be used during speaking practice activities or for everyday classroom language; train your learners to use English in these situations;
- we should always try to use English first, whenever possible;
- we should reduce the use of the mother tongue as our learners' English improves;
- the mother tongue can be used as a **learning resource**.

"If you talk to a man in a language he understands, that goes to his head. If you talk to him in his language, that goes to his heart."

Nelson Mandela

Part B – Literacy

What does Part B cover?

Part B of this book covers the topic of early **literacy** (learning to read and write). It has been written with the English language in mind, but many of the concepts and methods described will also apply to early literacy in the child's **mother tongue** and will be useful to teachers who teach the mother tongue in primary years 1 – 3.

What can I expect to learn in Part B?

In *Part B* you can expect to learn about the three important stages to literacy learning, experiencing them through the eyes of two learners from Nigeria. You can expect to learn what phonics is, how and why it helps children to learn to read and write in English and how you can use phonics theory in your lessons. You can also expect to learn how you can better understand and help children who have difficulty learning to read and write and how the parents and the community can support early literacy learning. There is also a practical resources section at the end of *Part B* to give you simple, effective ideas that you can try out in your class.

B1 – Introduction to Literacy

In this chapter:

- Three phases of literacy
- Two case studies
- Practical task: Obi and Beatrice
- Commentary to practical task: Obi and Beatrice

Three phases of literacy

Learning to read and write (**literacy**) is probably the most important part of any child's education. Without these two skills, she or he cannot learn other subjects and cannot pass exams. Children learning to read and write in Africa face some of the greatest challenges in the world:

- large classes where learners often cannot get the individual help they need;
- few **learning resources** such as alphabet letter cards or resources for writing and drawing;
- few printed resources, such as children's books, **textbooks** or posters;
- some children have to learn to read and write in a foreign language, such as English;
- parents who sometimes cannot help because they cannot read or write;
- a curriculum that may demand faster progress than they can achieve.

All children need to pass through three important phases along the road to literacy:

- **The pre-alphabet phase:** what children need to learn before they are ready to start learning the letters of the alphabet
- **The alphabet phase:** how children learn to link written letters to spoken sounds in English
- **The sight word phase:** how children begin to read whole words and progress to full literacy

In this literacy module you will learn about these three phases in detail, and how **phonics** can be a useful tool to help learners to read and write in English. It is important to remember that English is one of the most difficult languages to learn to read and write because the relationship between the letters and the sounds is not always straightforward. While phonics is a useful tool, it needs to be balanced with meaningful reading and writing, focused on pleasure and enjoyment and not just on understanding words.

Two case studies

In order to understand how different the contexts of African teachers can be, let us look at two learners in two classes in two different parts of the same country, Nigeria. We will refer back to these learners and their teachers of English in this module of the book.

Case Study 1: Beatrice, from Awai

Beatrice lives in a small village called Awai in rural Nigeria. Her **mother tongue** is only spoken by 12,000 people in a few villages. She lives with four brothers and sisters, her parents, who are farmers, and her grandmother. At home she has no electricity, no desk to write on and no books. Her parents want her to do well at school, but they cannot read or write, and do not have enough money to buy what she needs. Like all children in the village she has to do many chores when she comes home from school. Beatrice walks three kilometres to her primary school each day, where she studies in year one. She has not attended nursery school. She is one of 38 children in her class.

Her teacher of English, Mr. Okoro, comes from a different part of Nigeria and does not speak Beatrice's mother tongue. He is a new teacher with very little experience. He teaches them everything in English, and although he tries to teach as well as he can, he cannot help them when they do not understand. His only reading resource is the English textbook. There are no other books or resources for him to use in class.

Case study 2: Obi, from Ibadan

Obi lives in the city of Ibadan, and speaks Yoruba, one of Nigeria's most common languages. He lives with his sister and his parents in a small house. His father works in an office in the town, and his mother works in a shop. Both can read and write well. At home, they have a desk to do homework on and interesting books to read. His father sometimes helps him with homework, and his mother often reads stories to him. He attended nursery school for one year, and is now in year one of a primary school near his house, where he is one of 56 children in his class.

His teacher of English, Mrs. Ekala, also speaks Yoruba. She has taught at the school for 18 years. When necessary, she explains ideas and gives instructions in Yoruba, which Obi, and most of the children in the class speak well. He is also learning to read and write in Yoruba at the same time. They have English textbooks, some useful posters and resources in the classroom, and there is a school library where the teachers can take children for reading lessons.

Practical task: Obi and Beatrice

Write a list of the advantages that Obi has, when compared to Beatrice, that may help him to learn to read and write more quickly. Write them in order of importance, with the most important ones first.

Commentary to practical task: Obi and Beatrice

Every child learns differently. Perhaps Beatrice will learn to read and write faster than Obi. However, research has shown that a child's success at school depends partly on environment, parents and other things that the teacher cannot control.[18] Obi has advantages in five important areas, in order of importance:

1. **Parents**

Obi's parents can read. They read stories to him and help him with homework. He understands that written language is an important means of communication and is used by his parents at work. He enjoys the stories they read, and wants to read them himself. Beatrice may not really understand what written language is or why it is important. She does not know that it can be enjoyable.

2. **Previous Education**

Obi has already spent a year studying in his mother tongue at nursery school, and enjoys learning. He can probably already recognise his written name, and remembers some of the letters of the alphabet. He has also learnt a little English, and knows that his father uses this language at work. Beatrice did not go to nursery school.

3. **Home environment**

Obi has time, energy, space, light, resources and help to do homework and reading properly. Beatrice often has to do small chores for her mother when she gets home, and so it is often dark before she can do her homework. Sometimes she cannot find her exercise book or a pen, and nobody can help her when she has difficulty.

4. **Teacher and Language**

Obi's teacher is experienced and she can communicate with her learners in the mother tongue when she needs to. Obi is also learning to read and write Yoruba, which helps him to understand literacy. Beatrice's teacher does not speak her language and she does not speak his. He is teaching her to read and write in a different language, called English, but she does not know why, or understand the words of this language.

5. **School**

Obi's class has plenty of useful books and resources for reading and writing at school. Although Beatrice has fewer pupils in her class, they have few resources. She is rather scared of school; she has heard bad stories from other children, and her older brother failed his exams and stopped studying.

These differences between Obi's and Beatrice's situation show us that two learners in the same country can face very different challenges. Beatrice may be very clever. Perhaps she enjoys school and wants to learn, but the road for her is much more difficult. In the rest of *Part B* we will learn about what both Obi and Beatrice need in order to learn to read and write in English. We will also learn about how both teachers, Mr. Okoro and Mrs. Ekala, can help their pupils.

---

18 Richter, "The Importance of Caregiver-Child Interactions for the Survival and Healthy Development of Young Children. A Review."; Okumu, Nakajjo, and Isoke, "Socio-economic Determinants of Primary School Dropout."

Conclusion

In this chapter we have learnt the following:
- Teachers of English face significant challenges when teaching their pupils to read and write;
- there are three key phases of literacy that learners must go through;
- two learners in the same country can face very different challenges;
- many different things can influence a child's progress in literacy.

B2 – The Pre-alphabet Phase

In this chapter:

- What is the pre-alphabet phase?
- How old are children during this phase?
- What do they already know about language?
- The four areas of literacy awareness
- Your learners' names
- The importance of the mother tongue at the pre-alphabet phase
- How long will the pre-alphabet phase take
- Practical task: Exploring language
- Commentary to practical task: Exploring language

 **Reflective task**

This chapter will answer two important questions:

1. *Why should we prepare children before starting to teach them the letters of an alphabet?*
2. *How can we prepare them?*

Before you read any further, what do you think the answers to these questions are?

What is the pre-alphabet phase?

The pre-alphabet phase is the first phase of learning to read and write. Learners at the pre-alphabet phase are starting to discover:
- why written language is important;
- the role of written language in society;
- the relationship between the language we speak and the language we write.

From research, we know that if we help children to understand the features of language and why it is important, they will learn faster than if we just teach them the alphabet.[19] This is necessary both in English and in the **mother tongue**.

How old are children during this phase?

Most learners are at this phase when they start year one of primary school. Children who have studied in nursery school or kindergarten will probably have made more progress through this phase, and they can help other learners in their class.

---

19 Riley and Reedy, "Communication, Language and Literacy: Learning through Speaking and Listening, Reading and Writing Jeni Riley, 65-100."

What do they already know about language?

When they start school, most children will probably know the following:
- there are different languages, some of which they cannot understand;
- the name of their own language and the names of some other languages including English;
- words are part of language (although they may not know exactly what they are or how to identify them);
- we can use written language to communicate, like spoken language;
- written language is important and useful in society;
- one reason for going to school is to learn how to read and write.

Do you remember Obi and Beatrice from the *Introduction to Literacy*? Obi probably understands all of this, but Beatrice may only understand a few of these things. Children who live in cities like Obi know more about televisions, mobile phones and computers, and how we use them to communicate. Obi will see his parents reading at home, and will understand how it can bring enjoyment. But children who live in rural villages like Beatrice may only know written language from newspapers, handwritten signs and documents. She may not think it is important or interesting, so she may not have much motivation to learn to read or write when she starts school.

It is a good idea to begin **literacy** learning with activities that check and explore what your learners already know about language. Here are some of the things you can do:

- Find out what they know about their own language; its name, the name of other languages in their community, and whether they know any words in these languages (English may be one of these languages, especially in larger cities).
- Get the children to bring to school things from home and the environment that have words on them in any language (e.g. old newspapers, empty food packages, plastic bags).
- Choose some of the most famous product packaging that they know (e.g. a famous washing powder package, a Coca Cola bottle, a biscuit wrapper) and take them to class. Ask the learners to find the big words on the packaging. Ask them what they think these words 'say' (usually this is the name of the product).
- Show them advertisements in newspapers and magazines. Ask them what they can see, what they think these things are and why they are there. After this, you can point at and read the words for them. Then ask what they have learnt from these words.
- Create a class poster with packages, wrappers and other examples of printed text that the learners have brought to class. Write the name of each product next to it.

The four areas of literacy awareness

At the pre-alphabet phase children need to learn about four areas of literacy awareness. They should start learning about these before they start learning the alphabet, and can continue to explore them for their first year of school. It is useful to explore areas one, two and three with the learners at the same time and then to explore area four after this.

1. **Awareness of the role of language in society**

Learners need to learn that:
- 1a. language helps us to communicate what we feel, what we want and what we are thinking;
- 1b. written language and spoken language are both ways of communicating;
- 1c. we can communicate with people who are far away, people we have never met and we can communicate through time (using, for example, mobile phones, newspapers, radio, the Bible and the Koran);
- 1d. as well as being useful, reading and writing can be enjoyable;
- 1e. English plays a specific role in society and it is important for their education and future;
- 1f. each language must be learnt, both the spoken and the written form, and that they are still learning their first language.

2. **Awareness of spoken language (phonological and phonemic awareness)**

Learners need to learn that:
- 2a. we learn to speak the language of our parents naturally;
- 2b. spoken language can be divided into words;
- 2c. these words are made up of separate sounds;
- 2d. we can break up the spoken words and say these sounds separately.

3. **Awareness of written language (graphological awareness)**

Learners need to learn that:
- 3a. a written text or sentence is made up of words which are separated by small spaces;
- 3b. each word is made up of written symbols called letters, which can be counted;
- 3c. there is a limited number of letters in a language (e.g. 26 in English);
- 3d. we read and write these words in a special direction; horizontally from left to right, then down and back to the left at the end of each line;
- 3e. each word is also read from left to right;
- 3f. books are read from front to back, and the spine is on the left of the front cover.

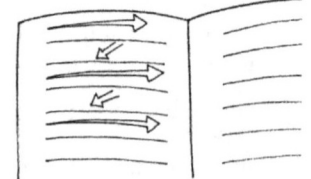

Fig. B2.1: READING DIRECTION

4. **Awareness of the relationship between written and spoken language**

Learners need to learn that:

- 4a. each spoken word can be written down and each written word can be said, both individually and in sentences;
- 4b. the letters in written words are the equivalents of the sounds in spoken words;
- 4c. each sound in a language can be written as a letter;
- 4d. each letter in a language makes a sound;
- 4e. we can combine these letters to make words that we can say.

Note that in a language such as English, **silent letters** and **digraphs** mean that 4c and 4d are not always true, but exceptions to these rules of thumb can be learnt later.

We will look at activities to help our learners learn about these four areas in the Practical Task below.

Your learners' names

The first word that every child should learn to recognise and to write is their own name. It is meaningful and important for them, and it will also be useful when they start to learn the alphabet. Every child should see their own name written somewhere in the classroom, for example on a wall chart, on a desk label or in an area of the classroom where that learner can show his or her work. You should also check that each learner's name is written clearly on their exercise books, either by you or their parents. You should teach the learners to point at it, to find it in a group of words and to write it. Of course, their writing will be far from perfect, and may be difficult to read, but this early practice is very useful. You can also help them to write their name on their work, and praise them for their efforts.

The importance of the mother tongue at the pre-alphabet phase

In order to learn about these four areas of literacy awareness, children need to build on their current understanding. They need to explore the language they already know – their mother tongue. Ideally, this exploration should take place in their mother tongue lessons. If this is not possible (for example if you are teaching English before they have started learning to read and write in their mother tongue), the exploration must take place in their English lessons, with the help of the mother tongue whenever possible. If you do not speak the mother tongue of your learners (like Mr. Okoro, Beatrice's teacher from *Chapter B1 – Introduction to Literacy*) it may be possible to ask for help from a member of the local community or a pupil from a higher class as a **language assistant** for a few lessons (see *Chapter B6 – Parents and the Community in Literacy Learning*). Teachers working in some large cities may find that their learners speak many different languages. In such situations, it is possible to raise parents' awareness of how they can help. For example, you could organise occasional evening workshops for parents and create documents to explain how they can help their children at this important phase in their education.

How long will the pre-alphabet phase take?

There are no clear lines between the three phases of literacy. The pre-alphabet phase slowly changes into the alphabet phase (the next phase), and this change will happen in different ways for each pupil at different times, depending on their age and whether they have studied at nursery school or kindergarten. Before you start to introduce the letters of the alphabet, you should spend at least two weeks developing your learners' literacy awareness until most of them have a good understanding of the four areas of literacy awareness described above. This can happen alongside their general language learning (e.g. learning their first spoken words in English). As they start to learn the letters of the alphabet, they should continue to learn about these four areas.

Practical task: Exploring language

Choose two of the four areas of literacy awareness above. Think of activities that the learners can do to help them to learn about the different ideas in each of the two areas. Draw and complete a table with your ideas, as in the following example:

Area of language awareness: _____		
Learners need to learn that ...	They could learn by doing this activity:	Resources needed:
e.g. 3a A written text or sentence is made up of words which are separated by small spaces.	e.g. Explore school posters and classroom signs that include short sentences. First the teacher can point at and count the words, then learners can stand up and count the words, and finally the learners can discuss and explain how they have separated the words.	e.g. A number of posters with large text written in short sentences, such as classroom signs, reading posters and information signs.

Commentary to practical task: Exploring language

There are many activities that you can do for each area of literacy awareness. Here are a few suggestions for you to try. These should all be done in the mother tongue whenever possible.

Learners need to learn that …	They could learn this by doing this activity:	Resources needed:
1a. Language helps us to communicate what we feel, what we want and what we are thinking.	Come into class one day with sticky tape over your mouth. Try to organise the learners and give an instruction with the tape over your mouth, making sounds, but also using gestures. Then ask a learner to remove the tape. Ask: "Did you understand my instructions? Why not?"	Some sticky tape.
1b. Written language and spoken language are both systems of communication.	The learners tell you the names of five animals – you write these on the chalkboard, then call in another teacher or a learner from a higher class to read the words **out loud**.	Chalkboard, another teacher or learner for a few minutes.
1c. We can communicate with people who are far away, people we have never met and we can communicate through time.	Take the resources to class, ask the learners questions about each one: "What is it? How do your parents use it? Who do they use it to communicate with?"	Mobile phone, radio, newspaper, the Koran and/or Bible, picture of a television, etc.
1d. As well as being useful, reading and writing can be enjoyable.	Show a storybook with pictures (e.g. a **Big Book**; see *Chapter B7*) and tell them the story. Afterwards ask: "Did you enjoy it? Why?"	A short storybook with pictures.
1e. English plays a specific role in their society and it is important to their education and future.	Ask the learners: "What do you know about English? Where does it come from? Where is it used? Do you know anybody who speaks it?" Show pictures of people who speak English (politicians, football players) and explain how and why they use English.	Pictures of famous people from the learners' country and community.
1f. Each language must be learnt, both the spoken and the written form, and that they are still learning their first language.	Show them some objects that they may not know the names of in their own language. Explain what they are and how we use them. Later in the lesson, find out if they remember the names. Ask: "What other words have you learnt recently?"	A few objects (e.g. from the school, parts of a bicycle or farming tools) whose names are new to the learners.

Learners need to learn that ...	They could learn this by doing this activity:	Resources needed:
2a. We learn to speak the language of our parents naturally.	If you have learners who speak different mother tongues at home, ask them questions about this language: "Where did you learn to speak it? Who taught you? How do you say 'mummy'/ 'school'/ 'hello'?"	None.
2b. Spoken language can be divided into words.	Sing a line from a song or **rhyme** they know in their mother tongue. Then sing more slowly and separate out the words. Get them to count them as you sing. Ask: "Can you explain the meaning of some of the words?"	None.
2c. Words are made up of separate sounds.	Take one of the words from the song, and sing it very slowly. Stop after different sounds and ask the learners: "What comes next?"	None.
2d. We can break up spoken words and say these sounds separately.	Choose a learner's name and say it slowly until you separate all the sounds. Get them to do this with their own names. Ask: "Can you count how many sounds are in your name?"	None.
3a. A written text or sentence is made up of words which are separated by small spaces.	Explore school posters and classroom signs that include short sentences. First point at and count the words, then learners can stand up and count the words. Finally ask: "How did you learn to separate the words?"	A number of posters with large text written in short sentences, such as classroom signs, reading posters and information signs.
3b. Each word is made up of written symbols called letters, which can be counted.	Write your name on the chalkboard in big letters, separated clearly. Count the letters. Ask the learners: "How many letters?" Do the same with a selection of their names.	Chalkboard.
3c. There is a limited number of letters in a language (e.g. 26 in English).	Write a simple sentence on the chalkboard. Use a different colour to circle one letter. Teach the name. Ask the learners: "Can you find the same letter somewhere else in the sentence?"	Chalkboard.

Learners need to learn that …	They could learn this by doing this activity:	Resources needed:
3d. We read and write these words in a special direction; horizontally from left to right, then down and back to the left at the end of each line.	Read a short text from a **Big Book**, or from the chalkboard, using your finger to follow your words. Ask a learner: "Can you come and show the direction of the words? Where should you go when you get to the end?"	Large text in Big Book or on chalkboard.
3e. Each word is also read from left to right.	Show a fruit. Ask for the name and write it on the chalkboard in large letters. Read it slowly, **sounding** out and pointing at each letter as you read: "m …a …n …g …o." Ask: "Where did I start? Which way did I go? Where did I finish?"	A few fruit.
3f. Books are read from front to back, starting with the spine on the left.	Put the learners in small groups and give each one a copy of a **textbook**. With your own copy show them the front, and explain how to put it on the desk correctly. Ask them: "Can you find the spine? Can you open the first page? The next page?"	A set of textbooks, any class, any level.
4a. Each spoken word can be written down and each written word can be said.	Ask the learners for the name of an animal. Write it on the chalkboard, saying the name as you do. Ask for more animal names, until you have four. Ask a learner to point at the word 'cat'? Then read the word she pointed at, even if it is a different word. Keep doing this until she points at the right word.	Chalkboard.
4b. The letters in written words are the equivalents of the sounds in spoken words.	Ask a learner with a short name for her name. Say it slowly to separate out the sounds. Write it on the chalkboard, sounding each letter. Then point at the separate letter and ask: "What sound did I say?"	Chalkboard.

Learners need to learn that …	They could learn this by doing this activity:	Resources needed:
4c. Each sound in a language can be written as a letter.	Show the pictures one by one. Point at the words, and ask: "What sound is he/she making? Let's read it slowly: 'Ha ha ha!'" Then ask them to think of a noise we make when we like food, or when we are tired, and write these on the chalkboard.	Several pictures of people and animals making noises, with written versions of these noises. E.g. 'Ha ha ha!' for someone laughing, 'Achoo!' for someone sneezing, etc.
4d. Each letter in a language makes a sound.	Give different **flashcards** to different learners, and ask them to come to the front. Tell individual learners to hold up their flashcards and say the letter sound when they do. Encourage them to say it with you.	Alphabet letter flashcards.
4e. We can combine these letters to make words that we can say.	Give three learners a letter each. Together the letters make a phonetic word (e.g. 'p-e-n'). Tell them to stand in different orders and sound the letters left to right, pointing as you do. Ask each time: "Is that a word?" Keep going until they get the right word order.	Alphabet letter flashcards.

Conclusion

In this chapter we have learnt the following:
- literacy learning begins before children start learning the alphabet;
- children already know some things about written language when they start school;
- some children will start primary school knowing more than others;
- there are four areas of literacy awareness that children need to learn about during the pre-alphabet phase;
- learners' names are very important to them, and they should learn to recognise and write their names during this phase;
- we need to use the mother tongue of our learners at the pre-alphabet phase if possible;
- the pre-alphabet phase changes gradually into the alphabet phase.

B3 – The Alphabet Phase and Phonics

In this chapter:

- When does the alphabet phase start?
- Using the mother tongue to help with English literacy
- Phonics
- The phonic alphabet
- Teaching a new letter using phonics
- Key skills in phonics
- Digraphs, sight words and the magic 'e' rule
- A suggested sequence for phonics teaching
- Handwriting in the alphabet phase
- Practical task: Our first story
- Commentary to practical task: Our first story

 **Reflective task**

What problems do your learners have when learning to read and write the English alphabet?

Think about:

- *letter names*
- *letter pronunciation*
- *spelling*
- *letter combinations (e.g. 'th', 'ee', 'sh')*

When does the alphabet phase start?

The **alphabet phase** of **literacy** learning starts when learners begin to understand the connection between the written letters of the alphabet and sounds in the spoken language. If they have learnt about the four areas of literacy awareness (see previous chapter), they should understand most of the following:

- written language is used to communicate;
- a text is made up of words which are themselves made up of letters;
- how to recognise their name as a written word;
- how we read sentences (left to right), texts (top to bottom) and books (front to back);
- a language has a limited number of written letters that we call the alphabet.

If you do not think your learners understand these ideas yet, try doing some of the activities from *Chapter B2 – The Pre-alphabet Phase* with your learners.

Using the mother tongue to help with English literacy

When we begin teaching children to read and write the English alphabet, it is important to think about how this relates to what they are learning about reading and writing using other written alphabets. In Africa, there are four possible situations:

- **Situation 1: English after mother tongue:** The children are learning the English alphabet after they have learnt the alphabet of their **mother tongue** (or another **community language** such as Kiswahili in East Africa).
- **Situation 2: English alongside mother tongue:** The children are learning the English alphabet at the same time as they are learning the alphabet of their mother tongue or a community language. Obi from *Chapter B1 - Introduction to Literacy* is an example of this.
- **Situation 3: Early literacy in several languages:** On some occasions, children may have to learn to read and write in three or more languages at the same time. In these situations learners will need extra support and more time to learn the different alphabets.
- **Situation 4: English as the first language of literacy:** The children are learning the English alphabet as their first written alphabet. Beatrice from *Chapter B1 - Introduction to Literacy* is an example of this.

Let us look at these situations in a little more detail:

Situation 1: English after mother tongue

Ideally, children should start to read and write in their mother tongue well before they begin to read and write in English. This enables them to learn the links between something new (written symbols) and something familiar (the sounds and words of their mother tongue) before they try to do this with an unfamiliar language. Thus, if you are teaching in situation one, you have a useful advantage. When learners meet a new letter in English, get them to tell you what it is called and what sound it makes in the mother tongue and also to think of example words that begin with this sound. They are then ready to notice similarities and differences in how this letter is used in English. This does not apply if they are learning a different written alphabet for their mother tongue (e.g. Arabic or Ge'ez alphabets; see below).

Situations 2 and 3: English alongside mother tongue/early literacy in several languages

Learning to read and write in English is difficult for all children, including those born in English-speaking countries. It becomes even more confusing for children who have to learn to read and write in two or more languages at the same time. Here are some of the problems that may occur:

- a letter can have different names in different languages;
- in the mother tongue each letter may have just one pronunciation, but not in English;
- sometimes a combination of letters is pronounced very differently in different languages.

It is important to help children with this confusion. They need to understand what is similar and what is different between the languages they are learning. Here are some activities we can do to help with this:

- If they are learning two languages which use the same or similar letters, plan lessons in which they compare the two alphabets. They can make two posters for the classroom; one poster shows letters that have similar pronunciation, and the other poster shows the different letters.
- When you introduce a new letter in English, ask the learners what they know about it in their mother tongue or any other shared language (e.g. How is the letter pronounced? What is it called? What words contain the letter?). You can then compare this to English.
- Show them words that they see every day on advertisements, shops and food packaging. Ask them which language the words are in and how they are pronounced (e.g. telephone, bank, Coca-Cola, bus, etc.).
- If the children learn other languages with a different teacher, discuss their learning with this teacher. You can plan together, and think of how to help them with the letters that the children find confusing.
- If learners are learning more than one alphabet at the same time (e.g. the Latin alphabet for English and the Ge'ez alphabet for Amharic in Ethiopia, or the Arabic alphabet in North Sudan), do activities where learners compare their own names written in the two alphabets to show them how a sound or a word can be written with different alphabets.

Situation 4: English as the first language of literacy

Some African children learn English as their first written language. This includes some children who live in cities where many different languages are spoken at home, and some children whose teacher does not speak their mother tongue, like Mr. Okoro, Beatrice's teacher. In some countries the government chooses to introduce English first.

This situation makes learning to read and write more difficult[20]. This is because the children have to learn to read and write in a language they do not know – the vocabulary, grammar and pronunciation are all new for them as well as the alphabet. If you are teaching in this situation, it is important to spend time helping the learners to understand the meaning of any new words you teach. There are two small advantages for teachers in this situation:

- your learners only need to learn one alphabet at this stage, not two;
- your learners will not confuse pronunciation of words in different languages.

Whenever possible, learners should learn to read and write in their mother tongue first.

Phonics

In English there is no simple relationship between the spoken words and the written words. Some letters have a range of different pronunciations and some sounds can be represented by a number of different letters or letter combinations. In addition to

---

20   Mehrotra, "Education for All"; Ferguson, "The Language of Instruction Issue."

this, traditional letter names in English can be very confusing for learners, especially the names of vowels. This is because the letter name is often different from its most common, or most logical pronunciation. For example, the letter 'a' in English, is often pronounced /æ/ (as in 'ant' or 'hat'), or the letter 'c' is often pronounced /k/ (as in 'cat' or 'cup'). These complexities make learning to read and write in English particularly challenging for learners.

Phonics is a method used widely in the UK, the USA and other countries to help to teach the English alphabet and basic literacy to children. Scientific research has shown that phonics helps children to learn to read and write in English more quickly than using non-phonic methods alone[21]. Phonics is also being used to help children in other countries to learn basic literacy in English as a foreign or second language, including several countries in Africa (e.g. Gambia, Eritrea). Even if your curriculum does not include phonics, you will probably find lots of useful ideas here to help your learners to read and write in English more quickly.

Phonics teaches the children to link letters in the English alphabet to sounds in spoken English and to put these together to make words. It starts by teaching words that have simple pronunciations and then gradually adds rules to enable children to cope with the complexity of English pronunciation more easily. To start with, children learn one common sound for each letter. Here are two vowel examples:

- The sound /æ/ (the first sound in 'ant') is taught for the letter 'a'
- The sound /e/ (the first sound in 'egg') is taught for the letter 'e'

Each consonant is learnt as an isolated sound (with two exceptions). Here are two examples:

- The sound /b/ (the first sound in 'bed') is taught for the letter 'b'
- The sound /l/ (the first sound in 'leg') is taught for the letter 'l'

Note the use of the forward slash sign '/' to show that we are writing phonetic symbols, not letters. Let us look at the whole phonic alphabet.

The phonic alphabet

Letter	Phonetic symbol*	Example words		
a	æ	ant	man	
b	b	bed	web	
c	k	cat	Africa	the same sound as 'k'
d	d	dog	sad	
e	e	egg	bed	
f	f	fat	if	
g	g	get	dog	
h	h	hat	hen	
i	ɪ	in	big	
j	dʒ	jump	just	

---

21 Ehri et al., "Systematic Phonics Instruction Helps Students Learn to Read."

Letter	Phonetic symbol*	Example words	
k	k	king	ask
l	l	leg	hill
m	m	man	am
n	n	not	sun
o	ɒ	on	dog
p	p	pen	stop
r	r	run	crops
s	s	sun	cats
t	t	tap	hat
u	ʌ	up	sun
v	v	vet	vest
w	w	wet	twin
x	ks	box	fix
y	j	yes	yet
z	z	zip	zebra

*The phonetic symbols are taken from the International Phonetic Alphabet and are similar to the symbols used in most English language dictionaries. If you have access to a computer and the internet and you would like to hear these sounds being pronounced, go to YouTube and search for: 'English phonic alphabet' or 'English phonic code'. You will find a link to this in the *Useful Websites and Online Materials* section at the back of this book.

Note the following
- the example words are all phonetic (i.e. they are pronounced using the sounds of the phonic alphabet);
- the letter 'q' is not included here (see Digraphs below);
- you can teach the learners that double consonants are pronounced only once in English (e.g. egg, hill).

Note for teacher trainers

This section on phonics presents a synthetic phonics approach, similar to those used in programmes such as **Jolly Phonics**. *It has been adapted from those used in the UK and the USA to draw on vocabulary that is both higher in frequency and more culturally appropriate for African learners who do not speak English as their first language. The IPA phonemes shown are taken from a standard British English phonemic set, and some (e.g. /ɒ/) will be slightly different in a standard American English phonemic set.*

Learning the phonic alphabet

Children often find it easier to learn the phonic alphabet before they learn letter names. If your learners have already learnt the letter names, no problem. Just explain that each letter has both a name and a sound, just like each animal has a name (e.g. 'cow') and a sound ('moo')!

Phonics encourages children to read and write whole words as soon as possible. For this reason, it is best to teach the letter sounds in groups that make lots of simple words. Here are the first four sound groups, which introduce 20 of the 26 letters in English. Each of these four sound groups may take between two and four weeks to learn. This depends on the speed of your learners and how much time you spend on phonics each week. The full table is presented later in this chapter.

Sound group	Teach the sounds for these letters	Use these words to practise reading and writing
1.	a n t h e m o	hat man hen ant hot ten mat men on at not am
2.	c i p s	cat can pen pot sit tin tap pet hit cap map pat pan top hop him it in
3.	k r u d	rat sad and dad run red cut cup hut nut sun hand desk up
4.	g l b f w	dog bag big soft bus egg pig bug wet went bat help old fat leg bed

Notice that all the words shown in this table are phonetic words, and can be pronounced using only the sounds of the phonic alphabet above.

Teaching a new letter using phonics

The easiest way to teach the sound for a letter is to show it, say it and get the learners to repeat after you. This method is useful, but we should combine it with other methods for the following reasons:

- it involves a lot of repetition, which is boring for the learners;
- it does not make a memorable connection between the written letter and the sound;
- young learners find it difficult to concentrate on something so abstract.

It is better to use a variety of activities to teach a new letter sound. For example, if you are introducing 'a', as well as using the method above, you can do some of the following:

- tell all the learners to point at the letter on a chart or in words written on the chalkboard;
- ask a learner to choose the letter from a set of letter **flashcards**;
- teach your learners a special action or movement for the letter (for example, to learn 'a', the learners can pretend to be a man sneezing: 'a-a-a-aaachoo!');

- tell all the learners to draw the letter in the air or on their desk with a finger (see Handwriting below);
- if one of the learners' names begins with the letter sound, you can get all the learners to associate the letter with this child, for example you can write the learner's name on an alphabet poster, or write the letter on the learner's name card;
- get the learners to draw or copy a picture of an object that starts with the letter (e.g. an ant or an apple) and write the letter ('a') next to it.

Fig. B3.1: 'A' FOR ANT

Some phonics methods even use stories and songs to teach the letters. For example **Jolly Phonics** uses a story and a song about a snake to teach the letter 's'. See link in the *Useful Websites and Online Materials* section at the back of this book. This combination of different activity types and ways of involving all the senses and movement will help children to learn the link between the letter and the sound more quickly.

 **Reflective task**

1. Which of the methods discussed above have you tried with your learners?
2. What other methods do you use to teach new letters to the learners?

Key skills in phonics

As soon as your learners begin learning the six letters in stage 1, they can start to do the following activities:

First letter awareness: *Learners identify the letter and sound at the beginning of a word*

Write some example words on the chalkboard, and ask the learners to say the sound of the first letter. Then say the word yourself like this: 'h-hat' or 'm-man' to show how this sound starts the word. You can also get the learners to match letters (on flashcards) with pictures. For example, they match 'd' with a picture of a dog.

Fig. B3.2: FLASHCARDS FOR MATCHING ACTIVITIES

Blending: *Learners read a word by saying (or **sounding**) the letter sounds and putting them together*

Write a phonetic word on the chalkboard and ask the learners to say the sound of each of the letters. Then say the sounds in the order of the word, repeating them faster and faster until they blend into one word. For example, say: 'a' ... 'n' ... 't', then 'a' 'n' 't', then 'a-n-t', 'a-nt' and finally 'ant'. Then get the learners to try blending. Start with easy words and get them to practise in groups and pairs. Remember to be patient and give lots of encouragement and **praise**. This is a very important skill.

Segmenting: *Learners write a word by saying it, separating the sounds and writing the letters*

Segmenting is the opposite of blending. First say a word at normal speed (do not write it), then say it more slowly, again and again until the sounds separate out. For example, say: 'ant', then 'aaanntt', 'aaa-nnn-t', 'aa ... nnn ... t'. Then ask the learners what sounds they heard and write these on the chalkboard as letters. Then get the learners to try segmenting and writing words they know. They will need to say the words several times to do this. Like blending, segmenting is a key skill. It will take time, encouragement and praise.

Letter ordering: *Learners put letter flashcards in the right order to spell a word*

Show the learners letter flashcards that make a specific word (e.g. the three letters of 'sun'). Say the word and ask them to put the letters in the right order. As they improve, you can show them a larger range of letters to select from, including extra letters that do not go in the word to make it more challenging. They can do this in groups too.

Completing words: *Learners hear words and write the missing letters*

Show the learners a word with one letter missing and say the word or draw it. Then tell them to write the missing letter. For example, you could write '_og' on the chalkboard, say 'dog' and ask one learner to write the letter. Then get them to do the same in groups or individually in their exercise books. You can do this with the first letter of a word (easiest), the last letter, or the middle letter (most difficult).

Digraphs, sight words and the magic 'e' rule

Digraphs

Digraphs are two letter combinations which have a specific pronunciation. They are usually taught with the phonic alphabet after the basic letter sounds (above) have been learnt. Here are the most important digraphs:

Digraph	Phonetic symbol	Example words
sh	ʃ	ship fish
ch	tʃ	chop which
voiced th	ð	this with

Digraph	Phonetic symbol	Example words
unvoiced th	θ	thin three
qu	kw	quack quick
ng	ŋ	thing sing
ai	eɪ	train rain
oa	əʊ	road boat
ee	iː	tree bee
ea	iː	leaf meat
or	ɔː	fork corn
long oo	uː	moon spoon
short oo	ʊ	book foot
ow	aʊ	how cow
ar	ɑː	car star
ou	aʊ	mouth sound
ay	eɪ	day hay

Note the following
- there are two different 'oo' digraphs, and two different 'th' digraphs – help the learners to separate them by writing them in different colours or always underlining one of them;
- most consonant digraphs (e.g. 'sh', 'ng') have only one pronunciation;
- some vowel digraphs (e.g. 'ai', 'oa', 'ee') can have two or more different pronunciations; teach the most common pronunciation first.

Sight words

Unfortunately for learners, there are many common words in English that are not phonetic. There is no logical connection between how we spell them and how we pronounce them. For example:

are   you   one   were   although   people

We call these words **sight words**. To help the learners to read sentences and stories, you should teach a few of these words every week. Choose common sight words that they often see in stories, on signs or need to write. Teach each sight word as a whole word. Do not ask the learners to blend the letters. Help them to link the visual word shape to the whole word pronunciation. To do this, you can use word flashcards (see *Chapter B7 – Resources and Activities for Developing Literacy*). You can also use the **look, cover, write, check** method, described under *Learning to spell* in *Chapter B4 – The Sight Word Phase*.

The magic 'e' rule

This is a rule we can teach the learners after they have learnt both the phonic alphabet and standard English letter names (/eɪ/ for 'a', /biː/ for 'b', etc.).

Look at the following words. They all have one syllable, and a silent 'e' at the end. But what else do they have in common? Think about the pronunciation of the first vowel:

        page   time   tune   home

In these example words, the first vowel is pronounced like the letter name (e.g. the 'a' in 'page' is pronounced /eɪ/, which is the same as the name of the letter 'a'). Explain to the learners that the final 'e' in these words is a magic 'e'. It is silent, but it makes the previous vowel 'say' its name. Note that the magic 'e' rule is most common with 'a', 'i' and 'o'. It is rare with 'u' (absent in American English) and very rare with 'e'. Other example words are given below under: *A suggested sequence for phonics teaching*. There are some exceptions to this rule (e.g. give), which you should teach as sight words.

A suggested sequence for phonics teaching

Now let us combine all these ideas together (the phonic alphabet, digraphs, sight words, the magic 'e' rule and simple sentences). Here is a 10-stage sequence that you can use when teaching using the phonics method:

Sound groups	Letters/ Digraphs	Example words	Useful sight words	Phrases and sentences
1.	a n t h e m o	hat man hen ant hot ten mat men on at not am a an		a hen an ant
2.	c i p s	cat can pen pot sit tin tap pet hit cap map pat pan top hop him it in	I my	I am (name) my pen
3.	k r u d	rat sad and dad run red cut cup hut nut sun hand desk up	one two three the is	The pen is in the tin. Two cups.
4.	g l b f w	dog bag frog big soft bus egg pig bug well wet went bat help old hill fat leg bed from	this your go no of small	This is my dog. I can run. A big frog.
5.	ee sh j or ck	tree sleep bee green sheep sweet fish wish dish jump jar jam storm for kick sock duck	he she they we you are to like her friend	I like cats. She likes dogs.

Sound groups	Letters/ Digraphs	Example words	Useful sight words	Phrases and sentences
6.	ng z x y	sing bring wing ring -ing (e.g. running, sitting) zebra zip box fox six yes yet	what eat play do give	What are you doing? I am singing.
7.	ch ea voiced th unvoiced th	with that those thing think chicken chips leaf meat each itch	has have some who his her three four five word	What do you have? She has a leaf. I have some sweets.
8.	ai qu long oo short oo	moon room spoon soon boot foot look good rain train snail queen quick	where there here which question was were	Where is the book? The book is here.
9.	igh ar oa ow	night light right fight car far hard arm farm star goat boat road soap cow how now	wrong come answer (days of the week)	Is it raining today? No. It isn't.
10.	magic 'e' ay ou	name make game home bike write fine time rice day hay say today mouth sound house	baby be mother father brother sister	I like games. My home is in …

Note the following

- this is a suggested order; the order you choose may be different – it depends on your curriculum, your learners' needs and interest, and your personal choices as a teacher;
- the amount of time you spend on each sound group will depend on your learners' progress;
- if possible, teach the names of the letters, and the traditional alphabet song after letter group 7 or 8;
- 'igh' is pronounced /aɪ/. It is the only three letter combination they need to learn during the alphabet phase;
- there are lots of resources on the internet that you can use to make this learning stimulating for the learners (see *Useful Websites and Online Materials* at the back of this book).

Note for teacher trainers

The order given above has been adapted from programmes for children in the UK and the USA to include more words that African children, as additional learners of English, may find easier and more useful to learn.

Reading simple sentences

As soon as your learners can blend simple phonetic words successfully and recognise a few sight words, you can get them to read short, simple sentences. It is a good idea to combine this with drawing. The picture can illustrate the sentence. For example, after learning sound group 3, your learners should be able to read sentences like 'The pen/duck/cat is on/in the desk/cup/hand', and draw a picture of this.

Lower case and upper case (capital) letters

Some phonics methods teach the lower case letters first, and introduce capital letters afterwards. Other methods teach them at the same time. Look at your teaching materials and also read the Teacher's Guide (if you have one) to help you to decide which method to use. If you are not sure, begin with lower case first, and start to introduce capital letters at Stage 6, adding them to flashcards and using them to start sentences.

Handwriting in the alphabet phase

When children begin to learn to write, they need to practise the following five skills:
1. making the letter shapes (including the right movements and making them in the right order);
2. controlling the muscles in their hands (called **fine motor skills**);
3. holding the pencil/crayon/pen correctly;
4. supporting the paper with the free hand;
5. writing on a line and between writing lines.

Before they write with a pen or pencil, they should practise writing with their finger in the air. Show them how to do this by doing examples with your back to the class, so that your letters are the same way round as theirs. Explain what you are doing and then get them to try. Write very big at first (50 cm letters), and gradually reduce size as you practise. Then they can practise the same shape with their finger on the desk, or with a stick in the sand outside (if you have sand in the playground). Get them to write smaller and smaller before they try in their exercise books. This helps to develop their fine motor skills gradually.

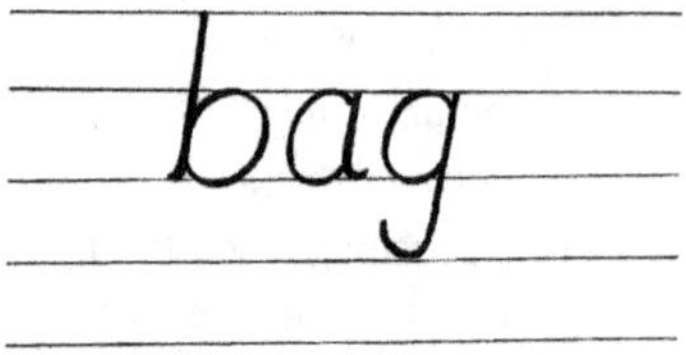

Use writing lines on the chalkboard (see Fig. B3.3) to show them the different strokes for a letter separately. Explain what you are doing (in the mother tongue if you can). Then check they remember the order and direction of all the strokes before you let them practise. They can practise writing with chalk on the chalkboard or on a concrete floor before they write in their exercise books.

Fig. B3.3: WRITING LINES

When learners begin writing, allow them to choose whether to use their left or right hand. Check every child is holding their pencil/pen correctly in the **tripod grip** (see Fig. B3.4), and show them also how to support the paper with their other hand. Right-handed learners should turn the paper 45° anticlockwise and left-handed learners should turn the paper 45° clockwise so they can see what they are writing more easily. Remember, if possible, to sit left-handed learners on the left of right-handed learners to avoid elbows bumping.

It is a good idea to practise letters that have similar shapes together. For example you can start with 'c' and then do 'a', 'g' and 'd', as these all have the same first stroke. Avoid practising letters that learners may confuse at the same time (e.g. 'b' and 'd'). When they have written a letter successfully, tell them to say its sound. Do not forget to provide encouragement and **praise**!

Fig. B3.4: THE TRIPOD GRIP

Practical task: Our first story

As soon as children can read sentences in English, they can also read stories. Stories are enjoyable and motivate learners, especially when they are illustrated. They can be very short and simple. You can start using them while your learners are learning the phonic alphabet.

Read this simple story and complete the tasks that follow:

Toto and the Hen

1 Toto is my dog.	2 Toto likes eggs.
3 A hen sits on three eggs.	4 Toto jumps on the hen!
5 The hen runs and Toto licks the eggs. Mmmm! Toto eats the eggs – one, two, three.	6 They are good eggs, Toto thinks! But the hen is sad. She has no eggs!

Tasks

1. Underline all the phonetic words in the story.
2. Draw circles around all the sight words.
3. Decide when you can use the story in the *Suggested sequence for phonics teaching*.

4. Think of three or four activities you can do with this story written on the chalkboard.
5. Think of three or four ways you can use pictures on flashcards to help you to tell this story.

Commentary to practical task: Our first story

1 and 2:

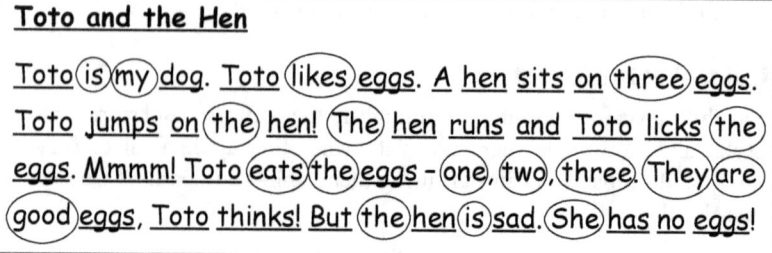

Fig. B3.6: PHONETIC WORDS UNDERLINED AND SIGHT WORDS CIRCLED

Note: Several circled words (eats, good) in the example answer could be considered phonetic words after the relevant rules have been learnt (e.g. after sound group 8) and several of the underlined 'phonetic' words are not completely phonetic (e.g. 'has' ends with the /z/ sound).

3. This story can be taught after sound group 7.
4. Here are some ideas. You can probably think of more:
   - Point at the words while you are reading the story;
   - Ask a learner to come and point at the words. You say the word she points at;
   - You say any word from the story. One learner comes to the front and points at the word;
   - You point at any word. The learners say the word;
   - Get a group of confident learners to come to the front. Together they read the story.
5. There are many possibilities. Here are some:
   - Read a sentence from the story. Get the learners to identify the correct picture;
   - Say a word from the story. Get the learners to point at the right object in the pictures;
   - Point at an object in a picture, get the learner to find the word in the story;
   - Put the pictures in the wrong order. Get the learners to put the pictures in the correct order while you tell the story;
   - Get the learners to retell the story from the pictures;
   - Get the learners to copy one sentence from the story and draw their own picture.

Conclusion

Phonics can help your learners to read and write in English more quickly. Once they learn to blend and segment words well, they can try to read or write any words. Of course, they will make mistakes with words that are not phonetic, but these mistakes are a natural part of learning, and with your help they will learn more and more about the English spelling system every day. Although phonics may seem technical, remember that every child who learns to read and write in English has to build up this complex relationship between sounds and letters in their brain, with all the rules and exceptions described above. Phonics simply provides clear, careful guidance for this learning.

In this chapter we have learnt the following:
- when the alphabet phase begins;
- how the learners' mother tongue can help them to read and write in English;
- how phonics can make learning the alphabet easier;
- the sounds of the phonic alphabet;
- how to teach a new letter using a variety of activities;
- key skills for phonics teaching (e.g. blending, segmenting, 1st letter awareness);
- what digraphs are, and when to teach them;
- what sight words are, and how to teach them;
- the magic 'e' rule, and how it can help learners;
- a possible sequence for phonics teaching;
- how to help learners to begin writing during the alphabet phase.

B4 – The Sight Word Phase

In this chapter:

- What is the sight word phase and when does it begin?
- Reading in the sight word phase
- Writing in the sight word phase
- Learning to spell
- Practical task: Planning a topic-based lesson
- Commentary to practical task: Planning a topic-based lesson

 **Reflective task**

The three underlined words in sentence A below are invented. Can you work out their meaning and pronunciation?

A. I need to <u>quiffle</u> my <u>bovlip</u> because the <u>gorling</u> has just broken.

Now read sentence B below. There is just one invented word. Can you guess its meaning now?

B. I need to sharpen my pencil because the <u>gorling</u> has just broken.

1. How did you guess the meaning of the unknown word in B? Why is it impossible to guess the meaning of the three words in A?
2. How did you work out the pronunciation of the three words?

What is the sight word phase and when does it begin?

Let us imagine that Beatrice (who we met in *Chapter B1 – Introduction to Literacy*) has learnt all the letters and digraphs in the phonic alphabet. Now she can read new words slowly by **blending** the letter sounds and write words she already knows by **segmenting** them. Her Teacher of English, Mr. Okoro, gives her regular reading practice three or four times a week. She can easily read many of the **sight words** that were difficult for her just a few months ago, and she recognises the most common phonetic words quickly just by seeing their shape (e.g. 'and', 'in', 'not'). In total, she has over 50 words that she can recognise on sight without needing to sound and blend the individual letters. Beatrice has begun to move into the sight word phase of **literacy** learning.

The **sight word phase** starts when a learner can read and write the most common words in English as **chunks**, rather than letter by letter. It will begin at different times for different learners, but it usually happens between 6 – 12 months after starting to learn the alphabet. It always follows the alphabet phase and will continue for Beatrice until she is fluent in reading and writing.

Reading in the sight word phase

As they move into the sight word phase of reading, learners continue to use their phonic understanding to blend and read new words, but they also learn a number of other strategies to read both new and familiar words. Let us look at several of the most common strategies, each with ideas for how we can help.

Words within words

What smaller words can you see within each of the long words below?

        hand   meat   Sunday   football

'Hand' includes 'and', 'meat' includes 'eat', Sunday includes 'sun' and 'day' and 'football' includes 'foot' and 'ball'. A large number of words are like this – they include whole other words which are often (but not always) pronounced the same. Learners quickly notice this, so when they want to pronounce a new word like 'hand', they notice the word 'and' first and then just add a 'h' sound at the beginning of the word. Every time your learners meet a word with a smaller word inside it, you can ask them questions like:

- What small word can you see inside this big word?
- What two words is this word made from?

You can do this with many words, but it is only useful if the 'inside word' is pronounced in the same way as they learnt it. For example, 'other' contains 'the' and it is pronounced the same, so you can show this to the learners. However, 'stare', contains 'are', but it is pronounced differently, so do not show this.

Word and morpheme shape

In this phase learners will often notice word shapes and bits of words that repeat regularly and have the same pronunciation, such as the '-ight' in 'light', 'night' and 'right', or the '-ing' in 'drinking' and 'jumping'. When our learners meet these words for the first time, we can ask them if they already know any other words that look similar, and how they are pronounced, or we can separate the two parts of the word and elicit the pronunciation of each part: 'eat-ing'; 'f-ight'.

Images

From the **pre-alphabet phase**, children quickly learn that images and text next to each other are often related. If they regularly see **textbooks** and storybooks with images, they will learn that a picture can help them to understand a word, and vice versa. We can help them to develop this skill both to learn new vocabulary and to understand the text.

    When a new word appears on a page, we can tell the learners to look at the picture as well as the letters to guess what it is. Here is an example for 'hospital':

Teacher: *That's a long word. What sound does it start with?*

Learners: *'h'*

Teacher: *Good. What does it finish with?*

Learners: *'l'*

Teacher: OK. *Can you see a building on the page that starts with 'h' and ends with 'l'?*

Learners: *'hospital!'*

We can also use images to teach learners to predict what they are going to read. When we come to a new page we can ask: *What can you see? Who is this? What is he doing? What do you think happens next?* Such questions encourage learners to predict words from the story before they read them, and also help with general comprehension of the story.

Images are also useful for teaching the meaning of a word if it is new to the learners. For example, if the word 'boat' is a new word shown in the picture, we can teach it before we read the text:

Teacher: *Oh look. Can you see the boat on the river?* (points at the image) *Can you all say 'boat'?* (learners repeat) *Let's find this word in the story … What sound does it begin with? …*

Using context, co-text and comprehension

Context is one of the most important ways that children understand any language, spoken or written. In the classroom, the school, and the local community, children learn to notice where words appears and try to understand why. For example, that word above the school gate is probably the name of the school. The word above each shop in the village is probably the name of the shop or the shopkeeper. The words on the front of a book usually tell them about what is inside the book. This can be called the **global context** of a written word, sentence or text.

Within the text, the words next to a new word will help the reader to guess the meaning of the new word. These surrounding words are called the **co-text**. Let us imagine Obi is reading the story Toto and the Hen (see *Practical Task* in Chapter B3 – *The Alphabet Phase and Phonics*), but does not know the word 'lick':

Toto licks the eggs. Mmmm! Toto eats the eggs.

Obi can see that 'licks' is something that the dog does to the egg (i.e. a verb), and that afterwards, the dog says "Mmmm!" and eats the eggs. When Obi thinks about what dogs do before they eat something, and looks at the picture next to the sentence, he can guess what 'licks' means. But Obi can only do this if his general comprehension of the story is high – he needs to understand at least 90% of the words to guess the meaning of the remaining 10%. We also saw this in the activity at the start of this chapter:

A. *I need to quiffle my bovlip. The gorling has just broken.* (27% of the words are new)

B. *I need to sharpen my pencil. The gorling has just broken.* (9% of the words are new)

Towards reading fluency

As Beatrice's sight vocabulary increases to over 100 words, she is able to read more quickly. She pauses mainly to sound out unusual content words (nouns, verbs, adjectives and adverbs), and she recognises most short **grammar words** (articles, prepositions, conjunctions, etc.) on sight. She is learning many new words each week from the teacher, from her classmates, from pictures and from context and co-text as explained above. In order to improve towards **reading fluency**, she needs the following:

- regular **shared reading** sessions, when the teacher reads stories from **big books** and **class readers** while the learners follow the text and answer the teacher's questions;
- the opportunity to read interesting texts and stories on her own two or three times a week;
- group reading sessions, when she reads with other children in groups of three;
- new vocabulary in her English lessons that the teacher explains, pronounces and writes down for Beatrice to copy to her vocabulary notebook;
- access to both fiction (e.g. stories in storybooks or in textbooks) and non-fiction texts (factual texts on animals, games, family life, etc.) on interesting topics.

Chapter B7 – Resources and Activities for Developing Literacy describes many of these activities in detail as well as other ideas that will guide both Beatrice and Obi along the road towards reading fluency.

Writing in the sight word phase

The sight word phase of writing starts later than the sight word phase of reading. When children start writing they will try to spell many words phonetically. For example, Beatrice may try to spell the word 'any' like this: 'eni'. This is natural, and caused by three main factors:

- **Writing is a synthetic process:** When we write, we build words letter by letter, and children will naturally do this using the phonic alphabet they have learnt.
- **The difficulty of English spelling:** Children try to avoid this by spelling words phonetically.
- **Choice:** In meaningful writing activities children choose what they want to write, and they may choose words they do not know how to write. Naturally they will try to write these words phonetically.

Here is an example of Obi's writing that he wrote at the start of the sight word phase:

I liv in sml house near skul wiv my mum, my dad and my sistu.

(I live in a small house near the school with my mum, my dad and my sister.)

Notice the following:
- Obi has sometimes forgotten the vowels ('sml' for 'small');
- he has used 'v' instead of 'th' in 'with' (he cannot pronounce 'th' yet);
- he has also invented phonetic spellings for 'school' and 'sister'.

As Obi moves into the sight word phase, he will add more words to his sight memory (notice his successes with 'my', 'house' and 'near'), and learn the correct spellings of more and more words.

Helping learners with writing tasks

We can help learners to progress quickly at this stage if we do the following:
1. Begin with tasks where they label pictures that they have drawn
2. **Revise** important vocabulary before the writing task
3. Model the writing process
4. Give simple writing tasks that they can enjoy and **personalise**
5. **Praise** their success and avoid too much correction

Let us look at these ideas separately:

1. Begin with drawing and labelling tasks: Drawing and writing go together naturally for children, so begin with tasks where they label pictures they have drawn (e.g. 'a big lorry'). Once they can do this, you can get them to label pictures with sentences (e.g. 'This is my mother Chantal.') and then two to three sentence texts.

2. Revise vocabulary first: As the learners are writing in a foreign language (English), they must have sufficient vocabulary to be able to do the task. Try to do a reading activity on the same topic before the writing task. This can be followed by an exercise where they match words to pictures, or complete missing letters in words.

3. Model the writing process: It is important to show an example text or sentence before you ask the learners to write. Write this text on the chalkboard while the learners are watching and listening. You can pretend to think aloud to show them how to think when writing:

> I have 1, 2, 3 (count on your fingers) sisters, and 1, 2 brothers. Hmm ... How do I spell brother? Let's see ... 'b', then ... er ... /br/, I think there's an 'r' there. Yes, that looks right... Now, I've finished the sentence, so I need a full stop ... (etc.)

4. Give simple, enjoyable, personalised writing tasks: Let them choose what to write about if possible, so that they can make it personal to their interests and their world. Example writing tasks at this stage include:
- drawing pictures and labelling them. This can include pictures of their home (window, door, goat, etc.), their family (mum, dad, baby, etc.), their own body (arm, leg, head, etc.);
- writing about games, sports, food they like: *"I like playing football."* (to accompany a picture);

- labelling pictures of people they know doing things: *"My daddy is digging in the garden.";*
- writing about what they did at the weekend: *"On Saturday we went to the market."*

5. Give praise before correction: Even if your learners are making mistakes, always praise their first writing attempts. You can do this by writing a meaningful comment or a question at the bottom whenever you mark their writing:
- Good picture! Well done!
- Interesting. Who do you play football with?

Correction is also important, but avoid too much correction because this can demotivate the learners. If they are getting lots of reading practice, this will improve their spelling more than correction. As they progress through the sight word phase, they will replace invented spellings with learnt spellings from their sight word memory.

Learning to spell

The first word children should learn to spell is their own name. We can teach this at the pre-alphabet phase, but it will take more time before they understand the link between the letters and the sounds in their name. At the alphabet phase they learn to spell by separating the sounds of the spoken word, and writing a letter for each sound (segmenting). This helps them to write phonetic words, but does not help with non-phonetic sight words. Obi's example above shows that he has already memorised some common sight words (e.g. my, house), but has not yet learnt others (school, sister).

As they progress through the sight word phase, we can help them to improve their spelling in three ways:
- help the learners to memorise sight words;
- encourage the learners to try segmenting words they do not know how to spell;
- correct common errors, both individually and with the whole class;
- do spelling games and **groupwork** spell tests.

The **look, cover, write, check** method is a useful way to help learners to memorise the spelling of sight words. Here is how to do it:
1. Show the learners a word (either on the chalkboard or on a flashcard), and help them to notice important features (e.g. ask *"How many letters are there? What's the first one?"* etc.).
2. Cover or hide the word (if it is on the chalkboard you can rub it out or cover it with your hand).
3. The learners write the word from memory and check what they have written in pairs.

4. Show the word again and get the learners to check that they have written it correctly.

Segmenting is still useful during the sight word phase. Learners will make mistakes, and learn from them. When we encourage them to guess the spelling of a word, it helps them to be creative and also prepares them for the correct spelling which they will see when they next read the word, or when their work is corrected.

When you mark your learners' work, instead of correcting every error (which may take a long time), keep note of any words that many of the learners are spelling wrongly and practise these with the whole class. You can use the **look, cover, write, check** method, or the spelling games described in Chapter B7 – *Resources and Activities for Developing Literacy* below.

Both spell tests and spelling games can be used to improve spelling. Remember when doing spell tests that you do not always need to test learners individually. If you get them to do the test in teams of two to four, they will help each other. Teach them to **pass the pen** after each word, so that every learner in a group participates. Two enjoyable games 'Spellman' and 'Countdown' are explained *in Chapter B7*. Crosswords and word searches can also be useful at higher levels (see Fig. B4.1).

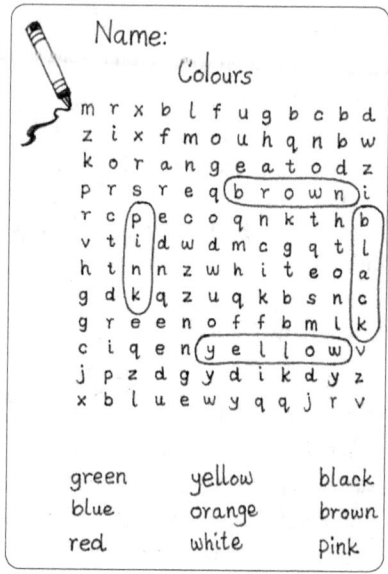

Fig. B4.1: EXAMPLE WORD SEARCH

Practical task: Planning a topic-based lesson

Write a brief lesson plan for a lesson that would help learners in primary year two or three (age 7 – 9) to improve both reading and writing skills on the topic of 'farm animals'. There is no need to write a full lesson plan with objectives, just note down the possible stages.

Commentary to practical task: Planning a topic-based lesson

Here is one possible outline of a lesson plan. Yours may be quite different:

Introduction	The teacher makes sounds of different farm animals. Learners guess the animals. (e.g. 'Mooo!' – cow)
Drawing	Learners draw different animals working in groups. Each picture is labelled with both the name and sound of the animal and then it is stuck on the wall for the whole lesson.
Shared story reading: The Angry Goat	The teacher reads from a **Big Book** and the learners listen and watch.

Discussion of the story using both English and mother tongue	"Did you like it? Why? Do you have a goat? Is it like the goat in the story?"
Quick game: Making animal sounds	Learners come to the front to make animal sounds. The others guess which animal.
Teacher models writing: My favourite animal	The teacher writes a short text: My favourite animal is a chicken. It eats corn and goes 'cluck, cluck, cluck'. I have three chickens at home.
Learner writing	Learners write a similar text and draw a picture of the animal.
Peer showing and reading	In small groups of three to four, the learners show each other their pictures and read each other's texts.

Conclusion

In this chapter we have learnt the following:
- how the sight word phase develops from the alphabet phase;
- we can use a number of strategies to help learners to improve their reading skills;
- images and context are as important as the letters in helping learners to read words;
- children need to be involved in a range of different activities during this phase to progress towards reading fluency;
- children can only guess the meaning of new words if they can understand 90% of the whole text;
- children will often invent phonetic spellings when they begin to write – this is nothing to worry about;
- how we can help learners with writing by making tasks interesting and personalised;
- how we can help learners to improve their spelling.

B5 – Children who Have Difficulty with Reading and Writing

In this chapter:

- Why do some children have difficulty with reading and writing?
- Practical task: Six causes
- Commentary to practical task: Six causes
- Early assessment of reading and writing
- How to help learners who have difficulty
- How can learners help each other?
- How can other family members help weak readers or writers?
- Activities for assessing reading and writing skills

Why do some children have difficulty with reading and writing?

We have all noticed that some children learn to read and write more slowly than their classmates. Many teachers think this is simply because they are less intelligent, but there are many causes. Here are six other reasons why a child may have difficulty with reading and writing:

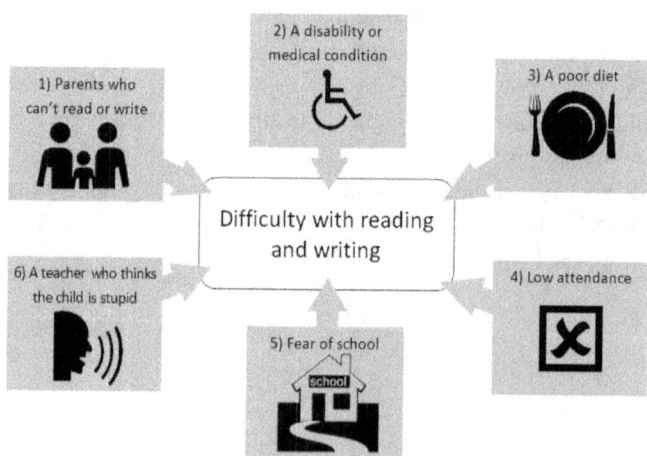

Fig. B5.1: THE SIX CAUSES

Practical task: Six causes

Read about the six situations below, and write one of the causes (given above) next to each name. An example has been completed for you:

B5 – Children who Have Difficulty with Reading and Writing

A. Alice <u>Parents who cannot read or write</u>
Alice's parents are farmers. They cannot read or write, and they have no books, pens or paper at home. Alice does not think it is important to read because her parents do not read.

B. Abdu _____
Abdu is the oldest child from a large family. Often at mealtimes, he allows his brothers and sisters to eat first, so he is often hungry. The food they eat is usually just rice or corn, so he does not get enough vitamins or protein. As a result, he is often tired at school, and cannot concentrate.

C. Joseph _____
Joseph is small and not very strong. In his class two boys often sit behind him and kick him under the desk. He is scared of telling the teacher, in case the two boys find out. He does not like school and cannot concentrate in class.

D. Tembe _____
Tembe cannot see very well, and needs glasses. However, her parents are not aware of her problem. At school she sits at the back of the class, from where she cannot read words on the chalkboard easily. As a result she finds reading and writing difficult and makes lots of mistakes.

E. Genet _____
Genet's mother is sick, so Genet often has to stay at home to help with the housework. As a result, she only attends school two or three times a week, and is often late.

F. Michael _____
Michael is the teacher of all the children above. In his view, all these children are less intelligent than their classmates, so he makes them sit at the back of the class, never asks them questions and punishes them when they make mistakes.

Commentary to practical task: Six causes

Solution:
- B – A poor diet
- C – Fear of school
- D – A disability or medical condition
- E – Low attendance
- F – A teacher who thinks the child is stupid

Notice that often one of these causes can lead to others. For example, because Joseph is scared of school, his attendance will probably fall. Think about one child in your class who has difficulty with reading and writing: What do you think the causes of his/her difficulty are?

Early assessment of reading and writing

Before you can help the learners in your classes who have difficulty with reading and writing, you need to find them, which is not easy if your classes are large. They may be quiet, or often absent. They may sit at the back and copy carefully from their classmates. You do not need to give exams or tests to identify these learners, and no special resources are necessary. Use the *Activities for assessing reading and writing skills* given at the end of this chapter.

How to help learners who have difficulty

As soon as you find the learners who have difficulty reading and writing, you can begin helping them. Here are four things you can do immediately:

- sit them near the front of the class – perhaps they cannot hear you or see the chalkboard;
- sit them next to a kind pupil who can help them (see below);
- give them a little more help during reading practice activities;
- give them lots of encouragement and **praise**.

You should also try to find the cause(s) of their problems if you can. Watch them more in class, talk to other teachers, and most importantly, talk to the learners themselves and their parents. Discuss the six causes given at the start of this chapter to find out if any apply to them. If necessary, seek advice from your head teacher.

Most of these learners will also benefit from individual help. Of course, the teacher is the best person for this, but you may be too busy to provide support to all the learners who need it. Let us look at two other ways these learners can get extra help:

How can learners help each other?

When you assess your learners' reading and writing ability, you will notice that some learners are stronger than others. Here are a few ideas to help you to make use of the stronger learners and to keep all the learners involved in reading and writing lessons:

- Create **reading pals** ('pal' means 'friend') between a strong reader and a weak reader who speak the same **mother tongue**. Give them time to read together each week and tell the strong reader to read to the weaker reader, like a parent reads to her children; showing the pictures, explaining words and following the text together.
- During group reading (see *Activities for developing literacy* in Chapter B7), sit one strong reader between two weak readers. The strong reader points at sentences in the text, and the weak readers take turns to read them. If the weak readers make a mistake, the strong reader should help them.
- Get strong writers to **monitor** their classmates during writing practice. The strong writers finish their own writing first, and then help their classmates by correcting mistakes or showing them how to write a letter or word.
- Train the strongest readers in your classes to become **reading assistants**. Tell them to watch how you help weak readers. Then ask them to help other

learners in a future reading lesson or during **English Club** if you have one at your school. Some learners will be better at this than others, so try different learners in the role of reading assistant. You will usually find a few who are good at it, and enjoy their extra responsibility.

How can other family members help weak readers or writers?

When you identify learners who are having difficulty with reading, you should organise to meet their parents. You should explain that it is natural and normal for some children in every class to have these problems. The child is not stupid, and must not be punished. Find out more about the child, discuss possible causes for the problem, and also find out if there is somebody in the family who can read and has time to help the child. Even if the parents themselves cannot read, there may be a brother or sister, a cousin, uncle or even a neighbour who can help.

You can also organise a workshop at the school for these 'helpers' once or twice a year and train the helpers in different skills such as **shared reading** (see *Activities for developing literacy* in *Chapter B7*), **sounding** out phonic words (see *Key skills in phonics* in *Chapter B3*) and using images to help learners understand new words (see *Reading in the sight word phase* in *Chapter B4*).

Activities for assessing reading and writing skills

Use the following activities regularly in your lessons – all are useful for learning as well as assessment. There may be similar ones in your class **textbook** which are also suitable. Remember the following tips:
- use the **mother tongue** to explain the instructions if possible;
- try to ensure learners do not copy from each other;
- at higher levels, learners can swap notebooks and mark each other's answers;
- keep note of each learner's marks, so you can help any who start to fall behind.

Assessment activity (year of primary school is given in brackets)	Reading or writing?
1. Matching letters to pictures *(year 1)* Write five letters on one side of the chalkboard and draw simple pictures of five things the learners know in English that start with the letters on the other side of the chalkboard (e.g. the letter 'd' and an image of a dog). Tell the learners to copy the letters and pictures into their notebooks and then to match them up using lines.	reading
2. From sounds to letters *(year 1)* Say 10 letter sounds from the phonic alphabet and tell the learners to write the correct letters in their notebooks.	writing

Assessment activity (year of primary school is given in brackets)	Reading or writing?
3. Drawing words (years 1 – 2) Write 10 words on the chalkboard and tell the learners to draw a picture of each word. Use only words that they know and can draw easily. Do not read out the words.	reading
4. Completing words (years 1 – 2) Write 10 words on the chalkboard with letters missing (e.g. 'd _ g'; '_at'). Learners copy the words. Say each word (don't spell or sound it) and tell the learners to write the missing letter.	reading and writing
5. Reading words (year 2 – 3) Write 10 words on the chalkboard. Tell the learners to copy them. Explain that you will point at a word and say it. Some you will say correctly. Some will be wrong. The learners must put a tick by the word in their exercise books if you read it correctly, and put a cross if you read it wrongly.	reading
6. Word dictation (years 2 – 3) Say five words and tell the learners to write them. Collect in books for marking. Give one mark for each correct letter in each word, and a mark if the letters are in the right order.	writing
7. Sentence dictation (years 2 – 4) Say three short sentences (e.g. "My dog is black." "I can swim."). Learners write each sentence. Speak slowly and repeat each one.	writing
8. Answering questions (years 2 – 5) Write five questions on the chalkboard. Tell the learners to read them and write down their answers (e.g. What is your name?; What game do you like?; What is your favourite colour?)	reading and writing
9. Individual assessment of reading (years 2 – 4) Once a week, begin by reading a text with the class (**shared reading** – see *Chapter B7*). After you have read it, tell all the learners to read it again in small groups. While they are doing this, you sit with one learner for two to three minutes and practise reading together. You can get him/her to read individual words, sentences or paragraphs.	reading

Conclusion

In this chapter we have learnt the following:
- there are many causes for problems with reading and writing;
- use early assessment to find children who are having difficulty with reading and writing;
- you do not need exams or special resources to assess your class, you can assess all the learners with just a chalkboard, chalk and paper;
- individual assessment of reading skills is also important;
- you can create 'reading pals' between strong and weak readers in your class;
- you can get members of the community to help the slower readers to improve.

B6 – Parents and the Community in Literacy Learning

In this chapter:

- Why are parents important when learning to read and write?
- How can parents help their children to read and write?
- Advice for literate parents
- Language assistants
- Bringing English into the community

 Reflective task

Read the following opinions. Do you agree with them? Give reasons for your answers.

1. "Parents who cannot read cannot help their children to learn to read."
2. "When children see or hear English in the local community, they understand why it is important to learn English at school."

Why are parents important when learning to read and write?

Children learn best from their parents. They want to do what their parents do, they understand why it is important, and play 'mummy and daddy' to practise the skills they will need for life. African children face two problems with **literacy** in this area:

- their parents may not be **literate**;
- the language of their home and community may be different to the language of school literacy.

Either or both of these problems may cause the children to think that reading and writing in English are not important skills. So how can we help the parents to help their own children?

How can parents help their children to read and write?

If a child's parents are literate, they can help them to read and write in several ways. The parents probably do some of the things mentioned in *Advice for Literate Parents* (see separate box). Parents who cannot read or write often think that they cannot help their children, but this is not true. Teachers can organise workshops for them at the school, and do the following:

- recommend useful picture books and storybooks and where to buy them;
- write the names of their children on a piece of paper for the parents to take away and learn, so they can recognise this important word when they see it on their child's work.

During the workshop, give the parents the following advice:
- show interest in what your children do at school. For example, look at their exercise books, ask what they learnt, what they found difficult and **praise** them for their successes;
- look at picture books and storybooks together – you can even pretend to read them (before your children start learning to read);
- encourage your children to draw and label pictures;
- if you have older children, get them to help their siblings with reading and writing for a little time every day;
- when your children start to improve, ask them to read to you; from their exercise books or **textbooks**, from food packaging, receipts or signs in the community – in any language;
- make sure your children always have a pencil, a pen and paper for school.

Advice for literate parents

You can help your children to learn to read and write by doing the following:
- buy storybooks for your children, both in **mother tongue** (if available) and English;
- read with your children every day, for example after school or before bed;
- enjoy reading with your children and do not tell them off for their mistakes;
- let them watch you writing and explain what you are doing and why;
- encourage them to draw pictures and label them;
- when they write, help them with spelling;
- look at their schoolwork – their writing, their pictures and their textbooks, ask questions about it and praise them for this work;
- when you read for your children, let them see the pictures and text you are reading, and move your finger over the text as you read it;
- ask them questions about the pictures and get them to predict the next part of the story;
- encourage them to read individual words, or guess a new word before you read it;
- if you are reading for them in English, read slower than you read in your mother tongue, helping them to understand difficult words through translation.

Language assistants

Research done in Africa and other developing countries tells us that children in primary school are able to learn better in their mother tongue than in a foreign language.[22] If possible, literacy should begin in the mother tongue. Any children who cannot do this have a disadvantage and will need extra help. One way to provide this extra help is through **language assistants**.

Let us recall the situation of Beatrice, the year one primary learner who we met in *Chapter B1 – Introduction to Literacy*. Her teacher of English, Mr. Okoro, is not from her community and does not know her mother tongue. Even if he wants to, he cannot explain anything to her in her first language, which creates a communication barrier between them. The only way that this barrier can be broken is through a language assistant in the class who speaks both English and the mother tongue well. The language assistant can be a member of the local community, another teacher in the school, or a child from a higher class. The amount of time the assistant can be with Mr. Okoro will depend on many factors, but even one lesson a week is useful. For the first two weeks of year one at primary school, it is a good idea to have a permanent language assistant in English lessons. She/He will be able to help the learners to understand about the *Four areas of literacy awareness* explained in *Chapter B2 – The Pre-alphabet Phase*, which will lead to faster learning in the future.

It is difficult to recommend exactly how to identify, train and make use of a language assistant. Each community where this communication barrier exists should develop their own solution depending on the situation. If you are a teacher working in such a situation, talk to your head teacher and community leaders about this. Having a language assistant at this important time can make a big difference to the future of the children's education and the future of the community.

Bringing English into the community

Children can learn English more effectively if it is used in the local community, not just in the school. How you do this depends on the role of English in your village, town or city. If English is widely used in your local community, this should be easy. Learners can listen to the radio, watch TV, practise using English with other community members and find books in English in local libraries. If English is not widely used, however, this may be more difficult. Here are some suggestions that may help:

An English club

A place where both children and adults can meet and speak English. The English club can invite **guest speakers** and organise special lessons, for example on computer and internet language, or understanding documents in English. It can also keep English language newspapers or show English television programmes.

An English section in the local library

This may exist already, but it can be made to welcome the local community by including books for learning English and a 'Learning English' booklet in the mother tongue to provide advice for adults and parents who want to improve their English and their children's English. Talk to your librarian; she/he may be grateful for some help with organising the English section and for recommendations of which books, DVDs and other English **learning resources** to buy.

---

22   Mehrotra, "Education for All"; Ferguson, "The Language of Instruction Issue."

English language films at local cinemas

It may be possible to show English language films with subtitles in the mother tongue. This can include not only American/European 'movies' but also African films in English (for example from Kenya or Nigeria), which are often easier to understand.

Local English radio

If there is a local radio station, it may be possible to make or broadcast some programmes in English, if this does not already happen. Talk to the people involved to find out if this is possible. Both adults and school children can be involved in writing and recording these programmes.

Theatre in English

This can include traditional plays performed in English, or plays originally written in English. School children will enjoy participating in these plays, and can help to write or direct them.

When we bring English into the community, children can communicate with each other and adults in English. This will help learners to understand how English can be important and useful outside school.

Conclusion

In this chapter we have learnt the following:

- all parents can help their children to learn to read and write;
- it is a good idea to organise workshops for parents on how they can help their children;
- if you do not speak your learners' mother tongue, a language assistant can help with early literacy in English;
- bringing English into the local community can help children to see how and why it is important, as well as helping adults to improve their English.

"It takes a village to educate a child."

African proverb

B7 – Resources and Activities for Developing Literacy

In this chapter:

- Resources for developing literacy
- Activities for developing literacy

Resources for developing literacy

Here are seven resources that can help you to develop your learners' reading and writing skills.

1. **Name tents**

See *Chapter C12 – 10 Essential Resources to Create* for instructions on how to make them. Useful at the **pre-alphabet phase** to help learners recognise their names and also to learn the individual sounds and letters in their names.

Fig. B7.1: A NAME TENT

2. **Alphabet letter flashcards**

Each card has a letter written on it. These are an important resource, especially during the **alphabet phase** when children are learning the phonic alphabet. You can make one set for yourself, and also have more sets in the school to use when you want to do **groupwork** with the **flashcards**.

You will need card and a marker pen or ink and a brush to make flashcards. Think carefully about how you will display them. Often folded flashcards, which can stand on a desk or hang on a **washing line** across the chalkboard, are most useful (see Fig. B7.2). Alternatively, if you have a pocketboard, you can create pocketboard flashcards (described in *Chapter C12 – 10 Essential Resources to Create*).

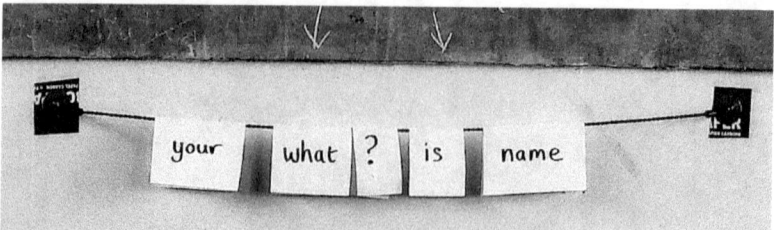

Fig. B7.2: A 'WASHING LINE'

Fig. B7.3: DIFFERENT TYPES OF FLASHCARDS

Each card must not be too wide, just a bit wider than the letter so you can put them together to make words that learners can read easily. Write lower case. It is a good idea to have two copies of each of the five vowels, and two copies of the most common consonants (t, n, s, h, r, d, l) in each set of flashcards. There is no need to write any example words or pictures on the flashcards.

Alphabet letter flashcards can be used for the following activities:

- **learning individual letters:** showing and saying; pointing at cards; choosing cards;
- **blending letters:** show the whole word, then sound out and blend the letters;
- **segmenting:** learners say a word, separate out the sounds and then choose the flashcards;
- **letter ordering:** give learners the letters that make up a word, tell them the word and get them to put the letters in the correct order;
- **spelling games:** say a word and get a learner to spell it by choosing the correct cards.

3. **Word flashcards**

Each flashcard has a word written on it in marker pen. You can write phonic words (e.g. hat, went) or **sight words** (e.g. are, do) on them. Keep the words you use in a box and reuse them regularly. They can be used for the following activities at the alphabet and **sight word phases**:

- **1st letter awareness:** show a word, elicit the first letter sound;
- **show, cover, write, check:** show a word flashcard to the learners for a few seconds, then hide it while the learners write it, and show it again to allow them to check their spelling;
- **say and draw:** learners get one word flashcard each (flashcards with objects or verbs only); they must say it and draw a picture of it on a separate card;

- **match cards to pictures:** take the words and picture cards from *say and draw* (above) and mix them up; other groups of learners have to match them again;
- **make a sentence:** each group gets a number of flashcards to make a sentence; they have to put the cards in the right order.

4. **Storycards**

Storycards have pictures from a story drawn on them. The sentences from the story can be written on a separate set of cards. They can be used at the alphabet phase and early sight word phase. (see *Practical Task: Our First Story* in *Chapter B3 – The Alphabet Phase and Phonics*).

5. **Wall frieze**

A **wall frieze** is a permanent alphabet displayed on the walls of the class, from A to Z. Each letter is shown in both lower case and capitals with an example word and a picture of that word (see Fig. B7.4). You can buy wall friezes or you can make your own using one sheet of A4 paper/card for each letter. Display it high on the walls so that the learners do not damage it, but low enough so that they can see the cards and you can point at them. Your learners or the school **English Club** may be able to help you to make a wall frieze.

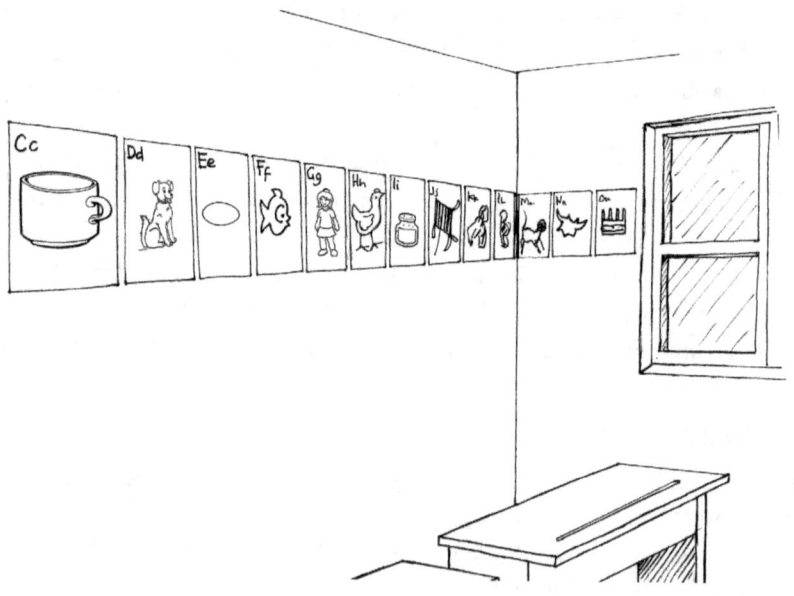

Fig. B7.4: A WALL FRIEZE

6. **Big Books, Class Readers and Reading Posters**

A **big book** is a very large easy-reader book with pictures. It is so large that the teacher can hold it and show the learners in a class, who can see the text and the pictures. They are designed for use in **shared reading** (see below). Class readers are sets of easy readers (e.g. Sunrise readers, described in *Chapter C11*). There are enough copies for all the learners to do individual or **pairwork** reading, and they can be used for shared reading or group reading (see *Activities for developing literacy* below). Reading posters are alternatives to big books or class readers for use in shared reading sessions (see *Chapter C12 – 10 Essential Resources to Create*).

7. **Children's literature**

Children need a range of books at a variety of different levels from easy to challenging. This becomes most important from the late alphabet phase and the sight word phase. The literature should include picture books for pre-alphabet and early alphabet phases, fiction (stories) and non-fiction (factual books about animals, food, places, etc.). The books should contain images and topics that are familiar to the learners. Most importantly, they should be interesting to the learners, so that they want to read them. Many schools cannot provide a library in each classroom, so it is important either to take your class of learners to the school library or to bring a box of books to the lesson regularly. If your school does not have any such books, discuss the following possibilities with your head teacher:

- organise for some money from your school budget to be spent on children's literature each year;
- arrange for the pupils in the higher level classes or members of your school English Club (if you have one) to make storybooks that the lower level pupils can read.

Activities for developing literacy

Here are 10 activities and games that your pupils will learn from and enjoy when they are learning to read and write. Note that the important techniques mentioned below (**blending, segmenting**, first letter awareness, etc.) are all described in *Chapter B3 – The Alphabet Phase and Phonics*.

1. **I spy …**

Phases: Pre-alphabet and Alphabet

Resources needed: None   **Preparation:** None

This game is very useful for awareness of initial letter sounds. Choose an object/thing in the classroom that all the learners know in English and can see (e.g. pen, window, door). This can include things on posters or on a **wall frieze**. Say:

I spy, with my eye, something beginning with …

And then say a sound from the phonic alphabet (e.g. /w/ for 'window' – do not say 'double-u'). The learners must try to guess what the object is. The child who guessed the word can choose the next word and say: *"I spy, with my eye …"* This game can also be played with traditional letter names as well as letter sounds.

2. **Point at …**

Phases: Alphabet

Resources needed: Letter flashcards   **Preparation:** None

This activity is very useful when teaching and revising letter sounds. It involves all the learners in a quiet activity that can also be used for formative assessment (see *Chapter C8 – Assessment*). Choose between four and ten learners. Give each one a letter flashcard. Tell them to stand along the walls of the class (some at the front, some at the back, some at the sides, etc.) and hold up their letter so that everybody can see it. Now tell the learners to point at one of the letter sounds:

"Point at /g/!"

All the learners in the class must point at the letter. Remember to use the sounds, not the letter names. Do this a few times, until they understand the idea, then **nominate** learners to say "Point at …". Do not forget to tell the learners who hold the cards that they should also point.

3. **Alphabet run-around**

Phases: Alphabet

Resources needed: Letter flashcards and playground   **Preparation:** None

This activity works best outdoors. It is enjoyable, but can be a little noisy! It is similar to 'Point at …'. Stand a number of learners in different parts of the playground. Give each one a letter flashcard to hold above their head. You say one of the sounds that they are holding, and all the learners must run to that sound. When they begin learning to segment words, instead of saying sounds, you can say words, and they must run to the letters in the order of the spelling. For 'pen' they would run first to 'p', then to 'e', then to 'n'. You can get them to hold hands with a partner to slow them down if necessary! This game can also be played in P.E. (physical education) lessons and the letters can be painted onto boards fixed around the playground.

4. **Rhyming words**

Phases: Alphabet and Sight word

Resources needed: Word flashcards   **Preparation:** None

Choose two pairs of words that **rhyme** (e.g. 'cat' and 'hat', 'hot' and 'not'). Display them so that all the learners can see them (e.g. in a pocketboard or on a **washing line**). Make sure you mix them up. Tell the learners that they make special rhyming pairs (you may need to explain 'rhyme' in their **mother tongue**). Either say the words yourself or get the learners to say them, then ask them which ones go in pairs. When they agree, get one learner to arrange them in their pairs. Practise saying the words that rhyme together. You can make up simple poems for them to say and copy into their notebooks:

"My cat wears a hat." "I'm not hot today!"

5. Spellman

Phases: Alphabet and Sight word

Resources needed: Chalk and chalkboard **Preparation:** None

This is a variation on the 'hangman' game (the hangman image is not appropriate for children). Think of a word they have studied and write one dash for each letter on the chalkboard. Ask the learners to suggest a letter (they can give sounds or letter names, depending on their **literacy** learning phase). If this letter is in the word, write it on the correct dash. If not, write the letter in a box on the side and draw one line of a stick man. Ask for another letter, and do the same. Continue until they have completed or guessed the word, or until you have completed the man (five lines for the two arms, two legs and the body, a circle for the head, one line or circle each for eyes, nose and mouth). If they guess the word first, they win. If you complete the man first, you win! See Fig. B7.5 for an example of Spellman.

Fig. B7.5: A GAME OF SPELLMAN

6. Countdown

Phases: Alphabet and Sight word

Resources needed: Chalk and chalkboard or letter flashcards

Preparation: None

Put the learners into teams of three to four. Write a word on the chalkboard with the letters in the wrong order (i.e. an anagram). For example, write 'kendoy' for 'donkey'. Say the correct word and give the learners 20 seconds to write it with the letters in the correct order in their notebooks. Give one point to each team if they spell it correctly. You can also do this using letter flashcards.

7. Alphabet hopscotch

Phases: Alphabet and Sight word
Resources needed: Chalk, concrete floor   **Preparation:** None

Fig. B7.6: ALPHABET HOPSCOTCH

This is a fun way to practise letter sounds and also **sounding**, blending and segmenting words. Draw a 5 × 5 chalk grid on the floor of the classroom and write the letters of the alphabet in the grid as in Fig. B7.6. The grid squares should be at least 20 × 20 cm. Choose two learners. Stand one on each side of the grid. Make sure other learners can see. Say a sound (e.g. /m/). The first learner to jump onto the correct letter wins. The other learner sits down. Another learner stands up. Repeat this with single sounds a few times. Then say the three sounds of a short phonic word in order (e.g. /m/, /a/, /n/). The two learners must race to jump on all three sounds without touching any other sounds. The winner stays, the loser sits down. You can then elicit from the class what word the three sounds make (blending). Alternatively, you say a word and they spell it by jumping on the letters. Alphabet hopscotch grids can also be painted permanently on concrete or tarmac surfaces in the playground.

8. Shared reading

Phases: Alphabet and Sight word
Resources needed: Big book, class readers or reading poster
Preparation: None

Shared reading is when a teacher or parent reads a story to children. It has many benefits for reading skills and also helps with story comprehension and creativity. Try to do shared reading at least twice a week with a class at the late alphabet or early sight word phase. You will need a Big Book, a set of class readers or a Reading Poster (see *Resources for developing literacy* above). The learners need to see the words that you are reading, and also to see the pictures. It is a good idea for someone (you or them) to follow the text with their finger, so that they can see which word you are reading. Read slowly and carefully. Pause before words that learners know and elicit these words. You can also get them to make predictions at a number of stages (e.g. you can look at the front cover together to predict the topic, characters, location, etc.). They can also search in the text for things they see in the pictures, and look for verbs that describe the actions they see. After a shared reading story, learners can do a number of activities. They can act out scenes from the story, retell the story to each other (speaking practice) or draw and label a picture from the story.

9. Group reading
Phases: Alphabet and Sight word
Resources needed: Easy readers or a variety of children's literature
Preparation: None
During the late alphabet and early sight word phase group reading can help learners to improve confidence and fluency when reading. Learners work in groups of three to four, ideally with one strong reader in each group. They take turns to read a sentence from the story, helping each other if necessary and correcting each other's mistakes if they notice them. The teacher **monitors** the whole class, intervening only if he hears a mistake or a learner having difficulty with a new word. After reading the story, they can do similar activities to those described above in *Shared reading*.

10. Individual reading
Phases: Alphabet and Sight word
Resources needed: Easy readers or a variety of children's literature, both fiction and non-fiction
Preparation: None
Individual reading is very important for all children. It can begin in the alphabet phase, but becomes most important in the sight word phase. You can use **textbooks**, but it is much better if the learners can choose the books they want to read from a range of interesting children's literature. They will need help to choose books, and should read new books that contain words they have not yet learnt, as well as easier books that they can read quickly. Reading a book that they have read before is also useful – it helps with **reading fluency**, with learning sight words and it also helps them to learn grammatical structures and collocations in English. Remember to include non-fiction in the individual reading sessions. As with Shared reading and Group reading, learners can do follow-up activities after reading a book. As they progress into the sight word phase and gain confidence in writing, you can teach them how to write book reviews. Their reviews can be displayed on a display board in the classroom. See Ideas for reading activities in *Chapter C6 – Teaching Reading* for more on book reviews.

Part C – Teaching Practice

What does Part C cover?

Part C of this book covers the practice of English language teaching, including the four skills of Speaking, Listening, Reading and Writing and the three systems of Grammar, Vocabulary and Pronunciation learning. In *Part C* of the book we will go into detail on how to teach English as a foreign/second language and as a language of education in African classrooms.

What can I expect to learn in Part C?

Part C builds on the theory of *Part A*, where we learnt why skills practice is such an important part of language learning, and the role of vocabulary, grammar and pronunciation in the learning process. You will learn how to structure and deliver lessons on all these aspects of English. You will also learn about how to assess learning and how to work with other teachers in your school to support the learning of other subjects in English. Almost every chapter in *Part C* contains example lessons for you to try out in class, and there are over 50 activity ideas that you can use and adapt for teaching, even if you have few resources and many learners.

C1 – Teaching Grammar

In this chapter:

- How should we teach grammar?
- An example grammar lesson
- Practical task: Introducing new grammar
- Commentary to practical task: Introducing new grammar
- Practising grammar
- Revisiting and revising grammar
- Ideas for grammar activities

 **Reflective task**

Which of these statements about teaching grammar do you agree with? Give reasons for your choice:

1. *"Teaching grammar is the most important part of an English teacher's job."*
2. *"Teaching grammar is important, but no more important than teaching vocabulary and the four skills."*
3. *"Children don't need to study English grammar. They learn it by using the language."*

How should we teach grammar?

In *Chapter A2* we asked the question, *How do children learn languages?* We now know that they learn less when we teach them the rules of grammar, and more when they use the language to communicate. Rules can be useful, but only if learners have opportunities to practise applying these rules through speaking, writing, reading and listening. Many teachers are worried that their learners will make lots of mistakes if they do not learn rules, but this is not necessarily true. Here are four guidelines for teaching grammar:

1. Only teach grammar that the learners need to communicate (speaking or writing) or to understand English (listening or reading). If they do not need it, they will not learn it.
2. Give the learners many opportunities to use the grammar, not just in written exercises, but also in meaningful speaking and writing activities.
3. Children can absorb grammar when reading and listening, so give them regular practice of these skills in your lessons.

4. Revise the most important areas of grammar regularly. This will create a strong base for future learning. Avoid teaching difficult grammar that they do not need.

An example grammar lesson

Here is an example grammar lesson for upper primary school level:

Lesson title: What did you do yesterday?

Lesson objectives: By the end of the lesson, the learners will be able to use 10 irregular verbs in the past simple tense to talk about the recent past.

Context of lesson: The learners studied the past simple of regular verbs (i.e. with '–ed' ending) last week, and did an activity on this for homework.

Time: 45 minutes   **Number of learners:** 62

Age of learners: 9 – 11   **Level:** Low intermediate

Stage	Time	Activities	Examples of language used*
1.	3 mins	Teacher greets learners. They play quick revision game on past simple of regular verbs.	T: "Leopard team: How do we say 'work' in the past?" L: "We think 'worked.'"
2.	4 mins	Learners check homework in pairs, then teacher elicits & confirms correct answers.	T: "Emmanuel and Alice, what did you get for number 3?" L: "Number 3. They played football last Saturday."
3.	1 min	Teacher introduces today's lesson.	T: "Today we are going to learn 10 important irregular verbs in the past."
4.	5 mins	Teacher writes 3 comprehension questions on the chalkboard and then tells a story about what happened to him yesterday. Answers to the 3 questions are checked afterwards.	1. Where did I go? 2. Who did I talk to? 3. What problem did I have?
5.	5 mins	Teacher writes 2 sentences from the story on the chalkboard. He elicits or gives the missing words (went, bought) and explains about irregular verbs in the past. Together they translate the sentences into the **mother tongue**.	Yesterday I _____ to my sister's house. On the way there, I _____ some coffee to give her as a present.

Stage	Time	Activities	Examples of language used*
6.	5 mins	Teacher writes 8 more irregular verbs from the story on the chalkboard. Learners copy and match to the infinitives, working in pairs.	Match the past simple to the infinitive: bought found went said go say find buy
7.	3 mins	Teacher drills the pronunciation of the new verbs. Learners repeat after the teacher.	T: "'bought', repeat everyone!" Ls: "bought"
8.	3 mins	Game: Teacher rubs the past simple forms off the chalkboard. He points at an infinitive and the teams compete to remember the past form.	T: "Elephant team: Can you remember the past for 'be'?" Ls: "We think: 'was' or 'were'."
9.	5 mins	Learners do a **gap-fill** activity based on the story, changing infinitive into past simple. They check answers in pairs before feedback.	When she _____ (see) the coffee, she ____ (be) very happy. She _____(say): "Thank you." and _____ (put) it in the kitchen … etc.
10.	8 mins	Teacher writes a question on the chalkboard and explains the speaking task. Learners speak in pairs, answering the question. Teacher **monitors**, helps and corrects errors.	Ask your partner this question. Answer in detail: What did you do yesterday? "Yesterday, I got up at 6 o'clock. I had breakfast and I went to school … etc."
11.	3 mins	The teacher asks 3 learners to tell the class what their partner did yesterday.	T: "David, what did Kora do yesterday?" L: "Kora got up at 6.30, went to fetch water …"
12.	2 mins	The teacher concludes the lesson. He asks learners for examples of irregular verbs in the past, **praises** them for their success and gives a homework activity.	T: "Well done guys! Very good lesson! So who can tell me: What did we learn today?" L: "Past simple irregular verbs." T: "Who can tell us the past simple of 'go'?" etc.

* *This includes what the teacher and learners said and also examples from exercises and boardwork.*

Note the following abbreviations are used above: T= teacher L= learner Ls= learners L1= 1st learner, etc.

Practical task: Introducing new grammar

In *Chapter A4*, we looked at different phases in a lesson. One of these is the **new language lesson phase** in which we usually do four things:
1. Provide EXAMPLES of the new language in context
2. Help learners to UNDERSTAND the meaning of the new language
3. Show learners how to PRONOUNCE the new language when speaking
4. Show learners how to FORM the new language when writing

Look at the lesson above. How does the teacher do these four things? Make notes and compare your ideas with another teacher if possible.

Commentary to practical task: Introducing new grammar

Provide EXAMPLES of the new language in context

In Stage 4 of the lesson shown above, the teacher uses his own life as a context. He tells the learners about what he did the previous day. This context is familiar to the learners, so it helps them to understand more about the new language and why it is useful. He then wrote two sentences from his story on the chalkboard to help the learners to notice the new language.

Apart from listening activities, we can provide context for grammar in other ways: a reading text, a dialogue written on the chalkboard, the classroom itself (e.g. for prepositions of location), the learners (e.g. describing physical appearance) or images on the chalkboard (e.g. for present continuous tense).

Help learners to UNDERSTAND the meaning of the new language

In Stage 5 of the lesson, the teacher uses explanation and translation of example sentences to help his learners understand the meaning of the new language. This is simple, fast and effective. The context of the story also helps the learners to understand the meaning. For example, the word 'yesterday' makes it clear that the teacher is talking about the past. He also helps the learners to remember the past tense verbs by using the game in Stage 8. For more help with understanding, the teacher could also ask questions like: *"Is this present or past?" "Which verbs in the story are regular? Which are not?"*. Other ways to make the meaning of new grammar clear include using pictures and drawings on the chalkboard, examples in the classroom and diagrams, such as time lines (see Fig. C1.1).

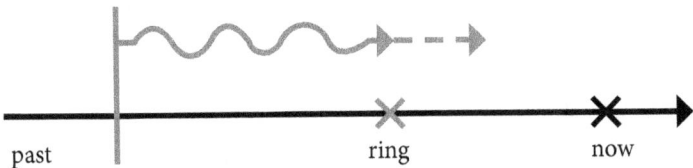

I was cooking dinner when my sister rang.

Fig. C1.1: EXAMPLE TIMELINE

Show learners how to PRONOUNCE the new language when speaking

In Stage 7 of the lesson the teacher **drills** the pronunciation. This means he says the new language (the past tense forms: went, bought, said, etc.) and gets the learners to repeat after him. It is usually best to begin with **choral drilling** (whole class) and then to do individual drilling, where you ask a few individual learners to say the new language to check they have got it right. Drilling is useful in small amounts, but notice that in the lesson it only takes three minutes. Do not drill pronunciation for longer than this. You do not need to drill every learner individually – this can take a long time in a large class and too many learners are left waiting. The teacher could also get the learners to practise reading the story **out loud**, working in pairs, to provide further pronunciation practice. This way he can monitor and provide individual help if necessary.

Show learners how to FORM the new language when writing

This happens in Stages 6 and 9 of the lesson. In Stage 6, he writes the past simple and infinitive forms of the verbs on the chalkboard and gets the learners to copy them and match them together. Then in Stage 9, they write the past simple forms of the verbs during the gap-fill activity. If you are teaching a more complex tense (e.g. present perfect continuous), or longer structures (e.g. conditionals), it is useful to study the form of the new grammar using a form table, as shown below. Contractions (more common in spoken language) are included in brackets:

Present perfect simple – form table				
positive (+)	subject He 	have/has has (He's)	past lost	participle his pen.
negative (-)	subject He 	have/ has not has not (hasn't)	past lost	participle his pen.
question (?)	have/has Has	subject he	past lost	participle his pen?

Second conditional – form table					
If If	subject they	past simple had a car,	subject they (they'd)	would would	infinitive drive there.

Practising grammar

Without practice, learners cannot learn new grammar, so it is important to spend time practising any new grammar that you teach. The example grammar lesson above provides two practice activities of two different types – **controlled practice** and **free practice**.

Controlled grammar practice

This is when we give the learners an exercise that helps them to focus on getting the form or the choice of the grammar right. In the lesson above, this happens during the gap-fill activity in Stage 9. Here are some examples of controlled practice activities:

Activity type	Example
Gap-fill activities	The Nile is the _____ river in Africa. (long)
Matching activities	Match the sentences to the pictures.
Choice activities	Mark plays/is playing the guitar every day.
Sentence completion activities	I went to the shop to _____.
Ordering activities	Order the sentences to create a story.

Free grammar practice

This is when we give the learners an opportunity to use the new grammar in speaking and writing activities. In free practice activities we provide a situation for them to speak or write and allow them to communicate freely. In the lesson above, the teacher does this by getting them to ask their partners: *"What did you do yesterday?"* To answer this question, the learners must use past simple verb forms. Here are some examples of free practice activities:

Activity type	Example
Role play activities	Role play a conversation in a shop.
Talking about your favourite things	Describe your favourite food to your partner.
Expressing opinions or debating in pairs or groups	What is the best form of transport?
Writing a letter	Write a letter to your pen friend about your weekend.
Creative writing	Write a short story about someone who loses something important.
Report writing	Write a report on the school sports day.

All of these activity types are explained in detail in *Chapters C4 – Teaching Speaking* and *C7 – Teaching Writing*. In grammar lessons it is important to provide both controlled and free practice of the grammar. Sometimes this is possible in one lesson (as in the example lesson above), and sometimes it is necessary to spread it over two lessons. It is logical to begin with controlled practice and then follow this with free practice. If you notice that the learners are finding it difficult or making lots of mistakes during the free practice activity, do another controlled practice activity and then try the free practice activity again.

Revisiting and revising grammar

All experienced teachers know that it is necessary to study an area of grammar several times before the learners can use it well. We call this **revisiting** the grammar. For example, most learners will need to revisit the present perfect tense three or four times over several years before they start to use it naturally when they are speaking. The first time you visit a new tense or grammar area, focus on the most common use of the grammar. Give learners opportunities to read it and listen to it. When you revisit grammar that they have already studied, you can focus on less common uses of the grammar, more complex rules, and also encourage more speaking and writing practice. This is summarised in the table below:

Visit	Skills	Complexity	Uses
Early visits to the grammar	Focus more on **receptive skills** (reading and listening)	Simple aspects of the grammar	Most common uses of the grammar
Later visits to the grammar	Focus more on **productive skills** (speaking and writing)	Complex aspects of the grammar	Uncommon uses of the grammar

Revisiting grammar involves adding more onto what the learners have already learnt, building on what they already know. In contrast, **revising** grammar involves refreshing their memories on something that they studied recently and may forget if we do not go back to it. Many teachers only use revision before examinations, which is not a good idea. Learners remember more when we revise 'a little and often'. Here are three suggestions to ensure that revision becomes part of your natural planning cycle:

- begin each lesson by revising what they studied last lesson, even if the two lessons are not linked;
- use the last lesson of the week to revise any grammar and vocabulary that you have studied during the week;
- include a **review week** in the middle of the term, in which you revise everything you have studied in the first half of term, and then a second review week at the end of term.

Many teachers think that with all this revision, they will not have enough time to get through the curriculum. However, as we learnt in *Chapter A3 – Child-centred Learning*, the opposite is true. If you follow these three rules for revision, your learners will learn the basics much faster, and they will be able to learn new grammar better in the future. Just like building a house, if you spend more time on the foundations, it will be stronger, and it will last longer as a result.

Ideas for grammar activities

Here are some ideas for grammar activities that can be done in any classroom. None of them require special resources, and they can be adapted to suit the needs of your learners and your teaching context:

1. Sentence jumble

Interaction pattern: Pairs or small groups

Materials needed: Chalkboard

You can do this enjoyable activity with any grammar, for controlled practice or revision at the start of a lesson. Think of an example sentence that contains the grammar you want to study. Draw a big box on the chalkboard, and write all the words from this sentence in the box mixed up. The learners must work in pairs or small groups to write the sentence in the correct order. You can give them the first word. Here is an example with the first conditional structure:

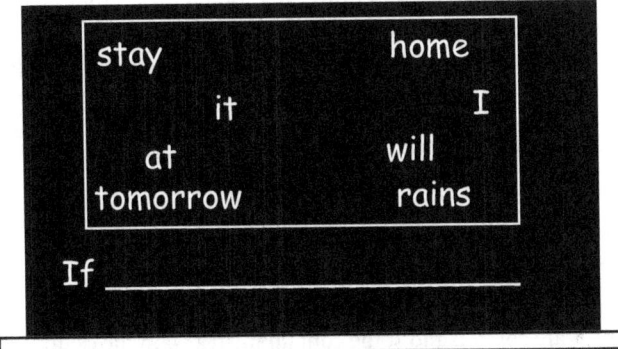

Fig. C1.2: SENTENCE JUMBLE

Solution: "If it rains tomorrow, I will stay at home." ('tomorrow' could go in other positions)

2. Grammar dictation

Interaction pattern: Small groups

Materials needed: Short text, notebooks

Grammar dictation is a good way to combine lots of skills together. It involves mainly listening, but learners also use writing, reading and speaking skills during a grammar dictation activity. It is usually best to use it for controlled practice during a grammar lesson.

Prepare or find a short text (40 – 80 words) that includes the grammar you want to study. Here is an example text for the present perfect tense at secondary level:

> Since 2005, mobile phones have become very popular. Many people have found that they are useful for contacting family and friends. Banks have introduced new technology to help people to send and receive money by mobile phone. What's more, since 2009 the cost of mobile phone calls has come down due to competition between large companies.

Organise the learners into pairs or small groups. Tell them that you will read a text **out loud**, and that they should try to write down as much as they can while you are reading it out. Read the text once, slowly but naturally. Pause only briefly and do not repeat anything. When you finish, each learner should have about half the words in their exercise book. Now tell them to compare what they have written in their groups. They must try to write one 'master text' from their individual notes. Different learners will have different words from the text which they can combine. There should be lots of discussion. Monitor carefully. After 3 – 5 minutes of **groupwork**, tell them that you will read the text again. This time, read the text a little faster, and again when you finish, put them back into groups to work on their 'master text'.

You may need to read the text a third time. When most groups have got most of the text correct (it does not have to be perfect), get one group member to write their master text on the chalkboard. You can then read the original text out again and elicit correction to make it 100% correct.

3. **Right or wrong grammar?**

Interaction pattern: Small groups

Materials needed: Chalkboard, paper

This is a useful grammar revision activity which you can use at the end of a week, or after studying an area of grammar. To prepare, write down several sentences. Some of the sentences are correct, and some contain mistakes. In the example below, there are six sentences on the grammar of 'verb patterns' (sentences 1, 3 and 6 contain mistakes). Write the sentences on the chalkboard, and tell the learners to work in small teams to decide which sentences are wrong. If they think a sentence is wrong, they should correct it. After five minutes, get a member from each team to write their team's opinions on the chalkboard. They can write them in a table, using a cross (✗) for a wrong sentence and a tick (✓) for a right sentence:

Sentence	Team A	Team B	Team C	Team D	Team E	Team F	Team G
1. I enjoy to play football.							
2. We decided to go to the market.							
3. I want that you help me.							
4. I love going to school.							
5. I am trying to improve my English.							
6. The teacher asked Christine clean the chalkboard.							

Check the answers and elicit correction for the mistakes. Get each group to work out how many they have got correct and write their total (e.g. 4/6) at the bottom of their column.

4. **Two-sided flashcards**

Interaction pattern: Whole class

Materials needed: Paper or card and marker pen

To prepare two-sided **flashcards** you need 5 – 10 pieces of paper and a marker pen. Write two words on each piece of paper and fold it. You can use two-sided flashcards for any area of grammar where words come in pairs. For example:

- write the verb infinitive on one side (go) and the past simple on the other (went);
- write an adjective on one side (hot) and the comparative form on the other (hotter);
- write a pronoun on one side (we) and a possessive on the other (our);
- write a positive sentence on one side (I live in Gaborone.) and the negative on the other (I don't live in Gaborone.).

Fig. C1.3: 2-SIDED FLASHCARDS – INFINITIVE AND PAST SIMPLE FORMS

In the lesson, show the first side of a flashcard to the class, and get the learners to say what is on the back. They can answer as a whole group, individually (raise hands) or in teams. Remember to use the flashcards again at the start of the next lesson for revision. You can also get learners to hold the cards.

5. **Human sentences**

Interaction pattern: Whole class

Materials needed: Paper or card and marker pen

This activity is useful for teaching grammar that has positive, negative and question forms, especially verb tenses:

positive sentence, e.g. Panji is playing volleyball.

negative sentence, e.g. Panji isn't playing volleyball.

question sentence, e.g. Is Panji playing volleyball?

To prepare for human sentences, write all the words you will need for the positive, negative and question sentences on separate pieces of paper. For example, for the three sentences above, you would need the following pieces of paper:

Fig. C1.4: CARDS FOR HUMAN SENTENCES

During the lesson, after you have shown the learners the form of the grammar, get several volunteers to come to the front of the class, and give each one a piece of paper. Ask them to stand in a line and show their pieces of paper. Tell the other learners to read the cards, and to direct the cardholders to stand in the correct order to make a positive sentence. After this, they can make a negative sentence, and then a question sentence. Sometimes one learner may need to stand to the side, for example the learner with 'isn't' in the positive and question sentences:

Fig. C1.5: HUMAN SENTENCE

6. **Who am I?**

Interaction pattern: Small groups of 4 – 6

Resources needed: None

This game is good for question formation. Bring one learner to the front of the class and whisper the name of a famous person (alive or dead) in his ear (e.g. Nelson Mandela). The other learners must ask him yes/no questions to guess who he is (e.g. "Are you from Europe?" "No." "Are you from Africa?" "Yes."). Once they guess who he is, put the learners into smaller groups of 4 – 6 and tell them to play again. This time they must take turns to choose a famous person themselves. You can limit the amount of questions to 20 if you like; the game is sometimes called 20 questions. They can choose nationally famous people, or even people who are famous in the local community, as long as all the learners know the person.

7. Animal comparatives

Interaction pattern: Small groups of 3 – 5

Resources needed: None

This game is good for practising comparative adjectives. Learners can play in groups. In each group, one learner must think of an animal. She must keep the name of the animal secret. She must describe the animal by comparing it with other animals until someone else guesses which animal it is. For example:

"It is bigger than a dog, but smaller than an elephant. It is slower than a goat but faster than a chicken. It is noisier than a sheep or a goat, and drinks much more water."

Solution: a cow.

8. Past tense pelmanism

Interaction pattern: Groups of 4 – 10

Resources needed: A set of the cards for each group, made from small pieces of paper

This takes a little preparation to make the cards, but once you have created them, you can use them again and again. Cut up lots of pieces of paper to create several sets of 20 small cards. For each set, you should write the infinitive of 10 common irregular verbs on 10 cards (e.g. go, do, see), and the past simple forms of the same verbs on the other 10 cards (e.g. went, did, saw). In class, show the learners how to play using one set of the cards. Put all 20 cards face down on a desk, so that the verbs cannot be seen. One learner turns over two cards at the same time and says the words. If they match (e.g. see and saw), the learner keeps the cards. If not, she turns them face down again. The next learner should do the same. Slowly, all the learners start to remember where each word is, and they will choose which cards they turn over carefully. The learner with the most sets at the end of the game is the winner. The learners can now play in smaller groups. You can also play pelmanism with irregular past participles (e.g. gone, done, seen), and you can get the learners to help you to make more sets of the cards, or add new verbs to the sets before they start playing.

9. What am I doing?

Interaction pattern: Small groups

Resources needed: None

This game is good for practising the present continuous tense. Put the learners into three or four teams. Ask one learner to come to the front. Whisper a verb action to him (e.g. "You are drinking water."). He mimes this action. The other learners watch and raise their hands if they know what he is doing. The first learner to provide the correct sentence (David is drinking water.) wins a point for their team.

Conclusion

In this chapter we have learnt the following:
- how to teach grammar effectively;
- what should happen in the new language phase of a grammar lesson;
- how we can provide learners with both controlled and free practice of grammar;
- why revisiting and revising grammar are both important;
- five activities for making grammar lessons enjoyable for the learners.

C2 – Teaching Vocabulary

In this chapter:

- How should we teach vocabulary?
- An example vocabulary lesson
- Practical task: Introducing new vocabulary
- Commentary to practical task: Introducing new vocabulary
- Practising new vocabulary
- Recycling and revising vocabulary
- Ideas for vocabulary activities

 **Reflective task**

1. How many words do you think your learners can learn in a week?
2. Do they sometimes forget vocabulary that you have taught? Why do you think this is?
3. Do you have any methods for helping them to remember vocabulary?

How should we teach vocabulary?

It takes a long time to learn a language, and most of this learning is vocabulary. When they start lower primary school, children can learn only about 5 – 10 new English words every week. This number increases steadily, so that by upper secondary school they can learn 20 – 30 words each week. When they finish secondary school, many learners will know over 3,000 words of English.

When we plan a new vocabulary lesson, we should choose the vocabulary we want to teach carefully, bearing in mind the following three points:

- the vocabulary we choose should be useful for the learners and the lesson;
- there should not be too much new vocabulary – remember how much they can learn;
- we should teach a variety of nouns, verbs, adjectives and **fixed expressions**.

One of the best ways to teach vocabulary is in **topic groups**. A topic group includes all the words the learners need in order to talk or write about that topic.

For example, the topic group of food includes the names of food that our learners eat (rice, cassava, meat, bananas) and also any verbs, adjectives and **collocations** that they need to talk about food ('like', 'hate', 'cook', 'peel', 'delicious', 'hungry', 'set the table', etc.). Other example topic groups include animals (including words to describe what animals do), and sports (including words to describe objects and verbs in these sports). When we teach new vocabulary in topic groups, the learners can practise this vocabulary together. For example, they can discuss questions on the topic, sing songs on the topic and play games using words from the topic group.

When we teach vocabulary, we should always get learners to record it by writing it down in their notebooks. It is a good idea to get them to use a separate notebook for vocabulary, or to write new vocabulary in the back of their notebooks, so that they can find it easily for **revision** activities (see below). They will find it useful to write a translation in their **mother tongue** next to the word. This will provide them with a simple dictionary that they can use in the future, for example when revising for exams.

An example vocabulary lesson

Here is an example vocabulary lesson for lower secondary level:

Lesson title: Our clothes

Lesson objectives: By the end of the lesson, the learners will be better able to talk about the clothes they are wearing and express their preferences and opinions about clothing.

Context of lesson: The learners can already use the present continuous tense and know the names of a few items of clothing (trousers, shirt, shoes, etc.).

Time: 40 minutes   **Number of learners:** 46

Age of learners: 12 – 13   **Level:** Intermediate

Stage	Time	Activities	Examples of language used*
1.	4 mins	Learners play a quick game in small groups to revise present continuous tense. One learner mimes an activity, then the others guess what it is.	L1: "What am I doing?" L2: "You are using a computer … What am I doing?" L1: "You are drinking water."
2.	1 min	Teacher collects in writing homework and introduces today's lesson.	T: "Today we will learn some new clothes vocabulary and do a speaking activity to use this vocabulary."
3.	3 mins	Teacher writes 12 new items of vocabulary on chalkboard. Learners copy into their notebooks.	dress (n); sandals (n); uniform (n); nice (adj); wear (v); suit (v); in fashion (exp), etc.

Stage	Time	Activities	Examples of language used*
4.	6 mins	Teacher elicits and explains the meaning of the new vocabulary, using clothes in the class and clothes she has brought to the lesson. She gives example sentences for some words.	T: "What am I wearing today? Is it a nice colour?" T: "This colour is in fashion this year. That means that it is a new style, and everybody wants to wear it."
5.	3 mins	Teacher models and drills pronunciation of the new vocabulary. Learners repeat. They then practise saying the words in pairs.	T: "Listen: 'uniform'. Repeat everyone, please." Ls: "Uniform!"
6.	2 mins	Learners play a quick team game. Teacher says a word and three learners, representing different teams, run to the chalkboard and write a translation in the mother tongue.	T: "wear" (learners run to chalkboard and write) T: "Who was first? Is it correct? Good! One point."
7.	10 mins	The teacher writes 7 questions for speaking practice on the chalkboard. Difficult questions are checked through translation into the mother tongue. The learners discuss these questions in pairs while the teacher **monitors**, noting down some of the mistakes she hears, but not interrupting the discussions.	1. What clothes are you wearing today? 2. What clothes is the teacher wearing today? 3. What clothes did you wear on Sunday? 4. What colours suit you? 5. What clothes do you wear for a wedding? 6. Do you think it is important to wear clothes that are in fashion? 7. "Girls are more interested in fashion than boys." Do you agree? (Give reasons)
8.	3 mins	The teacher gets feedback, asking 4 or 5 learners to tell the class what their partner said in response to one of the questions.	T: "So Dupe, what clothes did Mega wear on Sunday?" L: "Mega told me that she wore a dress, sandals and a bow in her hair."

Stage	Time	Activities	Examples of language used*
9.	4 mins	The teacher writes some of the mistakes on the chalkboard. She gets learners to correct them.	On chalkboard: I think the colour blue suits to me. T: "What is the mistake in this sentence?"
10.	2 mins	The teacher concludes the lesson by checking what the learners have learnt, giving them a homework task and praising them.	T: "So what have we learnt today?" L: "Vocabulary about clothes and fashion." T: "Good. Who can give me an example new word?"

* *This includes what the teacher and learners said and also examples from exercises and boardwork.*

Note the following abbreviations are used above: T= teacher L= learner Ls= learners L1= 1st learner, etc.

Practical task: Introducing new vocabulary

As in grammar lessons, we usually do four things when we introduce vocabulary in the **new language lesson phase**:

1. Provide EXAMPLES of the new language in context
2. Help learners to UNDERSTAND the meaning of the new language
3. Show learners how to PRONOUNCE the new language when speaking
4. Show learners how to FORM the new language when writing

Look at the example lesson above. How does the teacher do these four things? Make notes and compare your ideas with a colleague if possible.

Commentary to practical task: Introducing new vocabulary

1. Provide EXAMPLES of the new language in context

The teacher does this in Stage 4. She uses the vocabulary to talk about what she is wearing, and what the learners are wearing. In other lessons, she could use a reading text, such as a story or magazine article to provide examples of the new language in context. This stage shows the learners how to use the new vocabulary.

2. Help learners to UNDERSTAND the meaning of the new language

The teacher also does this in Stage 4. She uses real objects; clothes that she and the learners are wearing. She explains one fixed expression (in fashion). She also uses a translation game in Stage 6 to check understanding and help the weaker learners to understand more about the vocabulary. Here are the five techniques we can use to help learners to understand the meaning of new vocabulary:

Technique	Example from the lesson 'Our Clothes'
Use images	The teacher draws simple pictures of items of clothing on the chalkboard, or brings in photographs from magazines.
Use your body to mime the vocabulary	The teacher mimes a verb, like 'get dressed', 'take off', etc. She could also mime adjectives in her facial expression.
Translate	The teacher translates a word if there is an equivalent in the first language (e.g. tie) or if it may be confusing (e.g. the verb 'to suit').
Use real objects (called **realia**)	The teacher brings in items of clothing, or uses items that the learners are wearing.
Explain or describe the new vocabulary	The teacher explains what 'in fashion' means, and how we use it. This method is more useful at higher levels.

3. **Show learners how to PRONOUNCE the new language when speaking**

The teacher does this in Stage 5. The easiest and most effective way is to drill the pronunciation. The teacher says a word, and the learners repeat it. They can all repeat it together (called **choral drilling**) or individually (called **individual drilling**). It is best to start with choral drilling, and then check a few individuals. There is no need to individually drill every learner in the class. In the example lesson, the teacher also gets the learners to practise saying the new words in pairs. At this stage she can monitor and provide individual help to learners who need it.

4. **Show learners how to FORM the new language when writing**

The form of any vocabulary item is its spelling. We should write it on the chalkboard, or show it in a **textbook**, and give learners time to copy the spelling. If it is a long word, we should also mark the stressed syllable (e.g. by underlining it: 'imp<u>o</u>ssible'). We can also note whether it is a verb (v), noun (n), or adjective (adj), and tell the learners if it has any irregular forms (e.g. irregular past tense and past participle, such as take/took/taken; or irregular plural, such as mouse – mice).

Practising new vocabulary

The best way to learn new vocabulary is to use it. We can get learners to practise new vocabulary in two ways: **controlled practice** and **free practice**. Controlled vocabulary practice helps learners to understand how to use the vocabulary in sentences. Free vocabulary practice is an opportunity for the learners to use the vocabulary more naturally in speaking and writing activities.

Examples of controlled vocabulary practice activities:

Activity type	Example
Gap-fill activities	A policeman _____ criminals. (steals/arrests/sentences)
Matching activities	1. A hoe is used for … a. … carrying water. 2. A jerry can is used for … b. … digging the earth
Picture-word match activities	Draw a line to match each of the words on the left to a picture on the right.
Sentence completion activities	The kitchen is the place where _____.
Writing or saying model sentences using the vocabulary	"Write down example sentences using the following three adjectives: 'excited', 'angry', 'confused.'"

Examples of free vocabulary practice activities:

Activity type	Example
Personalisation questions *learners use the new vocabulary to talk or write about themselves*	What is your favourite sport? How often do you play it?
Describing games *learners have to describe something and classmates guess what it is*	Describe an animal to your partner. Your partner will guess which animal: "It's very big, grey and has big ears." "Elephant!"
Role play activities *learners have a conversation, pretending they are in a different situation*	Role play a conversation between a doctor and a patient.
Debates and discussions *learners express their opinions on a topic*	Do you think boys are better than girls at sports?
Project work *learners use English to work on a specific topic, with the aim of creating a poster or giving a presentation*	Six groups create posters on different forms of transport in the classroom.

At higher levels, controlled vocabulary practice is not always necessary; the free vocabulary practice is more important. This is why the teacher in the example lesson shown above spends most of the practice time on the seven questions for **pairwork** speaking practice. These questions are a combination of **personalisation**, describing and discussion questions. See *Chapter C4 – Teaching Speaking* for more on role plays, personalisation questions, debates and discussions.

Recycling and revising vocabulary

Recycling vocabulary means finding an opportunity to re-use vocabulary that has been studied recently. The more we recycle vocabulary, the more likely it is that learners will remember this vocabulary. For example, if we have studied the topic of 'the media', any activities relating to this topic will recycle this vocabulary, including:
- a reading text on the history of the newspaper;
- a listening activity in which the teacher describes how to use a radio;
- a writing activity in which the learners write about different media in their community;
- a story about a girl who becomes a journalist.

Just like grammar revision, vocabulary revision activities and games should take place regularly:
- at the start of a lesson, revise any vocabulary that was introduced in the previous lesson;
- at the end of a week, revise any vocabulary that was introduced during the week;
- twice a term, organise a revision week, when you revise all grammar and vocabulary learnt so far.

Without revision and recycling, learners can easily forget the new vocabulary they have learnt, thereby making all your teaching effort go to waste!

Ideas for vocabulary activities

Here are some good ideas for vocabulary activities. None of them need special resources and they can be adapted to work in any teaching context. There are other ideas in other parts of this book, including *Spellman (Chapter B7)*, the *Vocabulary Box (Chapter C12)* and *Define and Guess (Chapter C4)*.

1. Word spidergrams

Interaction pattern: Individuals or small groups

Resources needed: Notebooks, chalkboard

Word spidergrams (also called **mind-maps**) are diagrams that show the relationships between words. They are useful for helping learners to remember new vocabulary, especially topic groups and collocations (e.g. verbs that collocate with 'money'). They make notebooks look more interesting and can be illustrated with pictures. We can also produce spidergram posters for the classroom. An example of a word spidergram for food is given in Fig. C2.1. The best way to do a word spidergram activity is for you to begin the diagram on the chalkboard, and once there are a few examples, tell the learners to continue, working in small groups, adding all the words they know. After a few minutes, they can come to the chalkboard and add their words to your spidergram.

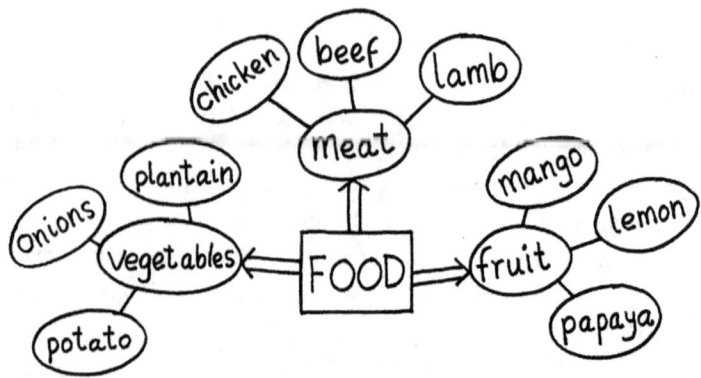

Fig. C2.1: WORD SPIDERGRAM

2. **Memory games**

Interaction pattern: Whole class or groups

Resources needed: None

Memory games are games where learners remember a number of vocabulary items within a topic group. Here is one example, *"I went to the farm and I saw …"*:

The teacher begins by saying: *"I went to the farm and I saw a cow."*. She tells one of the learners to continue. The learner repeats the sentence and adds another animal: *"I went to the farm and I saw a cow and a goat."* The next learner repeats this and adds another animal: *"I went to the farm and I saw a cow, a goat and a dog."* This continues around the class until the list of animals is very long! The learners enjoy trying to remember all the words. It can also be done with food: *"I went to the market and I bought … (some potatoes)"*, with furniture: *"Our auntie Mary has a big house, and inside she has … (a big bed)"* or with countries: *"Our uncle Paul has travelled all round the world. Last year he visited …(Brazil)"*. The game can also help learners to memorise grammar structures (e.g. present perfect and past simple in the last example above).

3. **The alphabet game**

Interaction pattern: Groups of 4 – 6

Resources needed: Paper

This is another good activity to do when there are many items of vocabulary associated with a topic group. Each group of learners writes the letters of the alphabet in two columns on a piece of paper. For each letter they must think of a word from the topic group that begins with that letter. The teams have a time limit (e.g. five minutes), and the team with the most words by the end are the winners. For example, for the theme of family members, they could have the following answers:

a – aunt, b – brother, c – cousin, d – daughter, e – elder, f – father, etc.

4. Describe and draw

Interaction pattern: Pairs

Resources needed: Notebooks, chalkboard

This is a fun game where one learner describes a picture carefully to their partner who has to draw the picture. Here is how to play:

Half of the learners must turn around so that they cannot see the chalkboard. They are not allowed to look at the chalkboard, but their partner is. Draw a simple picture on the chalkboard that includes lots of words from the vocabulary topic group. For example, if the topic group is Parts of the Body, you can draw a strange man with six arms, three fingers on each hand, five eyes, a long tongue, etc. When you finish drawing, the learners who can see the chalkboard must describe your picture to their partner. The other learners must listen and draw what their partner is describing. When they finish, they can display the pictures and choose a winner. They should then swap places and repeat the activity with a different picture.

5. Odd one out

Interaction pattern: Pairs or small groups

Resources needed: Chalkboard

This game is good for controlled practice and revision. It is also good for discussion. Write words in groups of four on the chalkboard. In each group, three of the words are from the same topic group, and the fourth word is unrelated. Here is an example:

    a) car bus monkey airplane

    b) truck chair table bed

    c) snake pigeon dog lion

Solutions: a) 'monkey' – the others are forms of transport; b) 'truck' – the others are furniture; c) either 'pigeon' because it is a bird and the others are animals, or 'dog' because it is domestic and the others are wild. Both answers are correct if the learners have a good reason.

6. Collocation challenge

Interaction pattern: Groups of 4 – 6

Resources needed: Chalkboard

This is a useful game for helping learners with collocations, especially at secondary level. Before the lesson, prepare a table with common verbs along the top and nouns along the side. Choose verbs and nouns that make collocations that the learners know or can guess. See Fig. C2.2 for an example table. In class, create teams (A, B, C, etc.) and draw the table on the board. Teams take turns to select a verb and noun collocation (e.g. 'make money'). They must provide an example sentence and an explanation/translation of the meaning. If the collocation exists in English, the team win the square. Write their letter in it. If it doesn't exist, they can't win it; cross out the square. The game continues until all the possible collocations have been found. The example in Fig. C2.2 shows the chalkboard after a game with 8 teams.

	make	do	take	pass
an exam		F	C	B
your homework	X	A		X
money	A		E	
time	F		D	B
a mistake	G	X		
a decision	D			X

Fig. C2.2: COLLOCATION CHALLENGE

7. **Anagrams**

Interaction pattern: Pairs or small groups

Resources needed: Chalkboard

This is a fast, simple vocabulary activity that you can use at the start of a lesson or the end of the week to revise vocabulary that the learners have already learnt. Write several words from the topic group on the chalkboard, but with the letters in the wrong order. Learners must work in pairs or small groups to put the letters in the right order. For example on the theme of weather, you could choose:

1. nusyn   2. yinar   3. dolc   4. dunther   5. gyfog

Solution:

1. sunny   2. rainy   3. cold   4. thunder   5. foggy

8. **Beep!**

Interaction pattern: Whole class or large groups

Resources needed: None

This is a game in which a learner has to describe a verb, and his classmates must guess the verb. Whisper a verb to the learner (or get him to think of a verb). He must say sentences that include the verb, but, instead of saying the verb, he must say 'beep!' (like a car horn). For example:

"Every day I BEEP! my face with soap and water after I wake up. I always BEEP! my hands after I visit the toilet."

The answer is 'wash'. After playing Beep! as a whole class, they can play it in groups, which is better in a very large class. They can think of their own verbs, or you can give them verbs from the vocabulary box.

9. **Back to the board**

Interaction pattern: Whole class in 3 – 5 teams

Resources needed: Chalkboard

Create 3 – 5 teams and stand one member of each team in front of the chalkboard. These learners must face the class and cannot look at the chalkboard. Write one word on the chalkboard. Any learners who can describe this word should raise their hand. Choose one. He should describe the word without saying it. The first team member with their back to the chalkboard who guesses the word wins a point for his/her team. Change the team members at the front and continue in this way.

10. **Guess the word**

Interaction pattern: Small groups

Resources needed: Small pieces of paper

Write the words you want to revise on small pieces of paper. Put the learners into small groups and give one learner from each group a piece of paper. This learner must not say or show the word. She must describe it, define it, or even mime it (mime is when you act it out) so that the other learners can guess which word it is. The first learner to guess the word wins a point. When they finish, you can give them new pieces of paper, swapping them round between the different groups.

11. **Board football**

Interaction pattern: Whole class in two teams

Resources needed: Chalkboard

Create two teams and draw a football pitch on the chalkboard about 1m in length, with a goal at either end. Draw the ball on the centre circle ready for kick off. Choose one team to start, and write a word on the chalkboard. Any learners who can explain this word should raise their hands. Choose one. She or he must explain its meaning or use the word correctly in a sentence. If s/he does, move the ball one step (about 20 cm) closer towards the opponent's goal (just rub it out and draw it again). Next write another word on the chalkboard for the other team. Again, one learner must raise their hand and use the word correctly in a sentence. If so, you can move the ball back to the centre circle. In this way, the ball will move back and forth, and eventually one team will score a goal. Keep going until you have revised all the words you need to. See Fig. C2.3 for an example of Board Football.

Fig. C2.3: BOARD FOOTBALL

Conclusion

In this chapter we have learnt the following:
- we should choose the vocabulary we teach carefully;
- we should teach vocabulary in topic groups;
- we should get learners to record new vocabulary in their notebooks;
- learners need to understand the meaning, form and pronunciation of new vocabulary;
- we can use both controlled and free practice activities to get learners using new vocabulary;
- we should recycle new vocabulary using a variety of different skills;
- we should revise all new vocabulary two or three times if we want learners to remember it;
- remember: "If they don't use it, they'll lose it!"

C3 – Teaching Pronunciation

In this chapter:

- What accent should I teach my learners?
- What other aspects of pronunciation should I teach?
- Techniques for improving learners' pronunciation
- Practical task: Sound advice
- Commentary to practical task: Sound advice
- Ideas for pronunciation activities

 **Reflective task**

Read the following opinions of three Kenyan teachers. Who do you think is right, and why?

"I want my learners to speak international English that people from any country can understand." — Paul

"I want my learners to speak British English, just like the kings and queens of England." — Grace

I want my learners to speak English with a Kenyan accent and be proud of it." — Judy

What accent should I teach my learners?

English is an international language, spoken all over the world, both as a native language and a second language. Within Africa there are many different varieties of English, and each one is as important as the varieties spoken in the UK and the USA. Teachers who speak English as a second language are sometimes worried that their **accent** is not a good model for their learners. However, this depends on the needs of your learners and the community in which they will use English. Many learners will benefit from learning the variety of English spoken in their country first, including the local accent, so, if you speak a local variety of English, your English accent may be the most useful one for them to learn.

What other aspects of pronunciation should I teach?

Most children will learn to pronounce English simply by listening to their teachers and any other speakers of English that they hear in their community, just as they do with their first language. In class we can help this process by giving them regular speaking activities that allow them to practise saying the sounds and the words of English in natural conversation. But we can also improve on this natural learning if we teach our learners about three important aspects of pronunciation:

- the sounds of English
- word stress
- connected speech

Let us look at each of these separately.

The sounds of English

Each language has its own sounds. Your learners will easily learn the sounds in English that are similar to their **mother tongue**, but they may have difficulty with the sounds that are different. For example, some Bantu languages have no difference between the sounds for 'l' and 'r'. So learners will have difficulty separating 'pray' and 'play' or 'long' and 'wrong'. Other African languages have no difference between the long 'ee' in 'sheep' and the short 'i' in 'ship'. Think carefully about the mother tongues of your learners and provide extra help with the sounds that are different in English. When you teach a new word with a difficult sound, spend some time showing the sound to your learners and explaining how it is pronounced (use their mother tongue to explain technical details if possible). You can also do **minimal pairs** work on this sound (see *Ideas for Pronunciation Activities*) below.

Word stress

In English, when we say words with two or more syllables, we usually say one of these syllables louder and make it a bit longer. This is called **word stress**, and it is very similar in most varieties of English. If we get the word stress right, it makes our English easier to understand. Notice that in the following three words, the stress falls on different syllables (the stressed syllable is underlined):

pho̱tograph	photo̱grapher	photogra̱phic

When you teach a new word, you can show the learners where the stress is by writing it on the chalkboard and underlining the stressed syllable. You can also emphasise the stress when you drill it.

If you have difficulty working out where the stress is, first try humming the word with your mouth closed. If this does not help, use a dictionary. It will usually show an apostrophe before the stressed syllable in the phonemic transcription:

impossible (adj) / ɪmˈpɒsɪbəl /

Notice that the apostrophe comes before /p/, so the next syllable /pɒ/ is stressed.

Connected speech

When we speak quickly, it often changes the way we say words. For example, in some varieties of English some short words almost disappear: *"a bottle of water"* becomes *"a bottle 'o' water"*, or *"salt and pepper"* becomes *"salt 'n' pepper"*. We can contract *"I am ..."* to *"I'm ..."* or *"must not"* to *"mustn't"*. Some expressions even seem to change from two or three words to one (e.g. *"I'm going to wait."* becomes *"I'm gonna wait."* and *"I've got to go."* becomes *"I gotta go."*). All of these are natural features of connected speech and are useful for learners to learn, especially if they hear them regularly in the community or on television. The best way to do this is to drill sentences, first slowly, then more quickly. We can also use poems, songs and **rhymes** to help learners improve their connected speech (see *Rhymes and Poems* under *Ideas for Pronunciation Activities* below). Intonation is another important part of connected speech. It refers to the music of our sentences, and is most obvious in questions. Think about how you would pronounce this sentence, first as a statement of fact, then as a question:

You've all done your homework! Good! You've all done your homework? Yes?

Always encourage your learners to notice and copy intonation patterns, especially when they are asking questions. To help with this, you can drill the pronunciation of the questions before a discussion activity.

Techniques for improving learners' pronunciation

Let us look at four simple techniques we can use to help improve our learners' pronunciation:

Drilling

Drilling is the simplest and the most important technique for improving pronunciation. We should always drill the pronunciation of new vocabulary and new grammar that we teach. The simplest way to drill a word or sentence is to say it yourself and get the whole class to repeat after you. This is called **choral drilling**. After choral drilling, you can choose a few individual learners to say the word or phrase to check that most have got it correct. This is called **individual drilling**. It is not necessary to individually drill every learner. If you want to listen to all of them, get them to practise saying the vocabulary or sentences in pairs, and walk round the class listening to the pairs. This way you can provide individual help more effectively if you hear any mistakes. Remember that drilling should be a quick activity (a few seconds for each word), and should always be followed by other enjoyable and meaningful ways of using the new language.

Showing and explaining

If your learners have difficulty pronouncing a sound or a word in English, it can be useful to show them how you are pronouncing it. Tell the learners to look at your mouth. Say the word or sound slowly with **exaggerated pronunciation** several times. Tell them to listen silently at this stage. You can then explain (in the mother tongue) what your lips, tongue, teeth and voice are doing. After this, give them a minute or two to practise in pairs, and **monitor**.

Awareness of word stress

As well as underlining the stressed syllable when you teach a new word, it is useful to ask the learners: *"Where is the stress on this word?"* You can ask them this question after drilling a new word, after hearing a mistake with word stress or when **revising** a word they have studied before. A learner can answer the question in three different ways:

- they say the word with exaggerated stress;
- they come to the chalkboard to underline the stressed syllable;
- they say "on the first/second/third syllable".

Reading out loud

When learners are practising reading as a skill, they should try to read silently (see *Chapter C6 – Teaching Reading*), but when we want learners to practise their pronunciation we can get them to read a text **out loud**. This is particularly useful with dialogues, short texts, poems and song lyrics. Although you could get one learner to read out loud while others listen, it is more effective to do this in pairs or small groups, so that everybody gets an opportunity to practise. While they do this, you can monitor, listen for errors and provide individual correction. Remember that when learners are reading out loud, they find it difficult to understand what they are reading, so choose **silent reading** if your aim is text comprehension.

Practical task: Sound advice

Here are three pronunciation problems. What advice would you give the teacher?

A. "My students cannot say 'won't' properly. It sounds exactly the same as 'want' when they say it."

B. "My learners often pronounce words with the stress at the end. They say 'doc<u>tor</u>', not '<u>doc</u>tor', and say 'tele<u>phone</u>', not '<u>tele</u>phone.'"

C. "My secondary school students all speak English well, but when they say sentences, the words are broken up. I want them to sound more natural."

Commentary to practical task: Sound advice

A. Many languages do not have the long /əʊ/ vowel sound in 'won't'. The two words 'want' and 'won't' are identical except for this vowel. Begin by showing and explaining in the mother tongue how to pronounce the two sounds. Next, drill the sounds and the two words chorally, starting with the word on its own, then using it in a short sentence ("I won't go."/"I want to go."). Follow this with individual drilling and then time to practise the pronunciation in pairs. Finish with a little more choral drilling. You could try playing *Odd one out* (see below) with the /əʊ/ sound in 'won't'.

B. In some languages words are stressed at the end, or near the end, but many long words in English are stressed on the first syllable. Begin by explaining and showing some examples of word stress, comparing the right stress and the wrong stress. Then, whenever you hear a stress mistake, ask the learners: *"Where is the stress?"* and drill the correct stress thoroughly. Try doing the *Count the syllables* activity below.

C. It sounds like these learners do not get much speaking practice. So the first piece of advice is to do more speaking practice activities (see *Chapter C4 – Teaching Speaking* for ideas). To help them improve their rhythm in connected speech, get them to practise reading short texts out loud in pairs or groups of three once a lesson, and also try doing some songs (see *Chapter C10 – Games and Songs*) and rhymes (see below) with them.

Ideas for pronunciation activities

1. Odd one out

Interaction pattern: Groups

Resources needed: Chalkboard

This activity is described in *Chapter C2* for teaching vocabulary. It can be adapted for pronunciation, and can be done with any sound that your learners are finding difficult. Write words of one syllable in groups of four on the chalkboard. Three of the words should have the same vowel sound, and the other should have a different vowel sound. The learners work in pairs to decide which word is different. Here is an example:

Odd one out

1. see hear week team
2. play cat game rain
3. put but cut hut

Solution: *The odd ones out are 1 – hear, 2 – cat, 3 – put.*

2. Rhymes and poems

Interaction pattern: Whole class, then in pairs

Resources needed: Chalkboard

Children love rhymes and poems in any language. They have natural rhythm that makes them easy to memorise. They help with word stress, connected speech, and also with learning grammar and vocabulary. Copy a rhyme or poem you know onto the chalkboard (or onto a rice sack or poster paper if you can). Say the rhyme once or twice. The learners should just listen. Remember to click your fingers or clap your hands as you say the rhyme. Then get the learners to say the rhyme with you. You can add actions, movements or special sounds to make it more enjoyable. Then get the learners to practise the rhyme in pairs. Remember to use the rhyme again soon. Here are two examples. *Old MacDonald* is fun at lower levels because the learners can say the animal sounds and pretend to be the animals. *My Pet Dinosaur*, a poem for children by Charles Thompson is easy to understand and has a strong rhythm that can help higher level learners with connected speech. If your learners enjoy rhymes and poems, you'll find links to many more in the *Useful Websites and Online Materials* section at the back of this book.

Old MacDonald

Old MacDonald has a farm, ee-ai-ee-ai-oh,
And on his farm he has some chicks, ee-ai-ee-ai-oh.
With a 'chick, chick' here and a 'chick, chick' there,
Here a 'chick', there a 'chick', everywhere a 'chick, chick'.
Old MacDonald has a farm, ee-ai-ee-ai-oh.

> Old MacDonald has a farm, ee-ai-ee-ai-oh,
> And on his farm he has a cow, ee-ai-ee-ai-oh.
> With a 'moo, moo' here and a 'moo, moo' there,
> Here a 'moo', there a 'moo', everywhere a 'moo, moo'.
> Old MacDonald has a farm, ee-ai-ee-ai-oh.

Note: This continues with other animals: the sheep says 'baa, baa', the dog says 'woof, woof', the duck says 'quack, quack', etc. Learners can pretend to be the animals when they say the sounds.

My Pet Dinosaur

My dinosaur
was getting thinner
and so I brought him
home for dinner.

*He ate as fast
as he was able:
he ate the food,
he ate the table.*

*He ate the fridge,
he ate the chair,
he ate my favourite
teddy bear.*

*He is a very
naughty pet.
He even ate
the TV set.*

by Charles Thompson

3. Pronunciation chase

Interaction pattern: Whole class, then in groups

Resources needed: Chalkboard, notebooks

This is a fun game for helping learners to improve their pronunciation listening skills. Write several words on the chalkboard that have similar pronunciation. See Fig. C3.3.

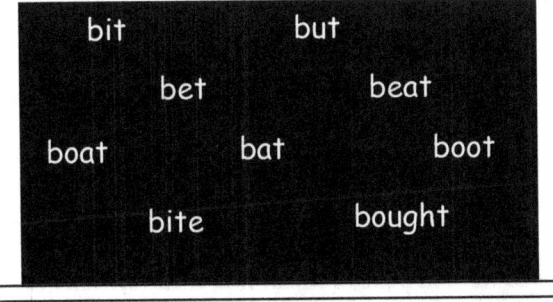

Fig. C3.3: BOARD FOR PRONUNCIATION CHASE

Divide the class into three or four teams and get a volunteer from each team to come to the front. They should stand next to each other two metres from the chalkboard. Say one of the words (do not point at it). The volunteers must run and touch the word that you said. The first one to touch the correct word wins one point for their team. Change volunteers and play again. After this, tell the learners to play the game in groups of three to four. They should copy the words from the chalkboard into their notebooks. One group member says the words. The others must touch the word on the page. You can also play this game using whole sentences. For example the following sentences, which practise 'can' and 'can't', have similar pronunciation when spoken quickly.

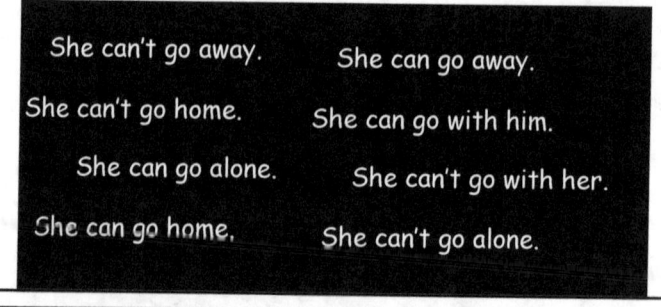

Fig. C3.4: PRONUNCIATION CHASE USING SENTENCES

4. **Syllables and stress**

Interaction pattern: Whole class, then in pairs

Resources needed: Chalkboard, notebooks

This is a useful activity for helping learners to improve their awareness of syllables and word stress. Choose a number of words that the learners have studied with different numbers of syllables and different stresses and write them mixed up in a box on the chalkboard. Then draw several columns under the box, with circles to represent patterns of unstressed and stressed syllables. For example:

| decide computer party country animal begin exercise |
| decision instrument children between together |

●● (e.g. listen)	●● (e.g. away)	●●● (e.g. probably)	●●● (e.g. unhappy)

Tell the learners to work in pairs to decide how many syllables each word has and where the stress is. Then they should write it in the correct column. For example, the first word in the box, 'decide' has two syllables with the stress on the second syllable, so it should go in the second column. 'Computer' has three syllables with the stress on the second syllable, so it should go in the last column.

Solution:

●● (e.g. listen)	●● (e.g. away)	●●● (e.g. probably)	●●● (e.g. unhappy)
party	decide	animal	computer
children	between	exercise	decision
country	begin	instrument	together

5. Minimal pairs work

Interaction pattern: Whole class, then in pairs

Resources needed: Chalkboard, notebooks

Minimal pairs are two words that are identical except for one sound. For example 'bad' and 'bed' or 'light' and 'right'. We can use minimal pairs work to help learners to hear and pronounce these sound differences.

Choose two sounds that your learners have difficulty pronouncing. Let's choose short /ɪ/ and long /iː/ as in 'ship' and 'sheep'. Write several minimal pairs in two columns on the board as in the diagram below:

A) long /iː/	B) short /ɪ/
sheep	ship
eat	it
reach	rich
seat	sit

First show the learners the difference between the two sounds using exaggerated pronunciation and then drill the words in the two columns. Next, tell the learners that you will say a word and they must shout out "A" or "B", depending on which column it is in. Do this several times, confirming the correct column after each one. Then get a few learners to say a word while their classmates identify the column. Finally, they should do the same in pairs, saying words for their partner, who identifies the correct column for each word, while you monitor.

Conclusion

In this chapter we have learnt the following:
- all varieties of English are equally important;
- you should not worry if you have a local **accent** – it may be a useful model for your learners;
- you should help learners with three important areas of pronunciation – sounds, word stress and connected speech;
- drilling is the simplest and most important way to improve your learners' pronunciation;
- when learners find a word difficult, show it carefully and explain how to pronounce it;
- use the question "Where's the stress?" to improve your learners awareness of word stress;
- reading out loud can help learners improve their connected speech.

C4 – Teaching Speaking

In this chapter:

- Why teach speaking skills?
- An example speaking lesson
- Practical task: Help!
- Commentary to practical task: Help!
- Speaking skills and the curriculum
- Controlled speaking and free speaking
- Ideas for speaking activities

 **Reflective task**

Read these opinions and decide which ones you agree with. Give reasons for your decisions:

1. *"Speaking practice is impossible in large classes."*
2. *"Speaking practice helps learners to remember the grammar and vocabulary that they have learnt."*
3. *"Speaking practice is a great way to motivate students."*

Why teach speaking skills?

There are several important reasons why we should include regular activities to practise speaking skills in our lessons:

- Speaking is probably the most difficult skill. It requires us to produce language quickly, without planning, so it needs lots of practice.
- Speaking activities get learners to use the vocabulary and grammar that they have studied. If they use this vocabulary and grammar, they are more likely to remember it.
- Speaking activities allow learners to express their opinion and share their ideas and their knowledge, which they enjoy doing.
- Whenever a learner is speaking, other learners are listening to him or her, so it also helps learners to improve their listening skills.
- When we can speak well in a foreign language, we feel a great sense of achievement.

We can see that speaking is challenging, useful, enjoyable and satisfying. Your learners will improve their English quickly if they get some speaking practice every lesson. Just 5 – 10 minutes is useful. You will find lots of ideas for speaking activities at the end of this chapter. Alternatively, if you want to plan individual lessons to practise speaking skills, this is also possible, and shown in the example lesson below.

An example speaking lesson

Here is an example speaking lesson for upper primary school level:

Lesson title: Role Play in a Food Shop

Lesson objectives: By the end of the lesson, the learners will have practised their speaking skills – buying food in a shop and discussing food.

Context of lesson: The learners studied food vocabulary earlier in the week.

Time: 40 minutes	**Number of learners:** 75

Age of learners: 9 – 10	**Level:** Low intermediate

Stage	Time	Activities	Examples of language used*
1.	1 min	Teacher greets learners and introduces the lesson.	T: "Today we are going to practise speaking skills by doing a **role play** in a shop."
2.	1 min	Teacher writes a short dialogue on the chalkboard between a shopkeeper and a customer.	Shopkeeper: How can I help you? Customer: Do you have any eggs? etc.
3.	1 min	Teacher models the dialogue by reading it **out loud**. Learners listen.	T: "Would you like anything else? … Yes. I also need some sugar. How much does it cost?" etc.
4.	3 mins	Learners read the dialogue in pairs. They play *Progressive deletion* (see *Ideas for Speaking Activities* in this chapter): Teacher rubs out a few words. Learners read dialogue again, trying to remember the missing words.	On chalkboard: Shopkeeper: How can I _____ you? Customer: Do you have any _____? Shopkeeper: Yes. How _____ do you want? Customer: I _____ 10 eggs, please.

Stage	Time	Activities	Examples of language used*
5.	2 mins	Teacher shows learners 5 common items of food and puts them on the table (plantains, onions, tomatoes, rice and mangos). She writes the role play synopsis on the chalkboard.	Role Play Synopsis: Student A: You need to buy 5 items of food to make dinner tonight. You only have 200/= shillings. Go to the shop. Student B: You are the shop keeper. Decide how much each of the items on the table costs. Student A will come to your shop to buy the items.
6.	4 mins	Two strong learners demonstrate the role play. Other learners watch and listen.	L1: "Good afternoon. How can I help you?" L2: "I need some rice. How much does it cost?" etc.
7.	7 mins	Learners role play conversation (shopkeeper and customer) in closed pairs. Teacher **monitors**, noting down any mistakes but not interrupting.	L1: "How much are the onions?" L2: "They are 10 shillings each." L1: "Oh that is too expensive. Lower the price, please!"
8.	4 mins	Teacher **praises** all learners and gets one pair who did well to perform their role play for the class. Other learners watch.	T: "Well done everybody! Good work! Now listen to Fatima and Kabelo. What does Fatima buy? How much does she pay?"
9.	3 mins	Teacher writes four common errors that she heard during **pairwork** role plays on the chalkboard. Learners discuss in pairs how to correct them.	1. How much is cost? 2. I don't want. Is too expensive! etc.
10.	2 mins	Volunteers come to the chalkboard to correct errors. Teacher praises them.	T: "Who can correct the first sentence? Bernard? Here, take the chalk."
11.	1 min	Teacher writes five **personalisation** questions on the chalkboard, on the topic of food and shopping.	1. How often do you go shopping? 2. Where do you buy vegetables/meat/eggs? etc.

Stage	Time	Activities	Examples of language used*
12.	5 mins	Learners discuss the questions in groups of four. One group member is the English monitor, and makes sure they all speak English.	L1: "I go shopping every Saturday with my mother." L2: "Me too. I also go on Wednesday, sometimes."
13.	3 mins	Teacher praises learners and gets feedback from several groups.	T: "Well done! Good speaking. So, in this group – who goes shopping most often?"
14.	1 min	Teacher concludes lesson by asking learners what skills they practised and how they will be useful in the future.	T: "So, what skills did we practise today?" L1: "We practised speaking – a conversation at the shop …" etc.
15.	1 min	Teacher praises learners and gives homework.	T: "Well done everybody! Now, for homework I'd like you to …" etc.

* *This includes what the teacher and learners said and also examples from exercises and boardwork.*

Note the following abbreviations are used above: T= teacher L= learner Ls= learners L1= 1st learner, etc.

Practical task: Help!

The following five teachers all have problems with speaking activities. Read the problems and think of some good advice to give each teacher:

"My classes are too big for speaking practice (70 – 80 students). Sometimes I try to make one or two students speak in front of the class, but they get very nervous and the other students get bored waiting for them to finish."

Daniel

"When I do speaking activities, some of the students speak in their mother tongue, not in English."

Rose

"When I do speaking in pairs or groups, the class gets too noisy. I'm worried it will disturb other teachers, or the head teacher will think I am not in control of the students."

Takwa

"Speaking is not in the exams, so it is a waste of time doing speaking practice."

Yussuf

"The students make lots of mistakes when they do speaking activities in pairs, and I can't correct them all."

Ondasi

Commentary to practical task: Help!

Daniel

Doing speaking practice in large classes: It is true that a large class can make speaking practice activities more difficult to organise and manage, but with regular practice, clear rules and lots of praise from the teacher, it is possible and enjoyable. Daniel should get his learners to do speaking practice in closed pairs or small groups, not in front of the class. This will allow all the learners to practise their speaking skills at the same time, and they will all get much more practice this way. See *Chapter A3* for more about how to do **pairwork** and **groupwork** and how to arrange the desks for this.

Rose

Learners' use of their mother tongue: This is a common problem, and there are several things Rose can do. It is often because they are enjoying the activity so much that they forget to speak English, so Rose should remind them before the activity that only English is allowed. If she hears the **mother tongue** during the activity, she can note down the names of learners who are using it most, and speak to them after the lesson, explaining why they must speak only English. After the activity, she should praise the learners who speak only English. This will encourage them all to speak more English next time. If she still has problems, she can try putting them in groups of three or four for speaking practice, and make one member of each group the **English monitor** who must make sure everyone in the group speaks only English.

Takwa

Too much noise: Some teachers think that noise in a class is an indication of bad behaviour but this is not necessarily true. Noise is evidence of communication which, in a child-centred class, is an important part of learning. Takwa can explain this to her colleagues. If the noise levels are so loud that her class is disturbing other classes, she can pause the activity and remind her learners to sit as close as possible to their partner(s) and to speak quietly.

Yussuf

It is not tested in the examination: Some teachers do not teach speaking because it is not in the exam. They have so many other things to do, and they think that speaking is a waste of time. But this is not true. Even though it may not be in their next exam, speaking activities provide learners with an opportunity to use all the vocabulary and grammar that they have learnt, helping them to **proceduralise** their knowledge. It is the fastest way to do this, and possibly the most effective because it is enjoyable, and learners learn more when they are enjoying themselves.

Ondasi

Correction during speaking practice: Many teachers worry that if they do not correct all their learners' mistakes, their English will get worse. While correction is useful, children learn correct language use from reading or listening and then trying out what they have learnt more than from having their spoken English corrected. It is more important to allow them to practise their speaking skills without too many interruptions. However, correction of common mistakes or mistakes with the new grammar or vocabulary can be useful. Ondasi should note down any mistakes that he hears from several learners while he monitors the activity. Then he can write them on the chalkboard afterwards and get the learners to correct their own errors as in the example lesson above.

Speaking skills and the curriculum

Some teachers do not do much speaking because they find that their curriculum emphasises grammar and provides few suggestions for communicative activities. Other teachers complain that their curriculum is very long and ambitious, and they feel that there is not enough time to do speaking. However, it is possible to create speaking activities that are relevant to the curriculum, meaning that the learners practise speaking skills while learning curriculum content at the same time. Here is how:

A. Take a piece of paper and write down the name of the grammar point or structure you are teaching – this is called the **target language**.
B. Think of a spoken conversation in which two people might use this target language and write down a few example sentences from this conversation.
C. Create an activity that will get your learners to produce these sentences. For example, they could role-play a dialogue (see *Ideas for Speaking Activities* below) which gets them to use this target language, or they could ask each other personalisation questions (also see below) that get them to produce the target language in their answers.

Here is an example:
- A. Target language: Present perfect simple
- B. Two people are talking about some of the interesting things they have done in their life: *"I have made my own dress." "I have played football for my school." "Have you ever made anything?" "Have you ever played a team sport?"*
- C. Work in pairs. Ask your partner these questions, and find out more if they say 'yes'.
  1. Have you ever made anything useful?
  2. Have you ever played a team sport?
  3. Have you ever travelled to a different district or county?
  4. Have you ever been to a wedding?
  5. Have you ever used a mobile phone or a computer?

With a little practice, you will find that you can do this quickly and easily. As well as providing an opportunity for speaking practice, this method will provide the learners with useful practice of the grammar that you have taught, helping them to learn it more effectively.

Controlled speaking and free speaking

There are many types of speaking practice activities. One way of categorising them is according to **control level**. This is useful because it enables us to see how easy or difficult they might be for our learners to do. Let us imagine three points on a line showing different levels of control:

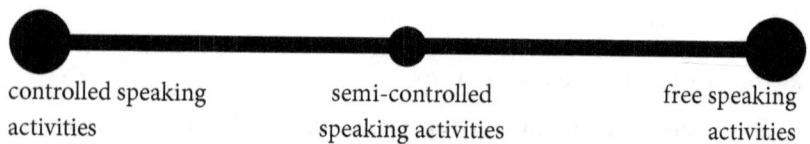

controlled speaking activities   semi-controlled speaking activities   free speaking activities

Fig. C4.1: CONTROL LEVEL

At one end of the line we have **controlled speaking activities**. For example, we can write a complete dialogue on the chalkboard and ask the learners to read it out, working in pairs. This is strongly controlled because everything the learners say is written on the chalkboard.

In the middle, we have **semi-controlled speaking activities**. For example, if we write only half a dialogue on the chalkboard, with just the questions of one of the speakers. This is semi-controlled because one learner is free to answer the questions as he or she likes.

At the other end of the line we have **free speaking activities**. For example, if we just describe a situation for a conversation on the chalkboard, but do not write down any specific sentences for them to use, they must create the whole conversation from their imagination.

Activities on the left of the line are easier for learners to do, and activities on the right of the line are more difficult. So, when we begin to do speaking practice activities with our learners, we should start on the left and move gradually towards the right, as shown by the arrow in Fig. C4.2 below:

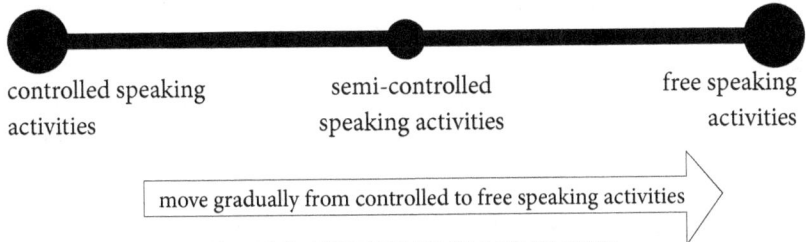

Fig. C4.2: CONTROL LEVEL MOVEMENT

Ideas for speaking activities

Here are some ideas for speaking activities that you can do. None of them require special resources, and there are many ways to do each one, so remember to adapt them to your teaching context. If you have never done speaking practice before, start with the more **controlled practice** activities. As the learners gain confidence, move onto the free speaking activities. Remember that all these activities should be done in closed pairs or small groups of three to four learners.

1. **Dialogues (controlled speaking activity)**

Recommended interaction: Pairs or **threes**

Materials needed: Dialogue written on chalkboard or in **textbook**

Dialogues are conversations between two people. You can sometimes find them in your textbook or invent your own and write it on the chalkboard. Here is a simple example of a greetings dialogue for lower primary learners:

    A: Good morning, Joseph.
    B: Good morning, Lydia. How are you?
    A: I'm fine. How are you?
    B: I'm not very well today. I have a cold.
    A: Oh dear! I hope you get better soon.
    B: Thanks. See you later!
    A: Bye!

If we get the learners to practise the dialogue as above, the activity is very controlled. To make it semi-controlled, we can leave a few blank spaces in the dialogue, for the learners to complete with their own names and ideas. For example:

    A: Good morning, _____.
    B: Good morning, _____. How are you?
    A: I _____. How are you?
    B: I _____. etc.

2. Progressive deletion (controlled speaking activity)

Recommended interaction: Pairs or threes

Materials needed: Dialogue, song or any short text written on the chalkboard

Progressive deletion (also called 'Rub out and replace') is a memory game that learners enjoy playing. First write a text of some kind on the chalkboard (e.g. a dialogue or a song). Then tell the learners to read it out loud in pairs once. Next rub out four or five words from the text and tell them to read it again. They should try to remember the missing words as they read. Rub out another four or five words and tell them to read it again. Continue until you have removed the majority of the text. Then ask them to tell you the whole text from start to finish, while you 'replace' it on the chalkboard. Here is an example – a song by the Beatles, called 'From Me to You.'

If there's anything that you want,	If there's that you ,
If there's anything I can do,	If 's anything I do,
Just call on me and I'll send it along,	call on me I'll it ,
With love from me to you.	With from to .

Fig. C4.3: PROGRESSIVE DELETION

3. Define and guess (semi-controlled to free speaking activity)

Interaction pattern: Groups of 4 – 6

Materials needed: Words written on small pieces of paper (several words per group)

Define and guess is a vocabulary describing game played in small groups. Each group receives a number of small pieces of paper from the teacher. On each piece of paper there is a word written in English. One learner takes a piece of paper and tries to define or describe the word without saying it. Her classmates must try to guess the word. The first one to guess it wins the piece of paper. Then another learner takes his turn. The learner with the most pieces of paper at the end is the winner. If you use a Vocabulary Box (see *Chapter C12 – 10 Essential Resources to Create*), you can take your words from it. Alternatively, you can get the learners to help; each group writes 10 new words from this week's lessons on pieces of paper. Then they give these words to a different group to play with.

4. Role play (semi-controlled to free speaking activity)

Interaction pattern: Pairs or small groups

Materials needed: Chalkboard

In a role play activity, learners pretend to be somebody else, somewhere else, having a conversation. They might be a seller and a buyer at the local market, or two parents at home organising their day. They could pretend to be a doctor and a patient in a hospital, or even pretend to be the president of their country and a journalist. In order to do a role play, the learners need a synopsis, which can be written on the chalkboard. Here is a simple example, similar to the one used in the example lesson earlier in this chapter:

> **Role play – In a shop**
>
> Student A: You are the shopkeeper of a food shop.
>
> Student B: You are a customer at the shop. You need to buy 10 eggs, a bag of sugar and a packet of biscuits. Make sure you do not pay too much!

Note that Student A will need to invent prices for the products based on his/her knowledge of the prices in real shops. Student B will need to decide if the prices are acceptable before buying. Here is another synopsis. It is more detailed than the first:

> **Role play – Buying a bus ticket**
>
> Student A: You would like to buy a bus ticket for tomorrow morning. You need to go to the capital city to attend an important wedding in the afternoon. You only have $5.00.
>
> Student B: You work in the bus ticket office. You have no tickets available for tomorrow morning, except on a private bus that costs $6.00. The cheaper bus ($4.00) leaves at 2 p.m. tomorrow afternoon.

This synopsis should inspire an interesting conversation, with lots of negotiation of prices and times. They will improvise, responding to what their partner says, just like in real life.

When you begin doing role play with your learners, it is a good idea to demonstrate how to do it, either with a strong learner or another teacher. This will show them how they can improvise and be creative. Here are some more ideas for role plays, including everyday situations and more creative role plays. You can probably think of lots more:

- a customer and a seller at the market/in a shop/in a post office;
- a customer buying a ticket at a bus station;
- a doctor and a patient in the hospital;
- a local person giving directions to a visitor or tourist;
- a person asking a neighbour to borrow some money;
- an old man giving advice to a teenager;
- a customer complaining in a café or a hotel;
- a young man proposing marriage to his girlfriend;
- a politician being interviewed by a journalist.

5. Personalisation (semi-controlled to free speaking activity)

Interaction pattern: Pairs or threes

Materials needed: Chalkboard

In personalisation activities, learners use English to talk about themselves and their world. They must provide real answers to the questions, answers that are different for every learner. There is a personalisation activity in Stage 11 of the example lesson above.

Write several questions with 'you' or 'your' on the chalkboard and tell the learners to ask their partners. Here is an example for a low level class:

My favourite things

1. What is your favourite food?   My favourite food is …
2. What is your favourite colour?
3. What is your favourite day of the week?
4. Who is your best friend?

You can write personalisation questions about any topic (e.g. animals, food, hobbies, family, sport, transport, holidays, the environment, etc.) Here is an example for the topic of animals, which can be used at intermediate levels:

Animals

1. What animals do you have at home? How many of each?
2. What is your favourite animal? Why?
3. Are there any animals that you do not like? Which ones?
4. What animals have you seen today? Where?

Notice the follow-up questions (How many of each? Why? etc.), which encourage longer answers. Personalisation questions can also be used to practise specific areas of grammar. For example, if you have just taught past tenses, you can get the learners to ask each other about what they did yesterday.

6. Discussions (free speaking activity)

Interaction pattern: Pairs, threes or groups of 4 – 6

Materials needed: Chalkboard

Discussions are speaking activities in which learners give their opinion on a topic. They are an effective way to provide free speaking practice. They can be done in pairs or in groups. Like personalisation questions, you can write discussion questions on

any topic, which can be linked to what they have studied recently, either in English or in other lessons such as social studies. Here are some examples of discussion questions:
- Which is the most important job in society? Why?
- What is the purpose of school?
- Which is the best form of transport? Why?
- How can we reduce crime in society?
- Do you think television is a good thing? Why? Why not?

We can even combine personalisation and discussion questions in the same speaking practice activity.

7. **Debates (free speaking activity)**

Interaction pattern: Groups of four or more, up to whole class

Materials needed: Chalkboard

Debates are similar to discussions. However, in a debate, each learner must agree or disagree with a statement (usually called a 'motion'). Here are some examples of motions:
- "Sport is a waste of time and energy."
- "Girls make better teachers than boys."
- "Money is the root of all evil."
- "We have a duty to protect the environment for future generations."

The learners are expected to present reasons (called 'arguments') for their opinion and to 'win' the debate by defeating their opponents. Sometimes the teacher chooses which learners support (or 'propose') the motion and which learners oppose the motion. Alternatively, we can allow them to decide whether they agree or disagree with a motion, so that they can express their own opinions.

Traditionally, debates are done as whole class activities, or even as part of an **English Club**, which takes place after school in the afternoon. This makes them exciting, but often in such whole-class debates only the strongest speakers of English will take part, and the majority of learners become listeners. To ensure that debates provide speaking practice for all the learners, we should reduce the group sizes, for example by creating groups of four to six learners. In each group two or three learners are for a motion, and the other two or three learners are against the motion. Before they have their debate, we should give them time to prepare for it, and we can also encourage them to speak English while preparing, to provide more speaking practice.

Conclusion

In this chapter we have learnt the following:
- why it is important to do speaking activities in our English lessons;
- how to do speaking practice in large classes;
- how to reduce use of the mother tongue during speaking practice activities;
- why noise is not a bad thing during speaking practice;
- how to correct mistakes made during speaking practice activities;
- how we can create speaking practice activities that fit into the curriculum;
- the difference between controlled and free speaking activities.

C5 – Teaching Listening

In this chapter:

- What can we listen to?
- Listening practice at lower levels
- Preparing for listening lessons
- An example listening lesson
- The grasshopper and the frog
- Practical task: A listening lesson activity cycle
- Commentary to practical task: A listening lesson activity cycle
- Three key stages for listening activities
- Ideas for listening activities

 **Reflective task**

1. Does your textbook include listening practice activities?
2. If 'yes', do you use these activities? Why/Why not?
3. If 'no', how do you provide listening practice for your learners?

What can we listen to?

Listening is one of the four skills. As such, it is an important part of language learning. Like reading, it can provide a way for learners to learn new vocabulary and grammar naturally. Although some textbooks include listening activities, teachers often do not use them because they are too difficult, or because they do not have the electronic resources (CD player, batteries, etc.). Because of this, many learners listen only to their teacher giving instructions or explaining grammar, which can be very repetitive and not very useful. However, many teachers forget that there are other ways to practise and improve listening skills. There are four basic types of listening activity that we can do in class:

1. Listening to the teacher's voice
2. Listening to each other
3. Listening to recordings
4. Listening to broadcasts

1. Listening to the teacher's voice

Your voice is a wonderful resource for listening activities. It is clearer than a CD or DVD. You can change the loudness, slow it down or speed it up, and even simplify the vocabulary. Best of all, your voice never runs out of electricity! Some teachers are concerned that their pronunciation may not be good enough for listening activities. Obviously, this depends on the needs of your learners. However, if you speak English with a local **accent**, by listening to you regularly, your learners will improve their ability to understand English used in the local community and on local television and radio. So your accent may be very useful to them!

Here are some ideas for how to use your voice for listening activities in class:
- tell the learners a story in English;
- read out a short, simple text from the textbook, or a listening tapescript;
- describe a place, a day in the past, your future plans or a member of your family;
- sing songs with your learners, or read poetry to them;
- pretend to be other people, such as a television newsreader, a shopkeeper or a businessman on the phone.

All of these things provide useful variety for your learners and enable them to hear different types of spoken English.

2. Listening to each other

Whenever learners are communicating with each other in **pairwork** or **groupwork**, at least half of them are listening. Dialogues, **role plays**, **personalisation**, discussion and all the other speaking activities described in *Chapter C4 – Teaching Speaking* are examples of this. This type of communicative listening is useful for several reasons:
- like the teacher's voice, the sound quality is good;
- it is easy for them to understand, as most learners in a class have similar levels of English;
- learners can **negotiate meaning** by asking questions or **paraphrasing** what they understood to check understanding;
- most importantly, it is enjoyable!

As well as pairwork and groupwork listening, learners can also listen to each other giving presentations to the class, reading written homework **out loud** or performing role plays and drama.

3. Listening to recordings

If your textbook has a CD, it is important to use this as much as possible because it provides access to a variety of accents, conversations and comprehension tasks, all related to the textbook topics and grammar. If you have access to a CD player and electricity or batteries, use these recordings at least once a week. If the listening activities are too difficult for your learners, try using the CD from a lower level textbook.

But what should teachers do if they do not have a CD player, electricity, or if the book has no listening material?

You can use the internet, mobile phones or MP3 players and portable speakers to provide your learners with listening activities. If you have internet access on your mobile phone, you can download listening activities and songs from English language learning websites (see *Listening resources* and *Song resources* in the *Useful Websites and Online Materials* section at the back of this book). If not, you can use a computer to download the recordings or transfer them from CD to MP3 player or mobile phone. You can find listening materials in many places:

- On the internet. Using a search engine like Google, you can search for "English listening practice" or "songs for children in English".
- You can transfer recordings from coursebook CDs to your mobile phone or MP3 player at an internet cafe. Ask for help at the cafe if you do not know how to do this.
- Local libraries may have songs and other recordings on CDs.

You can even use the voice recorder function on a mobile phone to record a conversation between yourself and another teacher or friend and play it back in class using audio speakers.

Special MP3 players designed for teachers and learners in developing countries are also being produced, for example the *Lifeplayer*, (see Fig. C5.1) which runs on solar or 'wind up' power. You can play MP3 audio files on such players using a USB connection.

4. Listening to broadcasts

In every country radio and television programmes are made to help children learn English. If you have a radio or television in your school, you can use these programmes. You can listen to them 'live' in class, or you can record broadcasts in the evening using an MP3 player, cassette recorder or mobile phone and play them in class the next day.

Listening practice at lower levels

Here are three ideas for listening activities that you can use at lower primary level (ages 5 – 8):

1. Total physical response (TPR) activities and games

This is when the teacher (or a learner) gives a command and the learners must do the command. We can say: "*Stand up, clap your hands, sit down*". If the learners do all three actions, they are showing they understand the command. We can extend this simple idea into games, such as *Simon says ...* or *Boys and girls* (see *Ideas for listening activities* below), and also use it to practise grammar through mime activities ("*I'm playing football ... Can you play football with me?*").

2. Songs with movements

Similar to TPR, but even more fun for younger learners, we can sing songs which have special movements or actions for the learners to perform as we sing. For example: "*The wheels on the bus go round and round ...*" (learners move hands in a circle); or "*If you're happy and you know it clap your hands ...*" (learners clap their hands). See *Chapter C10 – Games and Songs* for more on this.

3. **Describe and draw**

The teacher says: *"Draw a house with two windows."* or *"Draw a lion hunting a zebra.".* If the learners draw the right picture, it shows they understand the command. As they improve, you can do more detailed activities with several steps (*"… and in front of the shop, draw a man on a motorbike …"*).

Preparing for listening lessons

Always prepare carefully for a listening lesson to make it easier for the learners:

Disturbance from other noises

Plan listening lessons for the quiet times of the day. If possible, close windows. If there is a quiet classroom in the school, you may be able to swap classrooms with the teacher.

The listening source

The listening source (e.g. your voice; speakers; a learner doing a presentation) should be close to the learners and pointing towards them. It should also be loud enough for them to hear easily. If necessary, move learners closer to the source.

Fig. C5.1: LIFEPLAYER

Disturbance from the learners

In a big classroom, allow time for the learners to get ready before starting the activity. If the learners are not all silent and looking at you, they are not ready. Remind them not to make any noise during the listening.

An example listening lesson

Here is an example listening lesson for lower secondary school level:

Lesson title: The Grasshopper and the frog

Lesson objectives: By the end of the lesson, the learners will have improved their listening and speaking skills (telling traditional stories).

Context of lesson: The learners have recently studied question forms and food vocabulary.

Time: 40 minutes

Number of learners: 57

Age of learners: 12 – 13

Level: Intermediate

Stage	Time	Activities	Examples of language used*
1.	4 mins	Teacher greets learners. Learners **revise** food vocabulary through a quick game.	T: "Who can think of an orange vegetable?" Ls: "Carrot." etc.
2.	1 min	Teacher introduces lesson.	T: "Today, you are going to improve your listening and speaking skills by listening to and telling a traditional story."
3.	5 mins	Teacher **pre-teaches** vocabulary useful for understanding the story: (e.g. grasshopper, hop, dirty, etc.) and drills pronunciation.	T: "Watch me. What am I doing?" Ls: "You are jumping." T: "Yes. Or we can say I am hopping. Which animal hops?" etc.
4.	3 mins	Teacher draws pictures of grasshopper and frog on chalkboard. She asks learners questions about these animals and elicits answers.	T: "What does a frog eat?" Ls: "Insects and worms." T: "Good. What noise does a grasshopper make?" etc.
5.	2 mins	Teacher writes 5 comprehension questions on chalkboard. Learners copy into their notebooks.	1. Why does the frog get angry with the grasshopper? 2. Why does the grasshopper stop eating? etc.
6.	1 min	Teacher gets the attention of all the learners and provides a clear instruction.	T: "Listen to the story and write your answers to the questions in your notebooks. Work individually."
7.	3 mins	Teacher tells the story of the grasshopper and the frog using mime. Learners listen and make notes to answer comprehension questions.	T: "One day the frog invited the grasshopper to visit him for a meal: 'Why don't you come to have dinner with me tomorrow?' ..." (continues)
8.	2 mins	At the end of the story, learners discuss and check their answers to the questions in pairs. Teacher **monitors**, noticing how they have done.	L1: "What did you write for question 2?" L2: "I wrote 'he didn't want to disturb the frog.' Did you have the same answer?"

Stage	Time	Activities	Examples of language used*
9.	4 mins	Teacher tells the story again. Learners check in pairs again. Teacher monitors.	
10.	4 mins	Teacher elicits answers to comprehension questions from learners, checking others agree before confirming correct answers.	T: "Question 1: Who has the answer?" L: "He gets angry because …" etc. T: "Thank you. Does everyone agree? No? Why not?"
11.	7 mins	Teacher instructs learners to retell the story to their partner.	T: "Each of you should speak for 3 – 4 minutes. After one of you has finished, the other will tell the story."
12.	3 mins	One volunteer pair comes to the front to summarise the story to the whole class. Others to listen.	L: "One day a frog asked a grasshopper to come to his house for lunch …" etc.
13.	2 mins	Teacher **praises** all the learners, concludes the lesson, and gives a homework task.	T: "What did we learn today?" L: "We learnt a story – the grasshopper and the frog." T: "Good. For homework, ask your parents to tell you another traditional story."

* *This includes what the teacher and learners said and also examples from exercises and boardwork.*

Note the following abbreviations are used above: T= teacher, L= learner, Ls= learners, L1= 1st learner, etc.

Here is the whole story if you want to try this lesson with your class. Practise reading the story **out loud** and invent two different voices for the two animals to make it entertaining. You will find links to websites that have more stories like this in the *Useful Websites and Online Materials* section at the back of this book:

The grasshopper and the frog

One day the frog invited the grasshopper to visit him for a meal: 'Why don't you come to have dinner with me tomorrow?'

The next day the grasshopper arrived at the frog's house. They started eating, but as he ate, the grasshopper's legs rubbed together and made a very loud noise: 'CHIRP CHIRP!'

The frog got angry. 'Mr. Grasshopper, please stop chirping. I cannot eat with the noise,' he said. The grasshopper tried to eat without making a noise, but it was impossible. And each time his legs went 'CHIRP, CHIRP', the frog complained: 'Stop making that noise!' Grasshopper was so upset that he couldn't eat. He sat there hungry and watched the frog eating.

At the end of the meal he said, 'Mr. Frog, why don't you come to have dinner with me tomorrow?'

'What a good idea!' said the frog, greedily eating the last of the food.

The next day, the frog arrived at the grasshopper's home. The food was ready.

'Mr. Frog,' said the grasshopper, 'before we eat, let us wash our front legs in the river.' After this, they both hopped back to the sweet-smelling, delicious food. 'Oh, wait Mr. Frog,' said the grasshopper, just before the frog started eating. 'Your legs are dirty from hopping around in the mud. You should go back to the river to wash them.' The frog went and washed his front legs again, then hopped back to the food, where the grasshopper was already eating. But before the frog could eat any food, the grasshopper stopped him: 'Don't put your dirty feet into the food! Go and wash them again.'

'The frog was so angry: 'But I can't ... You know very well that I must use my front legs to hop about. They are always a bit dirty.'

'Sorry, my friend,' the grasshopper replied. 'But you did the same to me yesterday. You know I can't rub my front legs together without making a noise. Now you know how I felt yesterday.' The grasshopper finished the last of the food and licked his lips: 'Yum, yum!'

From that day the frog and the grasshopper were no longer friends.

The moral of the story is: If you want to be friends with someone, you must accept their faults, as well as their good qualities.

Practical task: A listening lesson activity cycle

In *Chapter A6 – Classroom Management and Behaviour Management*, we learnt that there are three stages to the **activity cycle**:
1. prepare the learners
2. monitor the activity
3. get feedback to the activity

Look again at the example listening lesson above and make notes on how the teacher of the lesson does these three things for the listening activity. If possible, compare your notes with another teacher before reading the commentary below.

Commentary to practical task: A listening lesson activity cycle

1. The teacher prepares the learners by doing three things:
   - pre-teaching important vocabulary;
   - engaging the learners;
   - providing a task and a clear instruction.

The teacher **pre-teaches** important vocabulary from the story. These are the most important words to help the learners understand the story (e.g. grasshopper, hop, dirty). She then draws the pictures of the grasshopper and the frog on the chalkboard to **engage** the learners. She asks questions to get the learners to think about what they already know about these two animals. In the third stage of preparation she writes a listening task on the board (five comprehension questions) for learners to copy and then gives her instruction. The task provides the learners with a reason to listen, and it provides the teacher with a way to assess how much they have understood during feedback. Here are some more ideas for listening tasks:

- Write true/false statements on the chalkboard. The learners listen to decide which are true and which are false.
- Write four to six sentences on the chalkboard that describe events from the listening activity. The learners must listen and put the sentences in the correct order.
- Draw a note table on the chalkboard, which learners copy into their notebooks. During the listening, they make notes in the table. Here is a simple example:

	His/Her opinion	Reasons
Speaker 1		
Speaker 2		
Speaker 3		

2. As this is a listening activity, the learners are doing the activity while they are listening to the teacher telling the story. She does not monitor during the listening itself, but after they have listened she gets them to check their

answers in pairs, and monitors at this stage. This gives them a chance to compare and discuss answers that they are not certain about, and it gives the teacher an opportunity to assess how well they have done. She can go round the class, listen to their discussions while they compare answers, and look at their notebooks. This gives her a good understanding of how well individual learners have done. Note that she lets them listen twice. They are likely to learn more during this second listening, as they will be familiar with the basic information and can concentrate on the details.

3. The teacher elicits the answers to the questions. She finds out if other learners agree before confirming the correct answer. Checking for agreement is useful because it provides the teacher with an evaluation of how well all the learners have done as a class.

Three key stages for listening activities

Let us summarise what we have learnt into three key stages for listening activities:

1. Before they listen	<ul><li>pre-teach useful vocabulary</li><li>engage the learners</li><li>give them a listening task</li></ul>
2. While they listen	<ul><li>let them listen two or three times</li></ul>
3. After they have listened	<ul><li>get them to check answers in pairs before feedback</li><li>check for agreement during feedback</li></ul>

Ideas for listening activities

1. **Live listening**

Interaction pattern: Whole class

Resources needed: Chalkboard and notebooks

Live listening is when the learners listen to a speaker 'live' in the classroom, rather than a recording. The speaker could be:

- the class teacher – you!
- two teachers (e.g. you and a colleague who visits your class for five minutes)
- one or two learners (e.g. a learner prepares a talk on a favourite topic)
- a friend of the teacher who speaks English (a **guest speaker**)

Live listening is easy to prepare, needs no special materials, and a speaker (the teacher) is always present. You can use it to provide listening practice of new grammar or vocabulary that you have studied. For example, after you study the present simple tense to talk about daily routines you can do a live listening activity where you tell the learners about your daily routines:

> "I get up at 6 o'clock every day. I wash and prepare breakfast with my children and husband. At 7 o'clock we eat breakfast. Then I walk with my children to the school where I work ..."

If you want, you can prepare by writing down what you are going to say. Alternatively, you can improvise it, which keeps your language more natural.

2. Storytelling

Interaction pattern: Whole class, then in pairs or groups

Resources needed: Chalkboard

Children love listening to stories. Storytelling is a natural way to use language and it can cover a wide range of topics. The example lesson above is based on a traditional story from West Africa, and includes two useful themes; animals and meals. Storytelling has several advantages:

- there are plenty of stories to choose from your local culture;
- preparation is fast; find the story, choose which vocabulary to pre-teach and think of a listening task;
- learners can retell the story in pairs or small groups after you have told it.

If you would like to find ideas for stories, use the internet. See *Resources for Listening* in *Useful Websites and Online Materials* at the back of this book. In half an hour you can find enough stories for a year and use each one as many times as you want!

3. Simon says …

Interaction pattern: Whole class

Resources needed: None

Simon says … is a popular game played around the world. If you like, you can change 'Simon' to a name from your country (the game is called "Sabah says …" in Eritrea, for example). It is even good for early primary learners. Here is how to play it:

Tell your learners that you will give them different commands. If you begin the command by saying 'Simon says …', they should obey the command. But if you do not begin by saying 'Simon says …', the learners should not obey the command. For example:

Teacher: *"Simon says 'Stand up'."*

The learners all stand up.

Teacher: *"Simon says 'Clap your hands twice'."*

The learners all clap their hands twice.

Teacher: *"Put your finger on your nose."*

Most of the learners do not put their finger on their nose (because the teacher did not begin with 'Simon says …'). Any learners who put their finger on their nose are out of the game. Either they lose a point, or they have to sit down and watch their classmates.

Other commands that you can use in the game are:

clap once/twice/three times; shake hands with another learner; smile; laugh; jump up and down once/twice/three times; turn around; touch your nose/ears/

knees/toes etc.; touch your partner's nose/ears/shoulder, etc.; pick up your pen/book/bag, etc.; put down your pen/book/bag, etc.

Once your learners are familiar with 'Simon says …', you can get them to play the game in groups of three to four. This game is really useful when your learners are tired. It puts a smile back on their faces!

4. Girls and boys

Interaction pattern: Whole class

Resources needed: None

This is a mime game, similar to 'Simon Says …', that you can use to practise action verbs and the present continuous tense. Here is how to play:

Tell your learners that you will say different sentences using the present continuous tense. Some sentences start with 'The girls are …', others start with 'The boys are …', and some start with 'Everybody is …'. If you start the sentence with 'The girls are …', only the girls should do the activity. If you start with 'The boys are …' only the boys should do the activity. If you start with 'Everybody is …', everybody should do the activity. For example:

Teacher: *"The girls are swimming."*

The girls pretend to be swimming.

Teacher: *"The boys are drinking water."*

The girls stop swimming and the boys pretend to be drinking water.

Teacher: *"The girls are playing football."*

The boys stop drinking water and the girls pretend to be playing football.

Teacher: *"Everybody is dancing."*

All the learners pretend to be dancing.

You can use "Girls and Boys" to practise any verb actions that the learners can mime, including eat, sleep, run, milk the cow, fish, prepare breakfast, chop wood, plough, wash their faces, clean their teeth, etc.

5. Role play performances

Interaction pattern: Whole class

Resources needed: None

In *What can we listen to?* (above), we learnt that the teacher can pretend to be other people, such as a television newsreader, a shopkeeper or a businessman on the phone. This 'pretending' is a form of role play. It is useful because it allows us to provide more variety to our listening practice activities. Remember to pre-teach vocabulary, engage the learners, and provide a listening task. For example, you can pretend to be a businessman on the phone, and use these questions:

1. Who is the businessman speaking to?
2. What are they talking about?
3. What problem does he have?

Remember to perform the conversation realistically. For the businessman role play, you can use your mobile phone as a prop, and perform only half the conversation, which makes it interesting and challenging for the learners:

"Hello. Is that David? (pause) *Hi David. This is John. How are you?* (pause) *Good. I'm calling about the delivery of the new computers ..."* etc.

In role play performances, the speaker could be the teacher, or it could be a group of learners who prepare their performance for the listening lesson. Here are some more ideas for role play listening performances – you can probably think of lots more:

- an old woman talking about how life used to be in the village;
- a group of teenagers arranging a party;
- two friends discussing a wedding;
- a journalist interviewing a famous football player or musician.

6. Listening to songs

Interaction pattern: Whole class

Resources needed: CD player, MP3 player or mobile phone with speakers

Songs are very useful for listening lessons. They contain grammar and vocabulary, and are enjoyable, so it is easy to memorise them. You need to get the song on your MP3 player, mobile phone or CD player. Think of a listening task. For example, you can copy part of the song (or all of it) onto the chalkboard, leaving a few gaps which the learners must fill as they listen. For example, 'You are not alone' by Michael Jackson:

Another day has gone.

I'm still all _____.

How could this be?

You're not _____ with me.

You never said goodbye.

Someone tell me _____

Did you have to go

And _____ my world so cold?

After you check the answers, you can play the song again and get the learners to sing along. You can also use songs that your learners like; this will motivate them to learn more English! See *Chapter C10 – Games and Songs* for more ideas about how to use songs.

7. Gap-fill dictation

Interaction pattern: Whole class

Resources needed: Notebooks

In *Chapter C1 – Teaching Grammar* we learnt that grammar dictation (grammar activity 2) can provide useful listening practice. Here is another dictation activity that you can do with your learners. First create a short, simple gap-fill activity, or find one in a textbook. Let us imagine the learners have recently studied superlative adjectives. Here is the gap-fill:

the largest the longest the fastest the most intelligent the highest

1. The Nile is _____ river in the world.
2. Addis Ababa is _____ city in Ethiopia.
3. Mount Kilimanjaro is _____ mountain in Africa.
4. The cheetah is _____ animal in the world.
5. The chimpanzee is _____ of all the animals.

In the lesson, write only the words in the box on the chalkboard. Do not write the five sentences. Tell the learners that you will dictate five sentences with gaps. They must write what you say and choose one word from the box to go in each gap. For example, you dictate the first one like this:

   "Number one. The Nile is GAP river in Africa."

Just say "gap" to indicate the gap. Remember to read slowly, pause after each sentence and then repeat it once. After you finish, let them compare answers in pairs or small groups before checking the answers.

Conclusion

In this chapter we have learnt the following:
- we can use our own voice to provide listening practice for our learners;
- learners can listen to each other;
- we can use mobile phones and MP3 players if we do not have CD players;
- listening activities at lower levels should be enjoyable and interactive;
- we should prepare learners carefully for listening lessons;
- learners should usually listen two or three times;
- learners should check answers in pairs after each listening;
- we should check for agreement during feedback to listening activities;
- we can use live listening, stories, role play, songs and dictation to vary how we practise listening skills.

C6 – Teaching Reading

In this chapter:
- Why read?
- What can we read?
- We do not have anything to read!
- An example reading lesson
- An example reading text – Let's talk about teeth!
- Practical task: Comparing reading and listening lessons
- Commentary to practical task: Comparing reading and listening lessons
- Different reading tasks
- Ideas for reading activities

> English language **literacy** is covered in *Part B* of this book. For help on how to teach children to read letters, words and simple sentences, look at *Part B*. This chapter focuses on improving reading skills after three to four years of learning to read in English.

 **Reflective task**

*Michael, a year five primary school teacher (learner age 9 – 10), does not have enough copies of the **textbook** for his classes. Whenever he has reading lessons, he copies the necessary texts onto the chalkboard at the start of each lesson, and gets his learners to copy it into their notebooks. Then he begins the lesson.*
 1. What problems do you think Michael has?
 2. What advice would you give Michael?

We will return to these questions later in the chapter.

Why read?

Reading is a very important part of education. Children who cannot read well will have difficulty reading textbooks in other lessons, such as social studies, science or maths. If these subjects are taught in English, the teacher of English plays an important role in helping learners to perform well in all subjects. But reading is also important for learning English. Here are three reasons why teachers of English should include regular reading activities in their lessons:
 1. Reading provides learners with information that they can discuss, recall and write about, which enables them to practise speaking, listening and writing skills.

2. Reading texts provide a natural way for children to learn and **revise** vocabulary and grammar.
3. Reading is enjoyable, especially story reading, and can develop children's imagination and motivate them to learn English.

Remember that to practise their individual reading skills, learners should read silently (sometimes they may need to whisper the words quietly to themselves). Reading **out loud** is useful for developing literacy skills (recognising and **sounding out** words – see *Chapters B3 and B4*), and for practising pronunciation (see *Chapter C3*). However, learners often find it difficult to focus on the meaning of a text if they are reading out loud, so if you want them to practise reading comprehension, use **silent reading**.

What can we read?

The English textbook (usually called the Pupil's Book or Student's Book) for your learners is the most important book for practising reading skills. It contains texts that build the learners' grammar and vocabulary slowly and carefully, **recycling** what they have already learnt and providing context for new learning. It also contains activities for learners to do while reading. If you do not have enough copies of your English textbook, see *We do not have anything to read!* below.

As well as the class textbook, you can use other books for reading activities:

Library books

If your school has a library, your learners can spend one or two lessons a week reading books of their own choice for pleasure. They can write reviews on the books they have read, and put their reviews on the classroom display board (see *Ideas for Reading Activities* below).

Class readers

Some schools have short stories called **class readers**, such as the Sunrise Readers described in *Chapter C11 – Learning Resources*. These books use simple English and are short enough to read in one or two lessons. If there are enough copies of each title, the whole class can read and discuss the same book in a lesson. See *Chapter C11* for more on class readers.

Big Books

Some schools have very large books that can be used in **shared reading** activities. The text and pictures are so large that only one copy of the book is needed. The teacher shows and reads at the same time. See *Chapter B7 – Resources and activities for developing literacy* for more on Big Books.

Fig. C6.1: TEACHER AND CHILDREN READING A BIG BOOK TOGETHER

Other textbooks

In addition to the English textbook for your year, your school may have other textbooks in English. You may be able to use these books to provide variety in reading lessons. For example, you may find older English textbooks in the school storeroom, which often have interesting and useful reading activities. If the reading texts in your English textbook are difficult, try using textbooks from a lower level – the learners will learn more if they understand more.

Authentic reading texts and the Newsbox

Authentic texts are texts written for newspapers, magazines, information leaflets or library books such as novels. They provide authentic reading practice to motivate and challenge your learners. Because they contain a wide range of vocabulary and adult themes, they are usually more suitable at secondary level, but this will depend on the type of text you choose and your learners' level of English. Some teachers like to collect second-hand newspapers, cut out the most interesting articles, stick them onto card and add a glossary of difficult words at the bottom. These articles can be stored in a **newsbox**. Learners can also contribute articles to the Newsbox or practise their dictionary skills by adding the glossaries for you. Try doing this during **English Club** if you have one in your school.

We do not have anything to read!

Some teachers only have one or two copies of the English textbook. Here are two ideas to help such teachers:

- Choose a learner in each class as the **writing assistant**. This learner should have good writing skills, so that he/she can copy a text from the English textbook onto the chalkboard before a reading lesson. Plan reading lessons for after breaks, or at the start of the day, so the writing assistant has time to copy the text. Then you can use the version of the text on the chalkboard for your reading lessons. Change the writing assistant regularly.
- Create **Reading Posters** for your school. A reading poster is a text copied onto a poster or rice sack. Full details of how to create and use reading posters are given in *Chapter C12 – 10 Essential Resources to Create*.

An example reading lesson

Here is an example reading lesson for upper primary or lower secondary school level:

Lesson title: Let's talk about teeth!

Lesson objectives: By the end of the lesson, the learners will have improved their reading skills (reading for gist and for detailed understanding) and speaking skills (giving advice). They will also have learnt new vocabulary related to teeth and health.

Context of lesson: The learners have recently studied 'should' and 'ought to' to give advice.

Time: 45 minutes **Number of learners:** 65
Age of learners: 10 – 12 **Level:** Intermediate

Stage	Time	Activities	Examples of language used*
1.	3 mins	Teacher shows the learners a toothbrush, and asks several questions, finding out how often they brush their teeth.	T: "What is this?" L: "It's a toothbrush." T: "Good! What do we use it for?" etc.
2.	1 min	Teacher introduces the lesson.	T: "Today we are going to read about our teeth, and find out why they are important."
3.	5 mins	Teacher **pre-teaches** 5 difficult words from the text (toothache, painful, bite, etc.). He writes them on the chalkboard, drills pronunciation and explains the meaning.	T: "The first word is 'toothache'. Everybody repeat it." Ls: "Toothache." T: "Toothache is a strong pain in your teeth."
4.	5 mins	Teacher writes 5 discussion questions on the chalkboard and asks learners to predict the answers. Learners discuss and take notes in small groups. Teacher **monitors**.	1. Why are teeth important? 2. How many types of teeth do we have? 3. What are teeth made of? etc.
5.	3 mins	Teacher instructs the learners to read the text quickly to find the answers to the 5 questions. He gives a 3 minute **time frame**.	T: "OK. Now read the text and find the answers to these questions. You have only 3 minutes to do this."
6.	2 mins	Learners compare the answers they found in pairs. Teacher monitors.	L1: "What answer do you have for question 2?" L2: "It says here 'we have 5 types of teeth'."
7.	2 mins	Teacher elicits answers from the learners, and checks for agreement before confirming or correcting any mistakes.	T: "Sanusi, what answer did you and your partner get for question number 3?" L: "We think teeth are made of enamel." T: "Thank you. Who agrees with Sanusi?"

Stage	Time	Activities	Examples of language used*
8.	5 mins	Teacher instructs the learners to read the text again and decide if 10 statements written on the chalkboard are true or false. He gives 5 minutes.	Decide whether the statements are true or false: 1. Brushing our teeth helps to prevent toothache. 2. The process of digestion begins in the stomach.
9.	4 mins	Learners compare the answers they found in pairs. Teacher monitors.	L1: "Number 2 is false. Look at this sentence, here." L2: "Ah, yes! I didn't see that. You are right."
10.	5 mins	Teacher elicits answers from the learners, and gets them to read the relevant sentence in the text that gives the answer.	T: "Why do you think number 2 is false?" L1: "Because it says here 'Teeth begin the process of digestion.'"
11.	1 min	Teacher instructs learners to work in groups and discuss how to look after their teeth.	T: "Think of 5 pieces of advice about looking after your teeth that you can tell your families after school."
12.	5 mins	Learners discuss. Teacher monitors.	L1: "OK. What is the most important piece of advice?" L2: "I think we should tell our families to brush their teeth every day. Do you agree?" L3: "Yes, but I think we ought to do it twice a day!"
13.	3 mins	Teacher gets feedback, writing some of the learners' ideas on the chalkboard.	1. We should brush our teeth twice a day. 2. We shouldn't eat too many sweets.
14.	1 min	Teacher **praises** learners, concludes lesson and gives homework.	T: "Well done! That text was quite difficult, but you all did very well. So what did we learn today?"

* This includes what the teacher and learners said and also examples from exercises and boardwork.

Note the following abbreviations are used above: T= teacher, L= learner, Ls= learners, L1= 1st learner, etc.

An example reading text – Let's talk about teeth!

Here is the full reading text if you want to use it in your lessons:

Let's talk about teeth!

Many people forget how important their teeth are until they get toothache. Have you ever had toothache? If you do, you will need to go to the dentist to get a filling. If the toothache is very painful, the dentist may remove the tooth!

Somebody who has good teeth has a beautiful smile. But teeth are also important for digestion. When we bite and chew food, it makes the pieces small so that we can swallow them easily. Smaller pieces digest faster, so chewing starts the process of digestion before the food gets to the stomach. Your teeth need to be very strong to chew the food you eat for years and years, so there are several layers to your teeth. The surface layer that you can touch is called enamel, and it is the hardest substance in your body – harder even than your bones! This protects the next layer, called dentine, and the nerves underneath. The reason toothache hurts so much is because the enamel has been damaged and sugar is decaying the dentine and touching the nerves. Ouch!

We get two sets of teeth in our lives. First the milk teeth (also called baby teeth) appear when we are very young. These are only temporary and fall out when we are between 6 and 10 years old. The adult teeth take longer to grow and are much stronger. By the time you reach adulthood you should have 32 teeth. How many do you have now?

Look at your teeth in a mirror. Can you see that there are several different shapes of teeth? The incisors are at the front and they are used for cutting and biting. Next to these are the canines. They are pointed like a dog's teeth and help with tearing pieces of bread or meat. The big flat teeth on the sides of our mouth are called molars and these are the teeth we use to chew food, along with the pre-molars, which are found between the molars and the canines. When you reach the age of 16 – 18, several more teeth usually appear at the back of your mouth. They are called wisdom teeth because they arrive when you finish school and are very wise!

So you see, teeth are very interesting and very special. Without teeth we cannot eat easily, and we even have difficulty speaking. We should protect them by not eating too much sugar and by brushing them after meals and before we go to bed.

Practical task: Comparing reading and listening lessons

Look at the structure of the example reading lesson above. Compare it carefully with the example listening lesson in *Chapter C5 – Teaching Listening*. Answer the following questions:

- What stages are similar in the two lessons?
- Why is it important to include these stages in reading/listening lessons?

Commentary to practical task: Comparing reading and listening lessons

There are several important similarities between the structure of the example reading lesson shown above and the structure of the listening lesson in *Chapter C5*. This is because reading and listening lessons are both **receptive skills** lessons (i.e. ways of receiving information):

1. The teacher pre-teaches any important or difficult vocabulary before the reading/listening activity. This will help the learners to understand more of the text.

2. Before they read/listen, learners have an opportunity to discuss and predict the content of the text (Stage 4 in both lessons). This prediction phase **warms up** the learners' knowledge of the topic, and helps them to prepare them for what they will hear.

3. The teacher gives comprehension questions to guide the learners while they read/listen. This gives them a reason to read/listen and enables them to practise a specific skill (e.g. reading for gist, listening for detailed understanding, etc.).

4. Learners always check in pairs after the reading/listening stages, before feedback to the teacher. This gives them confidence in their answers if they are right, and if they have made mistakes it allows for **peer-correction** (when the learners correct each other). It also allows the teacher to monitor and notice how well each pair or individual learner has done in the activity.

5. The teacher checks for agreement before confirming correct answers during feedback. This helps her to see how many of the learners have the same answer – an important part of assessing achievement of lesson aims.

6. Learners do a speaking activity after the listening/reading activity on the same topic. In the listening lesson they retell the story. In the reading lesson they think of several tips for looking after our teeth. This enables the learners to practise using the vocabulary from the activity. After receptive skills work, it is a good idea to get them to practise their **productive skills**; speaking and writing.

Different reading tasks

We can combine two or more of the following reading tasks in a reading skills lesson:

Reading for gist

The first reading task in the lesson above was easier and the time frame given was shorter (three minutes). We can call this type of task **reading for gist** or **skimming**. It helps learners to improve their ability to read a text quickly to pick up just the main points. It is a good idea to provide a gist reading task the first time learners read a text.

Reading for detailed understanding

The second task was more challenging (ten true/false statements) and the time frame was longer (five minutes). This type of activity helps them to **read for detailed understanding**, something we do naturally in our first language whenever we read an important text.

Analysing language used in the text

Sometimes we get learners to analyse grammar, vocabulary or other aspects of language used in a text. The text can provide a clear context for such language and help us to introduce something new or to revise something studied before. For example we can get them to identify and underline the past perfect tense, find linking words or adjectives to describe emotions. Alternatively, we could get them to analyse the structure, format or punctuation of the text (e.g. a formal letter or a CV).

Giving an opinion

We often enjoy providing our personal opinion on a text we read. For example, to say whether we agree with an opinion, or whether we like a story. This is a useful way of developing learners' evaluation skills (see *Chapter A2 – Your Learners* for more on **thinking skills**). Another good way to do this is to get them to write a book review (see below).

Look back at the *Reflective task* at the start of this chapter. What advice would you give Michael now?

Ideas for reading activities

1. Our questions

Interaction pattern: Groups of 2 – 4

Resources needed: A factual text

Sometimes learners enjoy thinking of their own questions for a text. This works best with factual texts (about animals, science, countries, etc.). Before they read, discuss the topic of the text with them (e.g. a text about elephants), drawing or showing some pictures, and getting them interested in it. Ask them to work in small groups to think of five questions about the topic that they would like to know the answers to. You can monitor and help the groups with their questions. Get some of the most interesting questions on the chalkboard. Then they read the text to find their answers. After they have finished, if there are any questions they still have not answered, they can find out the answers for homework. Here are five questions about elephants that a primary class thought of:

1. How big are elephants?
2. What do they eat?
3. Why do they have big ears and a trunk?
4. Do they have their own language?
5. Why are there no elephants near our village anymore?

2. Story prediction

Interaction pattern: Pairs or small groups

Resources needed: A story text

Children love predicting how a story will finish. They can predict either by looking at pictures, or by using their imagination. Next time you read a story with them, instead of reading it all the way through in one go, pause two or three times during the story and ask them to close their books. Say:

"What do you think happens next in the story? Tell your partner."

Let the learners discuss for a few minutes, get some predictions from them and then continue reading. Praise them if they guess correctly.

3. Jigsaw reading

Interaction pattern: Pairs or groups

Resources needed: Two or three texts on the same topic, or one long text

Jigsaw reading combines reading and speaking skills in an enjoyable two-stage lesson. There are many ways to do jigsaw reading. Here is how you can do it with two texts:

Divide the class into two groups: A and B. Give one text to learners in group A and the other text to learners in group B. Write a few simple comprehension questions on the chalkboard for each text, and get the learners to check answers in pairs when they have finished reading. Next, rearrange the learners so that each learner is sitting with a partner from the other group. Now they must tell each other about the text they have read (they cannot show their text). When they have finished, you can find out how well they have done by asking the questions about text A to learners from group B, and vice versa.

Alternatively, if you have a long text in your textbook, you can divide it into two parts and get the learners in group A to read the first part and the learners in group B to read the second part. After rearranging the learners, get them to tell each other about what they read and then work together to answer all the comprehension questions.

Two important tips when doing jigsaw reading activities:
- Choose texts that are easy for the learners – so that they can communicate the content successfully;
- Keep the comprehension questions simple – so you do not have to spend too much time checking the answers.

You can also do jigsaw reading at higher levels by using short articles cut out of newspapers (see the Newsbox idea above). If you have 10 articles, the learners can read them in 10 different groups. Then members of different groups can get together in new groups to summarise the stories they have read.

4. Book reviews and presentations

Interaction pattern: Individual, followed by class presentations

Resources needed: A range of library books or class readers

Book reviews and presentations are enjoyable project work for learners. All the learners choose a book that they are interested in; either from the library or from a selection of class readers. They read their chosen book in their own time (either at home or in the library) and write a review afterwards. Provide a Book Review template for them to use (see below) and an example of a completed review. The review is handed in for feedback and correction by you. The learner is now ready to give a presentation on the book.

Some learners will need more time than others to read their books and complete their reviews. This allows you to do a few presentations every week. They can be done at the end of lessons and only need to be a few minutes long each. The learner can read out their review, give their opinion on the book and recommend it if they like it. Some learners may enjoy drawing a few pictures to accompany their review. The reviews can then go on the class display board or they can be put into a 'review folder'. Book reviews can be used as part of a continuous assessment system. You can assess learners on both the written report and the spoken presentation.

5. Jumbled paragraphs

Interaction pattern: Groups of 3 – 4

Resources needed: A text with several paragraphs that are cut up

Some schools have copies of old textbooks that are no longer needed. This activity is a good way to use these textbooks. First choose a text with a clear structure (e.g. a story or a letter), and cut the paragraphs up. To make the texts last, you can stick the paragraphs onto paper or card. You will need one copy of the text per group. In class, give the 'jumbled paragraphs' to the groups. The learners must put the paragraphs in the right order. An example is given below. Can you work out the order of the paragraphs?

The greedy pig

A He called for help. First the rabbit tried pushing, then the other animals came and pulled, but no-one could free him. 'You'll have to wait here until you're thin enough to get out,' said the rabbit.

 B 'Oh, very well,' said the pig. He said goodbye to his friend and left. But he was so full he couldn't get out. He was stuck in the hole!

C One day the pig visited the rabbit for dinner. The rabbit lived in a hole underground, and although the pig was quite big, he was just able to squeeze into the hole and get into the rabbit's kitchen.

 D So the pig had to wait for three days before he could get out. Although he was very hungry, he learnt his lesson well and promised: 'I'll never eat too much food again!'

 E In the kitchen, the pig and the rabbit ate lots of food – bread, rice, biscuits and cakes. 'Yum, yum! What delicious food,' said the pig. 'I'll just have a little more.' 'I don't think that's a good idea,' said the rabbit. 'It's time for you to go home.'

Solution: *Correct order for The Greedy Pig: C, E, B, A, D*

Another way to create a jumbled paragraph text is to write your own story on a computer, print it and make enough photocopies of it for the class. Then cut it up in the usual way, and you can use it each year with each class you teach.

Conclusion

In this chapter we have learnt the following:
- reading is important not only to improve our learners' English, but also to help build their knowledge and understanding of the world;
- reading should be enjoyable, and can help learners to develop their imagination;
- silent reading is the best way to improve reading fluency while reading out loud helps more with pronunciation and early literacy;
- we can read many different types of books, such as library books, class readers, big books and authentic texts;
- even if you do not have many textbooks, you can still practise reading with your learners;
- reading and listening lessons have several important stages in common;
- there are many different types of reading tasks, such as reading for gist and reading for detailed understanding.

C7 – Teaching Writing

In this chapter:

- Why is writing important?
- Two types of writing
- Who should our learners write for?
- Collaborative writing
- Practical task: An example writing lesson
- Commentary to practical task: An example writing lesson
- Correcting learners' writing
- Ideas for writing activities

> English language **literacy** is covered in *Part B* of this book. For help on how to teach children to write letters, words and simple sentences, look at *Part B*. This chapter focuses on improving writing skills after three to four years of learning to write in English.

 **Reflective task**

What are the advantages and disadvantages of writing compared to speaking in the following situations:

1. when you want learners to use new grammar or vocabulary;
2. when you want learners to work together;
3. when you need to assess learners' ability to use English.

Why is writing important?

Writing and speaking are the two **productive skills**. They are both useful ways to get learners to practise using language and expressing their ideas, and both are essential to language learning. However, writing has several advantages over speaking, especially in large classes:

- when writing, learners have more time to think and to choose their ideas and words carefully;
- writing is quieter than speaking, and easier for the teacher to **monitor**;
- it is easy to see what they have produced and to use their texts for assessment (see *Chapter C8 – Assessment*);

- writing supports their literacy development, improving related skills such as handwriting and spelling.

Of course, writing and speaking can often be done as part of the same lesson or activity. For example, learners can plan what to write, they can compose a text together, and they can read and discuss each other's work after writing.

Two types of writing

We can divide classroom writing activities into two types. Both of them are useful:
- writing sentences
- writing whole texts

Writing sentences

Often we ask learners to write a sentence using grammar or vocabulary that we have just taught or **revised**. For example, if we have taught them the past continuous tense, we can ask them to write a sentence to describe what they were doing at seven o'clock this morning. Or if we have taught them vocabulary to describe appearance, we can ask them to write one or two sentences to describe somebody in their family. Sentence writing is an opportunity for learners to practise language. This is similar to many speaking practice activities and we can often follow these activities by getting learners to read out their sentences to their partner or to the class.

Writing whole texts

Sometimes we ask learners to write a complete text, such as a letter, a story or a birthday card. Because we also do these writing tasks outside the classroom, they can be called **authentic writing tasks**. After learners write whole texts we can get them to share what they have written with each other. Here are some more examples of authentic writing tasks:
- writing an email to a pen pal;
- writing a report on a football match;
- completing a questionnaire;
- writing a comic story with pictures;
- writing a book review;
- writing a poster for a school event.

There are many more types of authentic writing tasks. Your learners will benefit from practising the types of writing that they will need to do in the future, both in exams and after they leave school.

Who should our learners write for?

Sometimes teachers think that they have to read and correct everything that their learners write. This is not true. In Chapters *A3 – Child-centred Learning* and *C4 – Teaching Speaking* we learnt that learners can speak to each other in groups and pairs. In a similar way, learners can also write for each other:

Writing for their partner

After writing, learners can swap with their partner to read what their partner has written.

Gallery reading

After writing something, learners display their texts on the walls of the classroom; then they walk round and read a selection of their classmates' work.

Publishing

Learners can 'publish' what they have written, for example by creating a **class storybook** or a 'book review noticeboard' in the school library. If you have internet access they can even start their own blog.

Learners are very interested in what their classmates think about their writing, so we can also get them to provide peer-feedback on what they have read. They could write a comment or question at the bottom of the text, add another sentence, or evaluate their classmates' work by drawing a star on the one they like most. You can also participate in this activity, but you do not need to read every learner's work – just by reading a small sample you will see if they have completed the task well and you will be able to provide feedback and **praise** to the whole class.

Collaborative writing

Writing does not always have to be individual work. Learners benefit from doing some types of writing in pairs or **threes**. For example, if we ask them to write an essay analysing the advantages and disadvantages of television, or an article comparing life in the city with life in the village, the learners will benefit from working together and sharing ideas to produce a balanced piece of writing.

When they do a writing task in this way, the process of writing involves discussion, peer-correction and peer-reviewing, all of which are useful ways for learners to practise speaking and provide peer-correction. In this way, the process becomes as important as the product (i.e. the texts they write). Fig. C7.1 shows a typical model for a **pairwork** writing activity. Notice how the stages are all child-centred. The role of the teacher during pairwork writing is to organise the stages, monitor the pairwork and provide help when necessary.

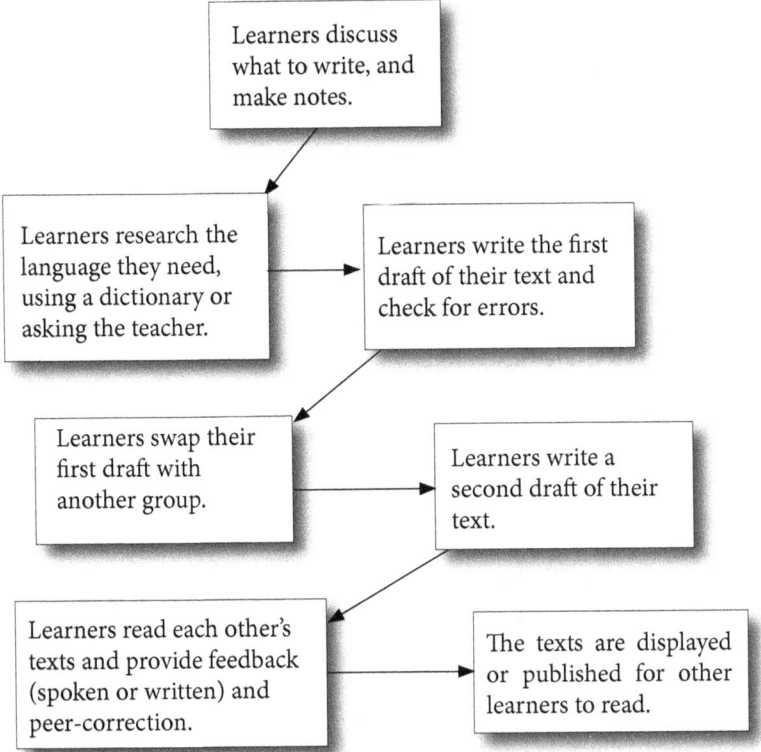

Fig. C7.1: MODEL FOR PAIRWORK WRITING

Practical task: An example writing lesson

Here is an example writing lesson for secondary school learners that involves pairwork writing. However, there is a problem! **The stages of the lesson are in the wrong order!** Try to figure out the correct order of the stages, using the model given above to help you. Stage A is the first one and Stage J is the last one.

Lesson title: The new oil refinery

Lesson objectives: By the end of the lesson, the learners will have practised their writing skills (writing a balanced essay) and their speaking skills (discussing and agreeing on how to compose their essay).

Context of lesson: The learners have recently studied vocabulary relating to the environment and environmental problems (e.g. pollution, deforestation, etc.) and the passive voice.

Time: 45 minutes

Number of learners: 49

Age of learners: 13 – 14

Level: Upper intermediate

Stage	Time	Activities	Examples of language used*
A	3 mins	Learners start the lesson by playing a vocabulary revision game in small groups.	T: "Write down 10 words about the environment. Then 1 student must explain the meaning of a word, while the others have to guess which word it is."
B	3 mins	Each pair swaps texts again with another pair, and provide peer-correction of mistakes they find in each other's texts.	L1: "I think there's a mistake here: 'The pollution will to kill many animals and birds.' The word 'to' is not necessary." L2: "Ah, yes. Thank you."
C	10 mins	Learners write the first draft of their essay, working in pairs or threes. Teacher monitors, providing vocabulary and ideas if needed.	L1: "How should we begin?" L2: "Let's write: 'New industry is always useful because it brings jobs to a community ….'"
D	5 mins	Working in pairs, learners discuss and make a list of the advantages and disadvantages of building the oil refinery.	L1: "OK. Let's start with the advantages." L2: "Yes. It will probably create lots of jobs …" etc.
E	5 mins	Each pair writes a second draft of their essay, including changes based on the peer-feedback they have received. Teacher monitors.	L1: "OK. So shall we change our conclusion?" L2: "I think so, but not everything, just the order of the ideas."
F	2 mins	Teacher writes the writing task on chalkboard, and explains it to the learners, saying how long their essays should be and giving a clear **time frame** for each stage in the lesson.	On chalkboard: A company wants to build an oil refinery near our town. Write an essay discussing the advantages and disadvantages of the refinery and finish with your own conclusion. Is it a good idea or not?

Stage	Time	Activities	Examples of language used*
G	3 mins	Learners check their **textbooks** and notebooks for any vocabulary they need for their essay. Some ask the teacher for help, or look for new words in the dictionary.	L1: "Mrs. Siaka, what do we call the big ships that carry oil?" T: "They're called 'oil tankers.'" L2: "Thank you."
H	8 mins	The learners stick their essays on the walls of the classroom for a gallery reading activity. They all stand and read 3 or 4 of their classmates' work, drawing a star on the one they like most, and adding a comment.	Written on one essay: "Very interesting, especially the effect of the refinery on tourism. Abdul." Written on another essay: "Good work! Did you write this from personal experience? Fatima."
I	4 mins	Each pair swaps their first draft with another pair. They work in groups of 4, reading each other's essays, discussing the ideas and providing peer-feedback.	L1: "This sentence is interesting. I think it should go first, before this one." L2: "Really! Why?" L1: "Because it is the most important point."
J	2 mins	The teacher concludes the lesson, praises the learners and gives homework.	T: "Well done everybody. I think we should include some of your essays in the school newsletter!"

* *This includes what the teacher and learners said and also examples from exercises and boardwork.*

Note the following abbreviations are used above: T= teacher, L= learner, Ls= learners, L1= 1st learner, etc.

Commentary to practical task: An example writing lesson

Solution: *The correct order of the lesson stages is: A, F, D, G, C, I, E, B, H, J.*

Correcting learners' writing

Error correction is a useful part of writing lessons. It is useful both for the learners and for the teacher to see what language they have and have not learnt. However, sometimes teachers can correct too much (called **overcorrection**) which can demotivate learners. Remember the following three tips:

1. As well as correcting errors, you should always praise learners for their work. Do not forget to include positive comments (for example; *"Well done." "Good point." "Nice use of grammar."* etc.).
2. Do not confuse correction with **summative assessment** (see *Chapter C8 – Assessment*). You do not always need to give a mark or grade to every piece of writing.
3. You do not need to correct every mistake. Learners can only notice a few corrections each time, so choose the most important mistakes to correct, ones which either make the text difficult to understand or ones which involve grammar that they have studied recently.

We all know that correction can take a long time, especially with a big class. Here are two suggestions that will help you to reduce the amount of time you spend correcting learners' work:

Self-correction and peer-correction

Before you collect in a piece of writing, get the learners to check it for mistakes. First, they should read through their own work (**self-correction**) to see if they can find any mistakes. Then they should give the text to their partner and let him/her check it (this is called **peer-correction**). Often they will be able to correct some of their mistakes without asking you. During this stage, you can **monitor** and answer questions. If they find an error in their own text or their partner's text, you can provide confirmation before they correct.

No need to correct all the time

Remember that teacher correction is not always necessary. The main reason learners need to write is to practise their English. The accuracy of their writing will improve naturally with time, as they read and listen, study grammar and vocabulary. Although the correction is useful, the practice itself is more important. One teacher in Eritrea, Tesfahannes, has the following strategy in his class of 60 learners:

"I usually give them writing three times a week. Each time I only correct the work of 10 learners, and I keep a careful record of whose work I correct each time, so I correct one piece of writing for each learner every two weeks. But I never tell them whose work I am going to correct, so they all try hard with every piece of writing they do!"

Have you ever noticed that your learners seem to make the same mistakes more than once? This is because they often do not notice their mistakes. Here are two activities that will help learners to remember their corrections:

Noting down mistakes

When you give back a piece of corrected writing to your learners, they should make a note of each mistake in the back of their exercise books by writing down the error, the correction and the reason why. For example:

Error	Correction	Reason
I enjoy to play football.	I enjoy playing football.	After 'enjoy', use verb + ing.
I putted it on the chair.	I put it on the chair.	Past tense of 'put' is also 'put'.

Remember, rewrite and check

When you give back a piece of corrected writing to your learners, give them a few minutes to notice their corrections. Tell them to choose three sentences that include corrections and to remember all three correct sentences. Then tell them to hide the text and write the three sentences on a different page correctly. After they have done this they check their work by comparing it with the text.

Ideas for writing activities

Most of these activities can be done either individually, in pairs or in small groups. You can follow the stages shown above for pairwork writing if doing them in pairs or small groups. Alternatively, learners can work individually, starting their text in class and finishing it for homework.

1. **Story writing**

   Interaction pattern: Any, although pairs are usually best

   Resources needed: Depends on the method

   Stories are one of the most important types of writing learners can do. They help them to develop their creativity as well as practise language use. Learners often find story writing easier when they are working in pairs or groups of three. They always need a little inspiration for their stories. Here are some ideas:
   - Collect pictures from magazines/newspapers. Put a selection on the chalkboard (e.g. 10) and tell learners that their stories must contain at least five of the things/people in the pictures.
   - Provide learners with the first or the last line of their story. An example first line might be: *"One day while walking in the forest, Seema noticed a small box under a tree."* An example last line might be: *"The leopard led the boys back to the village. 'Thank you,' they said. But the leopard was already gone."*
   - Give each pair of learners 10 words of vocabulary that they have studied recently. They must include five of the words in their story. If you have a vocabulary box (see *Chapter C12 – 10 Essential Resources*), you can use vocabulary from it.

   Learners always enjoy reading each other's stories, so remember to allow time for this. You could put the stories on the walls of the classroom, and allow learners to walk round and read each other's work, or put them together to make a **class storybook** that you can keep in the classroom or school library.

2. News articles

Interaction pattern: Pairs or small groups

Resources needed: A selection of articles from local newspapers

All learners are familiar with newspapers, and why they are important. If possible, begin a News article lesson by allowing them to look at some stories from a local newspaper. If you have a **newsbox**, you can use this (see *Chapter C6 – Teaching reading*). Then you can get them to write their own news articles. Here are two ideas:

- Write several interesting headlines on the chalkboard. Each pair must choose one headline and write an article based on it. Example headlines might include: *"Flying Elephant Seen over Nairobi"*; *"Uganda beat Brazil at Football 7:0!"*; *"Police Arrest Famous Pop Star"*; etc.
- For homework, ask the learners to find out the latest news in their family and the local community (e.g. weddings, babies, new businesses, etc.). They should take notes on all the details. Then, in the next lesson, they write their article.

Just like stories, learners always enjoy reading each other's articles. The best way to do this is to put them together in a class newspaper. Do not forget to think of a name for the newspaper! You can even add these articles to your newsbox.

3. Reviews and reports

Interaction pattern: Usually individual

Resources needed: None

The most common type of review that learners can write is a book review after reading a book or story. This is explained in *Chapter C6 – Teaching Reading*. Learners can also write reviews of films, dances, musicians and drama performances that they have seen. They can also write reports of other events, such as sports events, weddings, or even new shops opening in the local community. Reviews and reports are quite structured, usually with four parts:

1. Details of what is being reviewed – Name? Time? Place? Duration? Cost?
2. Description – Describe what you are reviewing, such as the story of a film, or what happened at an event.
3. Comments and opinion – What did you think of it? Was it enjoyable/interesting?
4. Evaluation – How many stars does it get out of a maximum of five?

Reviews can be displayed on a class display board, or in the school library. If your learners have access to computers and the internet, they could even post a review on a blog or website.

4. Chain stories

Interaction pattern: Desk groups

Resources needed: A few sheets of paper and a story idea

This is a fun game that can be played quickly at the end of any lesson. Learners work in desk groups. Give each group a piece of A4 paper. Write the title and the first sentence of the story on the chalkboard (choose a story theme related to something you have studied recently, e.g. travel, food, work, etc.). Learners should write a name for their group at the top of their sheet and below this they should copy the first sentence from the chalkboard. The groups now have two minutes to think of the second sentence to the story and add it beneath the first one. Now they pass their story to the next desk. They now have three minutes to read the story their classmates have written and add another sentence. The stories are passed around again, and another sentence is added. You can continue this game until the stories are concluded! Allow time for the learners to read the stories, especially the one they started! Here is an example:

A weekend in the city
On Saturday morning, Jeanette woke up very excited because she was going to visit her favourite aunt, who lived in the big city.
She caught the bus at 7 o'clock, and sat next to a tall, thin man in a grey suit and a tie.
At 9 o'clock the bus arrived in the city, but her aunt wasn't at the bus stop to meet her!
etc.

5. **Pen pals**

Interaction pattern: Individual

Resources needed: Pen pals in another school nearby, or in another country

Pen pals are individual friends who our learners write letters to (or emails if they have internet access). The pen pals could be in another school nearby, another school somewhere else in the country, or even in another country. The idea behind pen pal partnerships is that the learners write letters to each other regularly, giving information about themselves and asking questions. Whenever they receive a letter, they reply, and ask some new questions. The pen pals can stay friends for years, and even organise to visit each other in the future.

The most important part of a pen pal partnership is to make sure that the letters arrive successfully. If you can organise an international partnership, it is a good idea to collect all the letters, and send them in a single large envelope. If the partner school is nearby, you can deliver them yourself, or get someone in the village to take them for you. To find out more about international pen pals, type 'pen pal school partnerships' into a Google internet search.

6. **Greetings cards**

Interaction pattern: Individual or pairs

Resources needed: Paper and pens, coloured if possible

Learners love making greetings cards and enjoy receiving them even more! Learners can write a main greeting on the front (e.g. Happy Birthday), and another greeting or a short poem inside. You can get a whole class of learners to make "Happy Holidays!" greetings cards for important public holidays (e.g. Independence Day), or a "Get

Well Soon!" card for a classmate who is sick. Here are some other events for which they can write greetings cards:
- Father's Day and Mother's Day
- Birthdays
- Religious Festivals (e.g. Christmas or Ramadhan)
- Welcome Cards for new arrivals in the class
- New Baby Cards

Fig. C7.2: HOME-MADE GREETING CARDS

Conclusion

In this chapter we have learnt the following:
- writing is a useful alternative to speaking that is quiet and easier to monitor;
- writing gives learners time to prepare their ideas and choose their grammar and vocabulary;
- both sentence writing and whole text writing provide good practice for learners;
- learners can write for each other (not just for the teacher), and can provide useful peer-feedback and peer-correction;
- learners can write in pairs or even groups, and benefit from planning, drafting and reviewing texts together;
- it is not necessary for the teacher to correct all the writing tasks that our learners do;
- writing can be a great way for learners to express their creativity;
- learners should learn to write a variety of text types, such as letters, stories, reports, book reviews, articles, etc.

C8 – Assessment

In this chapter:

- What is assessment?
- Assessment for learning (formative)
- Assessment of learning (summative)
- How to assess for learning?
- Assessing achievement of objectives/lesson evaluation
- What is the difference between correction and assessment?
- Involving learners in their own assessment
- Continuous assessment
- Preparing learners for exams
- Practical task: Assessment blues!
- Commentary to practical task: Assessment blues!

 **Reflective task**

Make notes on the following two questions:

1. *What is the difference between assessment for learning and assessment of learning?*
2. *Why is each one important?*

What is assessment?

Let us begin with a simple definition of assessment:

"Assessment is checking what the learners have learnt."

Assessment helps the teacher to answer questions like:
1. Have my learners learnt what I wanted them to learn?
2. What should I teach them next?
3. Can I improve my teaching?
4. Have my learners learnt everything in the curriculum that they needed to learn?

Assessment is often divided into two types: assessment for learning and assessment of learning.

Assessment for learning (formative)

When we use assessment to answer questions 1–3 above, we are **assessing for learning**. This means that the purpose of assessment is to inform our planning and our teaching. All good teachers do this naturally. Whenever we ask a question or observe what our learners are doing, what we see and hear will help us to decide if they are learning effectively, and what to do next. We do not need to give marks to each learner, nor to correct their work when we are assessing for learning.

Assessment of learning (summative)

Assessment of learning helps us to answer the 4th question above (Have my learners learnt everything in the curriculum that they needed to learn?). It usually involves examinations or continuous assessment. Individual learners are given marks that help us to see their individual strengths and weaknesses in comparison with other learners and the curriculum content. Traditional assessment has often focused too much on written exams and placed a strong emphasis on grammar and reading. However, effective assessment of **language proficiency** should include all four skills (reading, writing, speaking and listening), and should place equal emphasis on grammar _and_ vocabulary.

Let us now look in detail at different aspects of assessment, with practical ideas for how to do it:

How to assess for learning?

In a child-centred class, we assess learning whenever we **monitor** the learners doing an activity. We can observe whether the learners have understood what they have studied, and how much more practice they will need. Sometimes we may decide that they are doing very well, and we can move on quickly. Sometimes we may decide that they are having difficulty, and will benefit from continuing with the same topic or area of language next lesson. Here are some ways to assess learners during the learning process:

- The learners are doing a speaking practice activity, giving their opinions on a topic in pairs. The teacher monitors, noticing if they are able to communicate well.
- The learners are working on a project, creating posters in groups of three or four. The teacher monitors, noticing if their posters are effective, and how well they are using English to discuss the project.
- The learners are doing a grammar practice activity in pairs. The teacher monitors, looking at their answers and listening to their discussions to notice which questions are most difficult for them.
- The learners are doing a reading comprehension activity individually. The teacher walks around the class, noticing how quickly they are reading, and how many correct answers each learner has.

Assessing achievement of objectives/lesson evaluation

Good teachers plan specific objectives for each lesson and for each week (see *Chapter A5 - Planning*). At the end of each lesson or week, we need to find out if they have achieved these objectives so that we can decide whether to continue or move on to something new next lesson. This is sometimes called **lesson evaluation** and is also assessment for learning. We can assess achievement of these objectives in a variety of ways:

- At the end of the lesson, the teacher asks learners questions about what they have learnt today. Individual learners answer and the teacher then checks for agreement before confirming: *What did we learn to do today? Why is this phrase useful? How can we use these expressions when writing?*

- At the end of the lesson, the teacher asks the learners for a 'thumbs up' for each objective. The learners have three options: If they feel that they achieved the objective they should indicate this by giving a thumbs up sign. If they found it difficult, they should use the thumbs down sign. And if they found some parts of it difficult, they point their thumbs horizontally (see Fig. C8.1). This works well in secondary school when the learners are capable of assessing their own achievement and being honest in self-evaluation.

Fig. C8.1: THUMBS UP AND THUMBS DOWN SIGNS

- At the end of the lesson, the teacher gets the learners to translate sentences that include the new language learnt from the **mother tongue** into English. If they translate them well, this is evidence of understanding.

- At the end of the week, the learners play a vocabulary **revision** game in small groups (e.g. *Define and Guess* from *Chapter C4 - Teaching Speaking*). Each group writes a list of difficult words and gives it to the teacher afterwards.

- For weekend homework, the learners write a short text using the grammar and vocabulary that they have learnt during the week. The teacher collects the texts on Monday to assess how well they have achieved the objectives.

- At the end of the week, the learners do a speaking activity in groups of three or four. Each learner speaks on a topic they have studied during the week for one minute. The teacher monitors the **groupwork** and takes notes on both how well they are using the new language and what errors are still causing problems.

- At the end of the week, the learners do a text translation exercise to test understanding of grammar, vocabulary and writing skills. After finishing, the teacher writes the correct translation on the chalkboard and the learners peer-correct any obvious errors. The texts are handed in for the teacher to assess achievement of objectives.

Notice that when you are assessing for learning it is not necessary to provide a mark for each learner. In assessment for learning it is important to make a general assessment of the learning of the class as a whole.

What is the difference between correction and assessment?

Some teachers think that they must correct their learners' work individually in order to carry out assessment. As shown above, in a child-centred class, you can assess for learning without providing any individual correction at all. While individual correction is useful and necessary, it does not need to happen every lesson and you should avoid correcting individual learners' work during the lesson itself, when the learners should be learning. If you want to provide individual correction, collect in their books at the end of a lesson and correct them after class.

Involving learners in their own assessment

Many teachers complain that it takes a long time to mark the books of a whole class. This is true if the teacher does all the marking! Such teachers forget that it is possible to enlist the help of the learners. Involving the learners in their own assessment has several advantages:
- it saves a lot of time for the teacher;
- it gives the learners responsibility for their own progress;
- it helps the learners to understand the importance of assessment.

Let us look at some ideas for involving learners in their own assessment:

Peer marking

After doing an exercise, learners give their exercise book to their partner. As you go through the answers, the learners mark (correct) their partner's exercise. This is very useful if you need to record marks for your learners in the register. If you are worried that some learners might cheat, swap pairs before you begin, so that they are not sitting with their best friend, and monitor the correction carefully.

Feedback columns

Get learners to do an exercise in small groups (four to six). Then divide the chalkboard into columns, one column for each group. Two members of each group come to the chalkboard to write their answers in their column (you will need several pieces of chalk for this). Then check the answers together. After this, a member of each group comes to the chalkboard to correct their group's mistakes and calculate their mark.

Blind marking

This is useful after individual writing tasks. Make sure learners work on sheets of paper and have not included their name. Collect in the sheets in order and write a number in the corner that will help you to identify who wrote which text (e.g. seating order). Then mix up and hand out the sheets, so that nobody knows whose work they are marking. They write a mark in the bottom corner.

At higher levels, you can even get the learners to decide on the criteria for assessment themselves. First explain a task (e.g. an individual writing task or a **groupwork** project), and ask them to discuss and then tell you what a good piece of work should include (e.g. a clear structure, attractive display, etc.). Agree on the five most important features of a good piece of work, and tell the learners that these will form the criteria for marking the work.

Continuous assessment

Continuous assessment is used in some countries as an alternative to examinations. In continuous assessment the teacher assesses a number of pieces of work for each learner over a period of time. It has several advantages over exams:

- there is no time pressure and learners are generally more relaxed;
- learning is often assessed over the whole year, rather than in one exam;
- the teacher, who knows the learners best, has more involvement in the assessment of his/her learners;
- communicative skills can be assessed gradually, with the teacher assessing a few learners each week.

Continuous assessment is a good way to test the four skills. Here are some examples of this. Notice that two skills can often be assessed together:

- **Speaking and listening:** Learners do the assessment activity in pairs. You provide a task (e.g. *'discuss the importance of education'* or *'role play a conversation in a shop'*) and assess each learner individually based on how they interact with their partner as well as their use of English.
- **Reading and writing:** Each learner reads a book and writes a book report on it.
- **Individual presentations:** Each learner prepares a three minute talk for the class on a topic of their choice. They must research their topic, which will involve reading skills.

Preparing learners for exams

Most teachers have to prepare their learners for important examinations at least once a year. These exams are assessment of learning. They are important for the learners, who all want to pass, and for the teachers, to show that they are doing their job well. This means that both teacher and learners can feel a lot of pressure when exams come close. Here is some advice to help you to prepare your learners for exams effectively:

- Do not rush through the curriculum just because the exam is coming closer. It is better to teach one thing well than to teach two things too quickly.
- Exam preparation should not take the place of learning. The two can be combined in a balanced curriculum, with new vocabulary and grammar

each week as well as exam practice. If you spend the final month or two doing only practice exams, you lose a lot of learning time, and the learners may get nervous if they find it difficult, which will affect their performance in the exam.

- Teach your learners about how to answer the different exam questions. For example, remind them that if they are doing multiple choice questions they should eliminate the answers they think are wrong first, and whenever they are not sure, they should make an educated guess.
- Revision can be child-centred. Learners can do past papers in pairs, or do revision quizzes in small groups. You can also get learners to prepare for and give presentations to the class on different areas of vocabulary or grammar. When learners revise together, the stronger ones often do a lot of peer teaching to their classmates, explaining correct answers and correcting mistakes. This is a type of **differentiation** that leads to improved marks for everyone. Sometimes you can allow your learners to refer to their notebooks and **textbooks** when doing practice exams or past papers. This is called an **open book exam**. It is a good way for the learners to revise what they have learnt, and to notice what is likely to be tested in the final exam.

Practical task: Assessment blues!

Read about the following three teachers, who all have problems with assessment. Think of some advice to give to each teacher, based on what you have learnt in this chapter. Compare your ideas with another teacher if possible.

Matida

"In our school we have to correct our students' work twice a week, including an end-of-week test, and record individual marks in the register. But I have over 50 students in each of my classes. If I do not do the correction in class, I have to take it home, and it takes hours to do!"

"I teach the final year of primary school. The head teacher is so nervous about the exam results that he makes me start exam practice six months before the exam. But we also have to complete the curriculum for the year, so I have to rush it, meaning the students get confused, panic and do badly in the exam."

Addison

Chantal

"When I assess for learning at the end of the week, I sometimes feel that my students need to spend more time on a vocabulary topic or an area of grammar. But I do not have time. The **scheme of work** tells me that I should start a new topic next week. So some of my learners are beginning to get lost and confused by the grammar."

Commentary to practical task: Assessment blues!

Here is some advice for the three teachers. You may have given different advice that is also useful:

Matida

This is a common problem, and one that causes many teachers to spend time correcting in class. Matida should involve the learners in the correction process. Perhaps she can get them to peer-mark each other's end-of-week test and provide the marks that she records in the register. She can then double-check the marks of a few of the learners to make sure no-one is cheating. She can also get them to blind mark each other's writing once a week. This leaves the rest of the week for learning.

Addison

There is an old saying in English: "You can't fatten a pig by weighing it." Addison is doing a lot of weighing and not much fattening! He should begin by talking to his head teacher. He should explain that the reason they are doing badly in the exam is probably because they are not spending enough time learning. Addison should stick to the normal curriculum, but instead of doing traditional practice activities, he should create practice activities that look like exam tasks, for example by changing reading comprehension questions. This will hopefully enable him to complete the curriculum and prepare the learners for the exam at the same time.

Chantal

Here are two suggestions for Chantal: Firstly, do a little work in the middle of each week on what they studied the week before. This could involve a homework task or a speaking activity at the end of a lesson. Doing revision like this will help them to remember what they have learnt. Secondly, it is sometimes necessary to adapt the scheme of work if it is too fast for your learners. Remember that if your learners forget what you have taught them, they have not learnt anything.

Conclusion

In this chapter we have learnt the following:
- there are two types of assessment: assessment for learning (formative assessment) and assessment of learning (summative assessment);
- we should assess for learning at the end of each lesson and at the end of the week;
- we do not need to correct learners' work to assess for learning;
- we should avoid correcting individual learners' work in class;
- we can involve learners in the correction of their *own* work;
- continuous assessment is a useful alternative to examinations, especially for assessing the four skills (reading, writing, speaking and listening);
- exam preparation can be child-centred; learners can revise and do practice exams together;
- we should not let assessment take the place of learning.

C9 – CLIL: Content and Language Integrated Learning

In this chapter:

- What is CLIL?
- Working together
- An example CLIL lesson
- Practical task: Analysing a CLIL lesson
- Commentary to practical task: Analysing a CLIL lesson
- Recommendations for teachers of content subjects

 **Reflective task**

Enock is a science teacher who works with junior school learners (age 13 - 14) in Malawi. Read about his problem and then discuss the two questions that follow:

"The biggest problem I face as a teacher is that my students do not understand enough English to study science in English. They don't understand the texts, so I have to translate them. They can't ask or answer questions in English, and they spend too much time talking in their mother tongue."

1. Do you know any teachers who have similar problems?
2. What advice would you give to Enock?

What is CLIL?

As English becomes more important in schools all over the world, more and more teachers have to teach in English. **Content teachers**, who teach other subjects (e.g. maths, sciences, social studies, geography, etc.) often find that their learners do not have enough English to be able to understand the vocabulary, or complete their learning tasks in English. Many content teachers have no experience of teaching languages, and may not know how to help their learners with this. So what can we do?

There is a solution – called CLIL.

CLIL stands for Content and Language Integrated Learning and is pronounced /klɪl/. It is a way of teaching both English (or any language) and content subjects (maths, social studies, science, etc.) at the same time. For example a science CLIL teacher does not only teach her learners science in English, she also teaches them the English they need to learn science in English. So the responsibility for teaching the learners

English is shared between all teachers who teach in English. Note that CLIL is not the same as EMI education. EMI stands for English as the Medium of Instruction, and indicates that English is the language of the classroom and the textbooks. It is a description of the language used, not a teaching methodology.

In a number of countries, schools are adopting CLIL as an official methodology, with materials and training for teachers to support the implementation of the new methods. Even if this is not happening in your school, you can work together with the teachers of any subject that is taught in English to improve learning and performance in all subjects. Let us look at some ways you can do this:

Working together

Teachers of English usually have a better understanding of how languages are learnt and better **explicit knowledge** of the English language. They can help content teachers in a variety of ways:

- English teachers can show content teachers how to teach new vocabulary, using the five methods described in Chapter C2 under *Commentary to practical task: Introducing new vocabulary*;
- They can show methods and games for learning and **revising** vocabulary, such as getting learners to record new vocabulary in their notebooks or using a vocabulary box (see *Chapter C12 – 10 Essential Resources to Create*);
- They can show content teachers how to teach reading lessons, as shown in *Chapter C6 – Teaching Reading*;
- They can give content teachers advice on how to get learners to speak English more in class, as shown in *Chapter C4 – Teaching Speaking*;
- If any of the content teachers lack confidence in their own English, the English teachers can give them English lessons once or twice a week;
- They can offer to help their learners with English vocabulary or grammar learnt in other lessons.

Children who are learning several subjects in English each day are learning a lot of English. If five different teachers give a learner 10 new words to learn for homework, the learner will have to learn 50 words that evening! So it is a good idea for content teachers to discuss the following issues with the English teachers of their learners:

The topics

The teacher of English may know what English words the learners do and do not know in a new topic area, and whether the topic has been studied in English before. Often social studies, science and other teachers cover topics that teachers of English also cover.

The learners

The teacher of English will know more about the strengths and weaknesses of each learner in English, and can give advice on how to help them, or how to organise pairs or groups to balance out these strengths. If some learners have learning difficulties, such as dyslexia, the teacher of English may also be able to help here.

The learners' workload

It is a good idea for content teachers to discuss any project work or challenging learning tasks that they are planning to give the learners with the teacher of English. For example, if they need to teach a lot of vocabulary for a reading activity, or give essay writing homework for the weekend. The teacher of English may be able to help by teaching essay writing skills or including useful vocabulary in the end-of-week revision game on Friday.

Difficulties with English

If content teachers notice that the learners are having problems with one area of grammar (e.g. passive tenses), or a specific skill (e.g. writing reports in English), the teacher of English can do an extra lesson on this area, or share useful materials with the content teacher.

An example CLIL lesson

Here is an example CLIL lesson for a secondary school geography class (age: 14 – 15)

Lesson title: Rivers and the Community

Lesson objectives: By the end of the lesson, the learners will:
- be able to give five reasons why rivers are important to communities;
- imagine how different their life would be without the local river;
- have learnt and recorded important vocabulary related to rivers and communities;
- have read a short text on the importance of rivers to the community.

Context of lesson: The learners are studying rivers this week. In the last lesson they studied basic river geography, and next lesson they will look at how river ecosystems can be damaged by pollution, overuse of water, overfishing, etc.

Time: 60 minutes **Number of learners:** 42

Age of learners: 14 – 15 **Level:** Upper intermediate

Stage	Time	Activities	Examples of language used*
1.	3 mins	Teacher introduces lesson, explaining her objectives to the learners.	T: "Today you will learn how rivers are important to the community. You will also imagine …" etc.
2.	5 mins	Learners help teacher to draw a large picture of the river in their community on the chalkboard (including fishing, irrigation, a factory, etc.).	T: "Could you draw fishermen on the bank, here?" L: "OK. How many should I draw?" T: "How many do you usually see there?" etc.

Stage	Time	Activities	Examples of language used*
3.	8 mins	Teacher elicits vocabulary associated with the river. This is written in a vocabulary column on the side of the chalkboard, explained and pronunciation is checked. Learners copy the vocabulary in the back of their notebooks.	T: "OK, so this small stream takes water to the fields. What do we call this process?" L: "Irrigation." T: "Good. What is the verb?" etc.
4.	5 mins	In small groups, learners discuss how the local river is important to their community.	Discussion task on chalkboard: Think of 3 to 5 reasons why the Congo River is important to our community.
5.	7 mins	Teacher gets feedback to the chalkboard, helping learners to improve their English, and noting any important vocabulary in the vocabulary column.	T: "So, what reasons did you think of?" L: "The river is like a road, if we want to get to Kinshasa." T: "Good, so what do we call this reason?" L: "Transport."
6.	4 mins	Learners read a text on the importance of rivers to different communities to see if their predictions were right, and to look for any more reasons.	T: "OK. Now I'd like you to read this text to see if the reasons we've put on the chalkboard are here, and also to look for any other reasons why rivers are important."
7.	3 mins	Learners compare their ideas in pairs. The teacher **monitors**, listening to the learners' discussions to notice if they have understood the text.	L1: "So, did you find any more reasons?" L2: "Yes, I found three." L1: "Oh, really? What were they?" etc.
8.	5 mins	Learners come to the chalkboard to add more reasons why rivers are important to communities. New vocabulary is added to the vocabulary column if needed.	T: "So how many more reasons did you find?" Ls: "Three." T: "OK. Who would like to write one on the chalkboard?"

Stage	Time	Activities	Examples of language used*
9.	12 mins	Learners work in groups to create a poster entitled: 'What would life be like without the river?'	L1: "OK. Let's write the title here." L2: "Yes. I can draw a picture of a dry river here." L3: "Good idea." etc.
10.	5 mins	Learners display their posters on the walls. The teacher tells the learners to walk round, look at the posters of other groups and ask questions about anything that is not clear.	L1: "What do the fallen trees show?" L2: "They show soil erosion." L1: "I see. Interesting!"
11.	3 mins	Teacher checks achievement of **learning outcomes** and concludes lesson.	T: "So what were our objectives for today? What new vocabulary did you learn?"

* This includes what the teacher and learners said and also examples from exercises and boardwork.

Note the following abbreviations are used above: T= teacher, L= learner, Ls= learners, L1= 1st learner, etc.

Practical task: Analysing a CLIL lesson

Answer the following questions for the example CLIL lesson above:
1. How does the teacher introduce new vocabulary for the lesson?
2. How do the learners use English in the lesson?
3. How does the teacher check the learners' understanding of the reading text?
4. How do the learners apply what they have learnt during the lesson?
5. How can the teacher use the posters to revise the lesson content and the English learnt?

Commentary to practical task: Analysing a CLIL lesson

1. The teacher uses a chalkboard picture of the local river, which is familiar to the learners, to teach the new vocabulary. She uses the picture to elicit vocabulary, and notes this vocabulary in a column on the side of the chalkboard. She also adds to this at other stages in the lesson (e.g. Stages 5 and 8). She makes sure learners record this vocabulary in their notebooks, and checks pronunciation by getting the learners to repeat after her (**drilling** the vocabulary).

2. Learners use English to practise all four skills during the lesson:
   - they speak and listen to English during Stages 4, 7 and 9 in a variety of discussion tasks;
   - they read English during Stage 6;
   - they write English during Stage 9, by creating a group poster.

   They may also use English to ask the teacher questions, note down meaning of vocabulary, and by listening to the teacher's instructions and explanations.
3. The teacher gives the learners a task to do while reading the text (to see if their ideas were right), and checks the answers afterwards by getting learners to add more ideas to the list on the chalkboard. She also monitors the **pairwork** discussions after the reading, which gives her an opportunity to assess the achievement of individual learners.
4. They apply what they have learnt by creating the posters in Stage 9.
5. The teacher can use the posters, firstly by keeping them on the walls for the duration of the 'Rivers' unit in the textbook. When vocabulary comes up that they have included on the posters, the teacher can refer to them to help learners to remember/revise the meaning. The posters could also be used at the end of the unit or at the end of the term to help learners to revise for their exams.

Recommendations for teachers of content subjects

Even if your school has not officially adopted CLIL, all content teachers who are teaching in English can help their learners to learn more by improving their English. Here are some recommendations for how you can do this in four areas of your teaching: planning, recording, learning and checking understanding:

Planning

Before each lesson, decide which items of vocabulary are most important for comprehension of the lesson (and also of related lessons in your **scheme of work**). Remember that verbs are often as important as nouns. Use the first 5 – 10 minutes of the lesson to teach this vocabulary to the learners. Pictures, examples and explanation are all effective, but remember that translation can also be simple, fast and clear.

Recording

Make sure that learners record new vocabulary somewhere. For example, they can keep a vocabulary list at the back of their notebook. Here is an example:

Science vocabulary list with English and Kiswahili words

English	Kiswahili
energy (n)	nishati
dissolve (v)	geyuka
magnet (n)	sumaku
combine (v)	unganisha
easily (adv)	kirahisi

Learning

Help the learners to learn new vocabulary. At least twice a week, get the learners to test each other on the vocabulary in pairs, by translating. They can also play games in groups or as a class using a vocabulary box (see *Chapter C12 – 10 Essential Resources to Create*). Remember that the key to learning vocabulary is using it. They will not learn the vocabulary if you explain it once and never revise it.

Checking understanding of reading texts

Good teachers avoid the question: Do you understand? They check that the learners understand by using comprehension questions. Here are some example questions for use with a text on the science topic of compounds:

- How many substances are there in a compound?
- Is it easy to separate a compound? Why?/Why not?
- How can you break a compound?

These questions can be used in different ways:

- write them on the chalkboard before reading and get the learners to write down their answers while they are reading;
- for discussion in pairs after the reading;
- ask them to the learners after the reading;
- for a prediction activity, where the learners predict the answers before they read, then read to see how many predictions are correct.

Translating the whole text may seem like a fast alternative, but it is not recommended. Provide your learners with the vocabulary that they need to understand the text in English. Each time you do this, their English will improve and your job will get a little bit easier.

Conclusion

In this chapter we have learnt the following:

- CLIL is a teaching methodology that can help all teachers who teach in English to teach more effectively;

- CLIL is not the same as EMI (English as the medium of instruction) education;
- teachers of English can help teachers of other subjects by showing them useful techniques and games, and by giving advice to them;
- other teachers can help teachers of English by discussing the topics they are studying, by sharing the workload and by discussing learners' difficulties together;
- content teachers should plan what vocabulary to teach the learners at the start of each lesson;
- learners in content lessons should record new vocabulary in their notebooks;
- to learn this new vocabulary, learners should revise it at least twice a week;
- content teachers should check understanding of texts in English using reading tasks.

C10 – Games and Songs

In this chapter:

- Why are games and songs important in language learning?
- Are games and songs only for small children?
- Introducing and inventing games and songs
- Games for vocabulary learning
- Games for grammar practice
- Games for skills practice
- Songs for younger learners (lower primary school)
- Songs for older learners (upper primary and secondary school)

 Reflective task

Decide whether you agree with the following opinions. Put a tick (✓) if you agree, a cross (✗) if you disagree and a question mark (?) if you're not sure or if you think it depends:

1. *"Children learn important social skills through play."*
2. *"Games during lessons waste important time that could be spent learning."*
3. *"Children can learn vocabulary and grammar from songs."*
4. *"Games and songs are only suitable at primary level."*
5. *"Learners enjoy repeating the same games and songs regularly."*

We will return to this task later in the chapter.

Why are games and songs important in language learning?

We all know that children love to play games and sing songs. However, not everybody knows that they are also two of the most natural and most important contributors to language learning among children[23]. Let us look at some of the advantages of using games in the classroom:

- games are social and interactive;
- games engage children's creativity and imagination, helping them to develop a greater range of **thinking skills** (see *Thinking Skills and Bloom's Taxonomy* in *Chapter A2 – Your Learners*);
- when they play games, children develop social skills, learning about teamwork, winning and losing;

---

23   Young, "The Negotiation of Meaning in Children's Foreign Language Acquisition."

- games can be played many times, so once you have taught your learners how to play a game, you can use it again and again to provide enjoyment;
- if learners like them, they may continue to play these games outside class, learning even when they are not at school.

Some teachers and parents think that because games are not serious, or because they are sometimes noisy, they are not proper learning. But this is not true. When we balance study activities with games that help them to remember what they have studied, we are creating the perfect balance and variety for children to learn quickly.

Like games, the main reason why songs are so useful for learning is because they are enjoyable. But songs also have a particular advantage for language learning because they contain words – words that we love to sing again and again. This repetition helps us to learn vocabulary and grammar when we memorise our favourite songs.

Although it is enjoyable to use CDs or MP3s to teach songs, we can teach and sing many songs just using our voices. We can also use songs which are being played on the radio at the moment, including songs which our learners like.

There are so many songs in English. It is often possible to find songs that relate to a topic you are teaching (e.g. *Heads, shoulders, knees and toes* for body parts), or songs that practise grammar that you have taught (e.g. *I still haven't found what I'm looking for* by U2 for the present perfect tense). Songs can also provide topics for discussion (e.g. *Imagine* by John Lennon).

Are games and songs only for small children?

Let us answer this question with another question: Do you enjoy playing games and singing songs? Hopefully, you answered 'Yes'. Games and songs can be played with learners at all ages, including adults. The types of games we play and our choice of songs change as the children get older, but they are always very useful for learning. Young children will often find games and songs that involve physical activity very useful, such as miming animals or making letter shapes with their bodies. This activity helps to improve their coordination and build their muscles. They also enjoy games or **rhymes** which involve repeating sentences, such as "*What time is it, Mr. Wolf?*". As they get older they will enjoy games that test their mental ability such as puzzles or guessing games. They will also become more interested in working together as they develop social relationships, so teamwork games are often successful in secondary school. At this age they will probably start listening to pop music in English, and will find it very interesting if you teach them the lyrics to their favourite songs on the radio.

Look back at your answers to the *Reflective task* at the start of this chapter. Did you agree with the advice given in the chapter?

Solution: *1. ✓ 2. ✗ or ? (they contribute to learning) 3. ✓ 4. ✗ (even adults enjoy them) 5. ✓ (as long as they're not played too much!).*

Introducing and inventing games and songs

When you learn a new game or song, try it out at two or three different levels. Do not forget to ask the learners afterwards if they enjoyed it. If they did, you can promise to play it again if they work hard tomorrow. You will find that some games or songs are best at one or two levels, and others are good for all levels!

The rest of this chapter is devoted to the many types of games and songs you can use in class. Remember that there are many other activities described in different parts of this book that are also games. Look in the following chapters for ideas:
- B7 – *Resources and Activities for Developing Literacy*
- C1 – *Teaching Grammar* (look at *Ideas for Grammar Activities*)
- C2 – *Teaching Vocabulary* (look at *Ideas for Vocabulary Activities*)
- C3 – *Teaching Pronunciation* (look at *Ideas for Pronunciation Activities*)
- C4 – *Teaching Speaking* (look at *Ideas for Speaking Activities*)
- C5 – *Teaching Listening* (look at *Ideas for Listening Activities*)

Games for vocabulary learning

In order to help children to learn vocabulary, we need to **revise** the same words many times. This can be boring if we just get the learners to read the words in lists or repeat them after us. There are a number of games described in the following two chapters:

Chapter B7 under ***Resources and activities for developing literacy*** *mainly for younger learners*	
• I spy	Learners guess an object in the room from its first letter.
• Alphabet run-around	Played outside. Learners run to letter **flashcards** for sounds or words.
• Spellman	Similar to 'hangman'; learners guess the letters of a secret word.
• Countdown	Learners rearrange letters in anagrams to spell words.
• Alphabet hopscotch	Learners play hopscotch with letters to spell words.
Chapter C2 under ***Ideas for vocabulary activities*** *for older primary and secondary learners*	
• Memory games	Learners recite spoken lists adding more items to make them longer.
• The alphabet game	Learners think of words that begin with letters A – Z on a specific topic.

•	Collocation Challenge	Learners find collocations in a table and give example sentences.
•	Anagrams	Learners revise vocabulary by rearranging letters in word anagrams.
•	Beep	Learners replace a secret word in an example sentence with 'BEEP!'
•	Back to the board	Learners try to guess secret words based on definitions by classmates.
•	Guess the word	Learners mime, describe or define secret words to each other.
•	Board football	Learners provide definitions of words to win a football match.

Games for grammar practice

Some aspects of grammar need lots of practice, such as question formation or learning irregular verbs. Games are useful in providing this practice. They make it enjoyable, which always leads to more learning. There are a number of games described in the following chapter:

Chapter C1 under ***Ideas for grammar activities***		
•	Sentence jumble	Learners order words mixed up on the chalkboard to make sentences.
•	Human sentences	Learners with **flashcards** stand in a line to make sentences.
•	Who am I?	Learners guess famous people by asking questions.
•	Animal comparatives	Learners guess names of animals described using comparatives.
•	Past tense pelmanism	Learners match cards with present and past tenses.
•	What am I doing?	Learners guess actions mimed by their classmates.

Games for skills practice

There are lots of game ideas for all four skills. Most are described in the relevant chapter:

      C4 – Teaching Speaking

      C5 – Teaching Listening

      C6 – Teaching Reading

      C7 – Teaching Writing

Here are a few more favourites that involve **integrated skills**:

1. **Quiz games**

Interaction pattern: Usually small teams of 3 – 6

Resources needed: It depends – often just notepaper or the chalkboard

Quiz games are great for revision. Small teams are usually best. Remember to get the groups to think of a name for their team (animals, fruit, adjectives, etc.), and also to keep score. There are two ways to prepare quiz games:

1a. Teacher prepares the questions

Prepare 10 questions based on what they have learnt. It is best to choose questions with short answers. In class, you read them out and the teams discuss and write down their team answer. Each team then sends two members to write their team answers on the chalkboard in feedback columns (see *Chapter C8 – Assessment* for more on feedback columns), followed by self- or peer-correction. This way of doing quizzes is good for practising listening and speaking skills.

1b. Learners prepare the questions

This works well with learners at secondary level. Instead of you writing the questions, you get each team to prepare 5 – 10 questions for another team. They use the textbook and spend 10 minutes writing questions in their teams. During this time, monitor carefully to help with errors. Then they pass their quiz to another team, who write the answers. This can be done either with open or closed textbooks. After this, a member of the team who wrote the quiz comes to mark their answers. If there are any mistakes, the marker can show them where the answer is in the textbook. This way of doing quizzes is good for practising all four skills together.

2. **Truth or lie games**

It may not sound like a good idea, but teaching learners to lie stimulates creativity and helps to practise writing and speaking skills! If necessary, you can explain that they are not serious lies, just 'fibs' (a fib is a small or trivial lie). There are many truth or lie games. Here are two examples. You should be able to think of ways of varying them:

2a. What did you do at the weekend?

Interaction pattern: Pairs

Resources needed: None

Each learner tells their partner what they did at the weekend. What they say should be mainly true, but they should include three facts that are not true. Their partner should listen carefully then guess which facts were untrue. This game improves both their speaking and listening skills, and can be used with a range of **personalisation** or discussion questions (see *Ideas for speaking activities* in *Chapter C4 – Teaching Speaking*).

2b. Call my bluff

Interaction pattern: Small groups of 4 – 6

Resources needed: None

You will need a few dictionaries (or copy relevant definitions from a dictionary before the lesson). Choose one English word from the dictionary for each group. Choose words that none of your learners know. In class, give the groups time to check the real definition of the word in a dictionary and also to invent two incorrect definitions for their word. Then each group presents their three definitions to the class. The other groups must listen and try to guess which is the correct definition. They score points if they guess the correct definition. This game is good for learning writing, speaking and listening skills.

3. Running dictation

Interaction pattern: Teams of two or three

Resources needed: A short written text

There are many ways to do running dictation, but remember that it is often quite noisy, so, where possible, take the learners into the playground where they will not disturb other classes. The learners usually work in pairs; one is the secretary (who writes) and the other is the runner (who runs, reads, remembers and dictates). Sit the writers down together, each with a pen and some paper. Tell them they are not allowed to move or to give the pen to their runner. Next, stick a short text on a tree or wall about 10 metres away from the secretaries. The runners must run to the text, remember a few words or a sentence, run back to their secretaries and dictate what they remember. The secretary writes it down and the runner goes back to the text to get a few more words. It is a race, so they can run if it is safe to do so. They continue like this until they have the whole text correctly written on their piece of paper. The first team to do this wins the game. If you like, you can get the runners and secretaries to swap roles half way through the game. Running dictation integrates all four skills, and can be done with almost any type of text. Remember to keep the texts quite short.

Songs for younger learners (lower primary school)

Very young learners enjoy doing songs that are accompanied by physical actions or dances. Here are some traditional favourites among teachers. If you do not know the music, ask your colleagues or check on the internet by searching for the name of the song on YouTube (https://www.youtube.com). Several links to song websites are also given in *Useful Websites and Online Materials* at the end of this book. It is a good idea to write the words to the song on the chalkboard, or create a class poster, and the first time you sing it, you can point at the words as you sing.

Heads, Shoulders, Knees and Toes

When singing, touch each part of your body as you sing the word. Start slowly, and speed up. Introduce the second verse only after they have learnt the first verse:

Heads, shoulders, knees and toes, knees and toes,

Heads, shoulders, knees and toes, knees and toes,

Eyes and ears and mouth and nose,

Heads, shoulders, knees and toes, knees and toes.

2nd verse (*optional*)

Ankles, elbows, feet and seat, feet and seat,

Ankles, elbows, feet and seat, feet and seat,

Hair and hips and chin and cheeks,

Ankles, elbows, feet and seat, feet and seat.

The Wheels on the Bus

Each verse has a different action, which you perform as you sing the words (e.g. rolling your hands in a circle when you sing *"round and round"*). You can find the actions by searching for the song on YouTube. Introduce the verses one at a time.

The wheels on the bus go round and round.

Round and round. Round and round.

The wheels on the bus go round and round,

All day long.

(Roll hands in a circle)

The horn on the bus goes 'Beep, beep, beep.

Beep, beep, beep. Beep, beep, beep.'

The horn on the bus goes 'Beep, beep, beep,'

All day long.

(Pretend to honk the horn like the driver)

The wipers on the bus go 'Swish, swish, swish.

Swish, swish, swish. Swish, swish, swish.'

The wipers on the bus go 'Swish, swish, swish,'

All day long.

(Move arms like windscreen wipers)

The baby on the bus says, 'Wah, wah, wah!

Wah, wah, wah! Wah, wah, wah!'

The baby on the bus says, 'Wah, wah, wah!'

All day long.

(Rub eyes like a baby crying)

The mummy on the bus says, 'I love you,

I love you, I love you.'

The daddy on the bus says, 'I love you, too,'

All day long.

(Point to yourself when you say 'I', touch your heart when you say 'love', and point to the learners when you say 'you'.)

The Hokey Cokey (called The Hokey Pokey in the USA and Canada)

It is probably best to play this outside. Start by standing in a big circle, with everyone holding hands. When you sing the first line, everybody takes a few steps towards the centre of the circle. This is repeated three times. The other actions are described in the song:

Chorus

Oh-ho, the hokey cokey

(sing three times, all stepping towards the centre of the circle holding hands)

Knees bend, arms stretch. Ra! Ra! Ra!

(raise both hands like you are cheering)

Verse

You put your <u>right arm</u> in

(everybody moves their right arm forward)

Your <u>right arm</u> out

(everybody moves their right arm back)

In, out, in, out, shake it all about

(move your right arm in and out quickly and then shake it)

You do the hokey cokey and you turn around

(everybody turns around on the spot)

That's what it's all about ... Hey!

(now hold hands and go back to the chorus above)

For the other verses you do the same, but replace the underlined part of the body with the options given.

Verse 2: You put your <u>left arm</u> in.

Verse 3: You put your <u>right leg</u> in.

Verse 4: You put your <u>left leg</u> in.

Verse 5: You put your <u>whole self</u> in (*in this verse, you jump in and out!*).

Songs for older learners (upper primary and secondary school)

With older learners, you can use authentic songs on CDs, MP3 or your mobile phone and play them in class. If you need the lyrics (the words), you can find them easily by searching on the internet, or from listening to the song yourself and taking notes (good practice for improving your English). The songs you choose with older learners will depend on three factors:

1. What songs are available – For example, if you have any songs on your phone, you could use these.
2. What songs the learners are interested in – If there is an English song that is popular on the radio, try to get it. Learners will be very motivated to learn it.
3. What the song is about – Some songs have interesting lyrics that can lead to a good discussion (e.g. *Blowing in the Wind* by Bob Dylan – see below). Some songs include stories that the learners can retell to their partner (e.g. *She's Leaving Home* by The Beatles). Some songs include grammar that you can analyse after listening to the song (e.g. *If I were a Carpenter* by Tim Hardin for the second conditional grammar structure).

Once you have chosen your song, there are several activities you can do when the learners listen to the song for the first time:

1. **Song gap-fill**

Write the lyrics on the chalkboard with some of the words replaced with gaps. Learners listen to fill the gaps or they fill the gaps first and then listen to check. You can remove single words or even phrases.

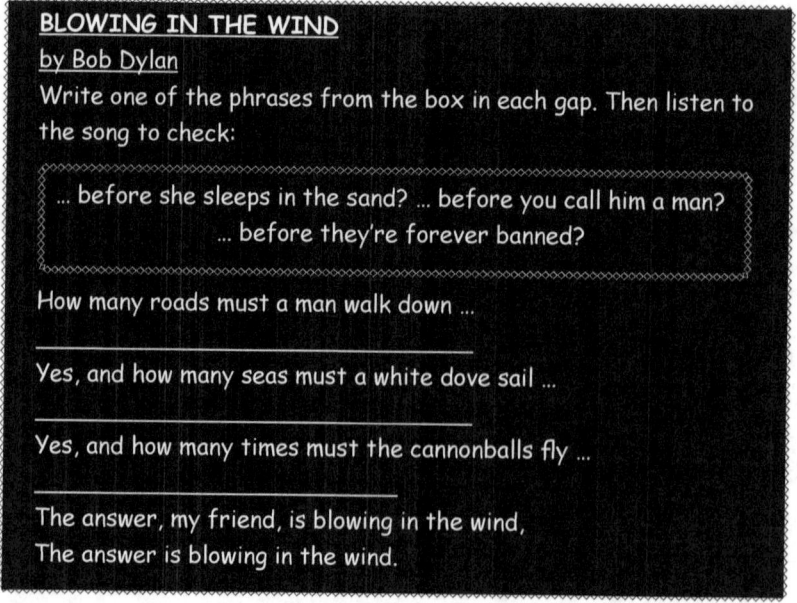

C10.1: EXAMPLE SONG GAPFILL

2. **Line ordering**

Write the lines of the song on the chalkboard in the wrong order. Learners listen to put them in the right order.

3. **Disappearing song**

Write the lyrics on the chalkboard. Listen once, letting the learners read and sing along as they listen. Then rub out five of the words. Learners listen again. This time they sing along and try to remember the missing words. Now rub out another five words and get them to listen and sing again. Do this again until most (or all) of the lyrics are gone. Each time they have to remember more and more of the song!

4. **Song discussion**

Write the lyrics on the chalkboard. Learners listen to the song, then discuss the meaning of the song, trying to understand why the singer is sad or happy, what problem they have or what advice they give.

Once the learners have done one of the activities above, listen again. This time both you and the learners should sing along. If learners really like a song, you can get them to create a class poster with the lyrics. This will help them to learn it off by heart, including all the vocabulary and grammar it contains.

Conclusion

In this chapter we have learnt the following:
- games are a natural part of learning for children, and can help them to learn faster;
- games help children to learn important social skills, such as teamwork;
- games and songs can be repeated many times, which helps learners to learn and reduces preparation time for teachers;
- games and songs are not just for small children – even adults love them;
- games can be used for learning vocabulary, grammar and skills;
- you can sing songs with very young learners and they will enjoy performing actions as they sing;
- older learners will prefer recorded songs, especially those that they hear on the radio and ones with an interesting message.

C11 - Learning Resources

In this chapter:

- What are learning resources?
- Why do we need learning resources?
- Seven types of learning resources
- Practical task: Any ideas?
- Commentary to practical task: Any ideas?

 **Reflective task**

1. Which of these do you think are learning resources?

the chalkboard	a photograph of your family
the **textbook**	pens and pencils
stones from the playground	the learners
posters on the walls	a receipt from a shop
a radio	

2. How many of these can you get for your lessons?
3. How many do you use?

What are learning resources?

Learning resources are tools that help learners to learn. They are sometimes called Teaching Aids or Pedagogic Resources. Many teachers feel that they cannot teach as well as they want to because they do not have enough learning resources. Even if your school does not have many 'bought resources' (i.e. resources made by companies for teaching and sold to schools), it is possible to replace these with resources that you have created yourself, with resources that are always present at the school or in the community, and with resourceful thinking.

Why do we need learning resources?

Learning resources make our job easier. They provide information, create context, allow communication, explain concepts and allow learners to participate actively in the learning process. Although it may take time to make or collect resources, this is time well spent, given that they will come in useful in the future.

Seven types of learning resources

We can divide the resources available to most teachers working in Africa into seven categories:

1. **Boards:** fixed chalkboards, portable chalkboards, mini-boards, **wall boards**;
2. **Printed resources:** the 'main' class textbook, other books in the course, **class readers**, dictionaries, etc.;
3. **People as resources:** the learners, the teacher, other school staff, school visitors;
4. **The school as a resource:** furniture in the classroom, the walls and the floor of the classroom, the school playground;
5. **Created resources:** posters, **flashcards**, pocketboards, **puppets**, etc.;
6. **Realia:** objects the learners bring to school, objects the teacher brings to school, objects in the school environment;
7. **Electrical and electronic resources:** computers, radios, audio players (CD players, cassette players, MP3 players), mobile phones, calculators.

Let us look at these seven categories in more detail:

1. Boards

All teachers need a chalkboard (also called blackboard) to teach effectively. It may be the oldest and the simplest resource in the classroom, but it is also the most important one. Chalkboards vary in size, quality, quantity, location and other factors that can all affect how useful they are. Some classrooms have two, one at either end of the room, which can be useful if we want to keep information on the chalkboard for a long time, or if we want many of our learners to use the chalkboard at the same time.

If a school also has several portable chalkboards, this can help us when we want to draw a table or picture and take it to several different classes, or when we want to hide and reveal information to the learners by turning it around. Portable chalkboards also allow learners more access to the chalkboard. They can be made by painting smooth wooden panels with chalkboard paint.

Mini-boards or 'slates' can also be useful. These are small pieces of chalkboard that are given with chalk to groups of learners to use as notepads. During feedback to an activity, the groups can hold up their mini-boards to show their answers at the same time. They can be made by painting A4-size pieces of wood with chalkboard paint. For a class of 60 learners, you will need at least 10 mini-boards. See *Chapter C12 – 10 Essential Resources to Create* for instructions on how to make and use them.

Some African schools (including schools in the UNICEF Child-friendly Schools project) also have **wall boards**. Wall boards are a simple idea in which the lowest metre of the side walls is painted with chalkboard paint. They are useful because they allow every child in the class to have their own chalkboard and chalk. The can use it to express their ideas, to practise writing and drawing and to compare and share what they are doing with each other.

If your school has chalkboard paint, chalk and wood, talk to your head teacher about making portable chalkboards, mini-boards or wall boards to try out in the classrooms.

Fig. C11.1: WALL BOARDS IN MALAWI

2. **Printed resources**

The most important printed resource is the class textbook. In most countries, there is a standard textbook for each year, which is often called the Pupil's Book or Student's Book. It is usually part of a set, called a 'course' that includes other books and resources:

- **Teacher's guide:** This provides learning objectives, lesson plans, answers to exercises and procedure for activities. Each teacher should have a copy of the Teacher's guide for each year they teach.
- **Class CDs, cassettes, audio material:** Traditionally, these are a set of cassettes or CDs containing the listening exercises for each level. The format of these in many countries is changing to digital, which means it may be possible to download them from the internet or transfer them via USB flash drive and use them as MP3 or WAV files in class (see Electrical and electronic resources on pages 236 – 237).
- **Homework book or workbook:** This provides more written exercises and activities for learners to do at home. It can be used in class for further practice (e.g. for reading).
- **Teacher's resource pack:** If your course has this, it can provide some useful ideas and possibly photocopiable resources to use with specific activities in the textbook. A lack of photocopying facilities may make it difficult to use the resource pack, but it can provide some good ideas that you can adapt and

use with your learners.

One of the most common difficulties that teachers working in public schools face is a lack of textbooks. Ideally, there should be one copy for every learner, but often teachers have fewer, meaning that learners have to share in pairs or groups. Occasionally there is only one copy per class. Some teachers who have a small number of textbooks have found a way to reduce this problem by organising desks and space carefully so that up to eight learners can read from one textbook (see Fig. C11.2). However, teachers who have only one copy of the textbook often spend a lot of lesson time copying exercises onto the chalkboard. One possible solution to this is to pre-prepare the board work, or ask a willing learner with good handwriting to do this for you (see *Chapter C6 – Teaching Reading* for how to do this). Another possibility is to use school funds to photocopy some of the most important pages of the book, such as reading exercises, grammar reference tables, etc. These copies are handed out at the beginning of the lesson, and collected in at the end of the lesson. For a class of 60 learners, you may only need 20 copies of each such page.

Fig. C11.2: SHARING A TEXTBOOK BETWEEN A LARGE NUMBER OF LEARNERS IS A POSSIBLE LAST RESORT

Some schools may not have a Teacher's guide for each year, which means that teachers may not be sure about how or why they are doing an activity, or what the correct answers to an exercise are. The only solution is to borrow the book from a different school and photocopy it, or, if there are very few copies available, it may be possible for your local Ministry of Education office to get hold of it, reproduce it and distribute copies to local schools.

Class readers are a very useful way to provide additional reading practice for your learners. They are specially written or adapted short stories with simplified vocabulary and grammar. They make reading enjoyable, and can provide inspiration for class discussions or writing and project activities. They can even form the basis for drama performances. In many countries, Sunrise Readers are very popular, as the stories are about African children and are illustrated to aid comprehension.

Fig. C11.3: CLASS READER BOOKS

Resource books such as atlases or dictionaries are usually kept in the staff room, but can be taken to class when needed. If you buy your own mini-dictionary, you can take it to every class with you. Choosing a learner to be the **dictionary monitor** each lesson can also be a good idea. Whenever learners need to check a word, they can ask the dictionary monitor what it means. This has the double advantage of giving the learners additional responsibilities and skills, and not putting you 'on the spot' with difficult questions. You can use either an English-only learner's dictionary (often better at higher levels), or a bilingual dictionary (often better at lower levels).

Two alternatives to published resources – reading posters and mini-readers – are given below under Created resources. How to make and use them is explained in *Chapter C12 – 10 Essential Resources to Create*.

3. **People as resources**

People are very useful resources that every teacher has access to. We can use the learners, ourselves, other teachers and staff, and even school visitors to help us to teach. The learners can help us in many ways. We can get them to provide a context for introducing new grammar. For example, if we want to teach comparative adjectives, we can stand two learners at the front of the class to demonstrate the sentence: *Merhawi is taller than Fortuna*. We can also use them to provide the inspiration for speaking and writing practice activities. For example, if we want the learners to practise describing items of clothing, we can ask them to describe to their partner what they are wearing. Teachers can use their own body to mime actions (swim, sleep), emotions (happy, angry) or even stories, and they can use their own voice to replace recorded listening material. We can also use other teachers when they have a free period, or other staff and visitors who speak English to provide the learners with an opportunity to try out their English. For example, we can get the learners to interview another teacher in order to practise speaking and listening skills.

4. **The school as a resource**

The school itself is a resource, including the furniture in the classroom, the walls and floor of the classroom, the playground and other outside spaces within the school compound. The furniture can be useful for providing a context for new grammar.

For example we can use a ball, a chair and a table to teach prepositions of location: *The ball is under the chair*. We can also get the learners to use their pens to practise the same language in pairs: *"Where is my pen?" "Your pen is on the bench."*

The walls can be covered with posters and other visual aids to make them more interesting (see *Chapter C12 – 10 Essential Resources to Create*), and the floor, if it is made of smooth concrete, can be used by the learners for chalk drawings. For example, we can give the learners small pieces of chalk, tell them to find a free space on the floor and ask them to draw and label a picture of their home. Do not worry about making a mess, the chalk soon disappears with walking and cleaning.

Fig. C11.4: CHILDREN IN RWANDA DRAWING ON CONCRETE FLOOR

Many classrooms in public schools are overcrowded, which often inhibits movement and reduces opportunities for language practice. However, most schools have plenty of space outside where learners can do **groupwork**, re-energise tired brains, explore the environment, and play learning games safely.

5. Created resources

Created Resources are re-usable resources that we make ourselves. The best created resources are ones that we use regularly; every day or every week. It is necessary to have certain basic materials to create your own resources. The only essential resource needed is paper. Marker pens are also useful, although coloured chalk, or traditional ink (see *Resource 3 – Flashcards* in *Chapter C12*) can be much cheaper. Other useful materials include card, scissors, glue, staples, needle and thread, fabric, rice sacks, string or banana rope and sticks.

Examples of created resources that most teachers can make easily and use regularly are visual aids, a pocketboard and flashcards, reading posters, mini-readers, sock puppets and masks, a class display board, a vocabulary box, a beanbag and name tents. Details on how to make and use each of these resources are given in

Chapter C12 – 10 Essential Resources to Create. The acronym **TALULAR** is used to refer to these created resources. It stands for Teaching And Learning Using Locally Available Resources.

6. Realia

Realia includes any real objects that we use to help learners to learn. For example the objects in the classroom or school environment, objects that we or the learners bring from home, and also objects that come from the community. Thus, if we are planning to teach the names of vegetables tomorrow, we can ask each of the learners to bring a few vegetables to tomorrow's lesson. If we are teaching possessive pronouns we can use the learners' pens to provide a context for the language (e.g. *"Whose pen is this?" "It's mine."*). If we are teaching the names of family members (brother, cousin, etc.), we can take a photo of our own family to show the learners. From the community, we can get hold of old English-language newspapers to provide **authentic text** reading practice, or collect pictures cut out from food packaging to replace real objects in a shop **role play**. Realia can make the introduction of new language clearer, the communication authentic and the lesson more memorable for the learners.

7. Electrical and electronic resources

Many teachers of English working in developing countries do not have access to electrical resources on a regular basis. However, as the 21st century progresses, we can expect that low-tech electrical and electronic equipment will become more easily available, including wind-up radios, rechargeable MP3 players (such as the **Lifeplayer**), digital cameras with video functionality and cheaper, tougher laptop computers, as used in the **One Laptop Per Child** (http://one.laptop.org/) project. As solar power becomes more available to power computers and to recharge batteries and other devices, even in remote areas, many teachers will be able to record MP3, video and radio programmes to use in class. They will be able to use MP3 players and portable speakers to provide listening practice for their learners, and also to use mobile phones to video drama performances or presentations and show these to their learners. As more and more schools get computer labs, teachers will also be able to facilitate computer-based English lessons for their learners.

Here are some ideas for how you may be able to use your own devices to help you as a teacher:

- If you have a mobile phone or MP3 player with a voice recorder, you can record a conversation between yourself and another teacher to play back in class as a listening exercise. Alternatively if you can get access to the internet, you can download recordings direct to your MP3 player. Although some mobile phones have quite loud speakers, you will probably need a portable speaker to increase the volume on playback.
- If you have only one or two computers in your school, consider training one of the more responsible learners in your class to use the English language learning programs on the computer. Then this learner can train other learners to use the program. Learners may be able to use the computer in small groups whenever possible.

- If there are English-language programmes on the radio or television in the evening, you could give your learners homework to listen to the programme. The following day it is possible to provide a follow-up lesson with comprehension or discussion questions and explanations of new vocabulary used.

Practical task: Any ideas?

Let us now try to think creatively about how we could use resources from the seven categories above. Imagine that some of your teaching colleagues are having difficulty coming up with ideas for their lessons. For each quote below, suggest one or two resources that the teacher could use and how they could use them:

I want to introduce and practise using superlative adjectives with my learners.
(learner age 11 – 12)

I want my learners to learn the names of six different parts of the body.
(learner age 7 – 8)

I want my learners to role play conversations buying food at a market.
(learner age 9 – 10)

I want my learners to improve their ability to give and understand directions.
(learner age 14 – 15)

I want my learners to learn to identify five colours.
(learner age 6 – 7)

I want to introduce and practise the question words 'How much' and 'How many' with my learners.
(learner age 8 – 9)

I want to set my learners a project that will lead to drama presentations at the end of the academic year.
(learner age 8 – 9)

Commentary to practical task: Any ideas?

There are many ways that resources could be used to teach in these lessons. Here are some ideas; you may have thought of others:

1. **"I want to introduce and practise using superlative adjectives with my learners."** (learner age 11 – 12)

Just as with comparative adjectives, the teacher can ask the learners in the class to participate as resources. She can ask three learners to stand at the front and teach sentences such as: *"Philippe is the tallest."* or *"Pierre is closest to Suzanne."* Practice could then follow this, with the learners working in groups of three to decide who is the oldest, the youngest, and who lives closest to the school within their group. Alternatively, the teacher could use atlases or a globe and ask learners to find the largest country, the longest river and the highest mountain on each continent. This could lead into a quiz, in which each team prepares several questions that include superlatives about the geography of the world for each other.

2. **"I want my learners to learn the names of six different parts of the body."** (learner age 7 – 8)

This teacher can use his own body as a resource to show the different parts of the body that he wants to teach. Alternatively, he could use a diagram on the chalkboard or a poster. He can then use the floor of the classroom as a resource by giving groups of learners one piece of chalk each and asking them to draw and label a picture of a body on the floor. He could also teach the learners to sing the song *Heads, shoulders, knees and toes* (See *Chapter C10 – Games and Songs*).

3. **"I want my learners to role play conversations buying food at a market."** (learner age 9 – 10)

In the previous lesson this teacher can ask each of the learners to bring in a few different items of food (realia) that we find at a market. Using this food, she can tell the learners to set up market stalls in different parts of the room. After a few examples, she can organise a whole class role-play in which some of the learners are customers and others are sellers at the market. Alternatively, she can collect packaging from different food items (packets of biscuits, noodles, cola bottles, cans, etc.) and create a shop using these resources from the community. The learners could work in pairs to write dialogues including the items they see and some pairs could perform their dialogue in front of the class.

4. **"I want my learners to improve their ability to give and understand directions."** (learner age 14 – 15)

Using a portable chalkboard, this teacher could prepare a chalk map of the village before the lesson. He could use this to teach/**revise** the language of directions. Working in pairs, the learners could then give each other directions to different places on the map. They could practise both speaking and writing in this way. The school environment could be used as a resource, by taking the learners outside and getting them to direct each other to different locations on the school premises.

5. **"I want my learners to learn to identify five colours." (learner age 6 – 7)**

This teacher could bring in a variety of different objects from home (realia) in the five colours, such as a green plant, a red cup, a yellow jerry can, etc. and use these objects to teach the colours. She could then ask the learners to look for these colours in other objects in the classroom, and teach them to ask and answer the question: *"What colour is this?"*

6. **"I want to introduce and practise the question words 'How much' and 'How many' with my learners." (learner age 8 – 9)**

This teacher could use realia from the school environment and the learners to teach 'How much' and 'How many'. First, he could ask some of the learners to go outside to collect stones from the playground. He could then teach them to ask and answer the question: *"How many stones do you have?" "I have seven stones."* After this, he could find out who has brought drinking water to the lesson, and then teach them to ask and answer *"How much water do you have?" "I have half a bottle of water."* The learners can then practise asking and answering these questions in small groups.

7. **"I want to set my learners a project that will lead to drama presentations at the end of the academic year." (learner age 15 – 16)**

This teacher could make use of published resources such as class readers to inspire her learners. Each drama group could read one book and choose a scene from the story to perform. Alternatively, the learners could use family members as a resource to find out about a traditional story within their local community. They could then translate this story into English before they learn and perform it.

Conclusion

In this chapter we have learnt the following:
- why learning resources are important and how they can help with learning;
- how we can replace 'bought resources' with created resources and resourceful thinking;
- how learning resources can be categorised into seven different types: chalkboards, books, people, the school, created resources, realia and electrical resources;
- how we can solve a number of common problems using simple resources available to teachers everywhere.

C12 – 10 Essential Resources to Create

In this chapter:

- TALULAR
- Three tips for resource creation
- Resource 1: Permanent visual aids on the walls of your classrooms
- Resource 2: A pocketboard
- Resource 3: Flashcards
- Resource 4: A beanbag
- Resource 5: A vocabulary box
- Resource 6: Reading posters
- Resource 7: Sock puppets
- Resource 8: Classroom display board
- Resource 9: Mini-boards
- Resource 10: Personalised name tents

TALULAR

TALULAR stands for ***Teaching And Learning Using Locally Available Resources***. TALULAR resources can replace the 'bought resources' that are not available in many African schools. This chapter presents ten TALULAR resources that any teacher can create for their learners. Although it will take time to create some of these resources, they can be used again and again to make your teaching more effective and your lessons more enjoyable. See *Resource Creation* in the *Useful Websites and Online Materials* section at the back of this book for more ideas.

Three tips for resource creation

1. Try to create one new resource every week or every month, rather than creating them all at once.
2. Remember that you have lots of learners who will be ready to help you – some of them can probably draw well, others can sew, and they will all be proud to see their own work used in the classroom.
3. Remember that for these resources to be available and useful, you will need somewhere to store them where they are easily accessible and safe from damage. If there is no space in your school for such resources, talk to your head teacher – all good teachers need resources, and all good resources need a home!

Resource 1: Permanent visual aids on the walls of your classrooms

Levels: All primary and secondary

Time to create: 60 minutes per visual aid

Materials needed: Poster card or used rice sacks, marker pens or traditional ink, nails or pins

Description: Permanent visual aids are posters fixed to the walls of the classroom. They can be made from either poster card (manila paper), or from used rice sacks. They are fixed to the walls using nails or pins. They display important information that we want the learners to learn by heart. For teaching English this could be a **wall frieze** with example words (see *Chapter B7 - Resources and Games for Developing Literacy*), important classroom language (all levels) or past forms of irregular verbs (at higher levels). As well as displaying important information, when they are on the walls of a classroom, permanent visual aids make the classroom an interesting and stimulating learning environment.

Ideas for lower primary levels: Alphabet chart, animal pictures with labels, food pictures with labels, pictures of classroom objects with labels, picture of a human body with labels, colours with labels, daily greetings, days of the week.

Ideas for upper primary levels: Preposition diagrams, pronunciation chart, a favourite song, a weather chart, pictures of common verbs with labels, classroom language, question words.

Ideas for secondary levels: Past simple and past participle forms of irregular verbs, example sentences of the important tenses in English, examples of different text types (such as a formal letter or a CV), important language for **groupwork** interaction, question formation chart.

How to make permanent visual aids: If you are using old rice sacks, which can usually be bought at local markets, first cut open the rice sack to maximise the size of the poster. Then seal the edges to stop them from fraying. This can be done by stitching them (seamstresses at local markets can often do this cheaply and efficiently) or by passing the edges quickly over a candle flame. Before you begin making your permanent visual aid, remember to plan it out on an A4 piece of paper. Remember to include a title, and to use different colours to make things clear. If you do not have the colour you need, it is possible to put glue onto the area

Fig. C12.1: EXAMPLE PERMANENT VISUAL AID

and sprinkle coloured chalk dust onto the glue. Write clearly and large enough so that all learners will be able to see. Then copy your plan onto the poster card or rice sack. Choose a good place to hang it in the classroom. This may need to be high up if you are worried about learners damaging it, but make sure it is visible to all learners. Use nails or pins to secure it to the wall. If you put them up carefully in the right place, these visual aids can last for many years.

Resource 2: A pocketboard

Levels: All primary and secondary   **Time to create:** 2 – 3 hours

Materials needed: A large piece of fabric (or two rice sacks), at least 1.5 m × 1 m, sewing needle and thread.

Description: A pocketboard is a large piece of fabric stitched together and hung on the wall to create a 'wall of pockets'. It can be used to display **flashcards**, pictures and even pieces of paper at the front of the class. A pocketboard is made of a single piece of fabric, so it is strong, cheap to make and easy to repair. It can be taken to each lesson and hung on nails, or it can be left in the classroom permanently. Teachers of English find pocketboards useful for displaying letters at low levels (e.g. when doing spelling activities), for displaying whole words at higher levels (e.g. when showing learners how to form questions or negatives), for matching activities (e.g. matching pictures with words), and for games (e.g. a noughts and crosses quiz with words to define on each card).

Fig. C12.2: TEACHER USING POCKETBOARD IN KENYA

Teachers can use pocketboards to make lessons more colourful and more interesting than if they used only the chalkboard, and also for involving learners in presentations and other activities. Some teachers in Kenya have found that they prefer to use the pocketboard more than the chalkboard, displaying the date and lesson title, creating flashcards with pictures and words drawn by learners, short sentences, images cut out from old **textbooks** or newspapers and they may even use their pocketboard to display real objects (such as leaves, flowers, learners' pens, etc.). The biggest advantage of preparing lessons for the pocketboard is that you can repeat the same lesson many times, so if you teach a lesson two or more times in a day or week, the pocketboard can save you a lot of time and energy in class.

How to make a pocketboard: Take a large piece of material (for example 1.5 m wide × 1 m high) and fold it to create several rows, as in Fig. C12.3. Each row should be at least 12 cm high. Pin these rows. Then create pockets by sewing vertical dividing lines between the columns, as in Fig. C12.3. Each pocket should be 7 – 10 cm wide. A useful pocketboard needs to be at least seven pockets wide, and five rows high. If your piece of fabric is larger, make it 10 pockets wide by 10 pockets high. Remember to sew a piece of fabric onto each of the four corners (straps), which you can use to attach the pocketboard to the wall of your classroom. You can either hang it on nails or tie the pocketboard to two poles or trees if you are teaching outside.

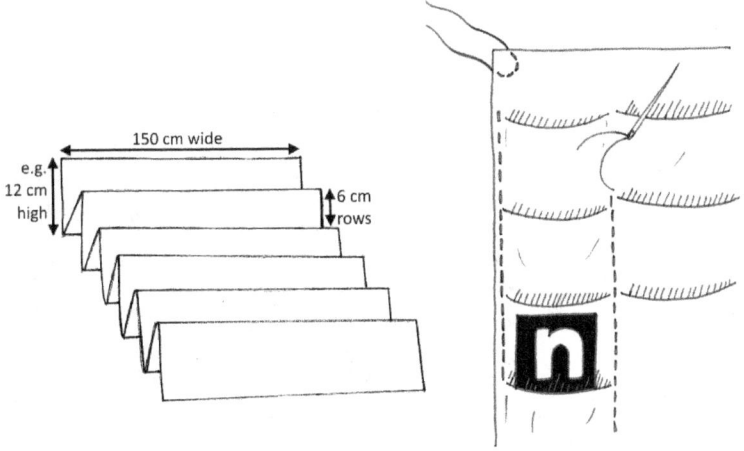

Fig. C12:3 HOW TO MAKE A POCKETBOARD

Resource 3: Flashcards

Levels: All primary and secondary **Time to create:** 1 – 5 minutes per card

Materials needed: Poster card, thick paper or old cardboard boxes, marker pens, brush and paint or traditional ink.

Flashcards are small pieces of card or paper with pictures or words written on them. The pictures/words are large enough so that all your learners can see them when they are shown at the front of the class, or displayed on a pocketboard. Marker pens, brush and paint or traditional ink (see page 245) are used to draw on the flashcards. They are useful for a number of reasons:

- they are easy to make;
- they can be reused many times;
- they provide variety and interest to the lesson for learners;
- they can be kept in a box and added to whenever needed.

For teaching vocabulary, double-sided flashcards can be made, with the word on one side and illustrations or translations on the back of the card.

If you have a pocketboard (see above), you can use it to display your flashcards. If you do not, you can make your flashcards out of folded pieces of card or paper, and stand them on a table or hang them from a **washing line** to display them.

Ideas for lower primary levels: Cards showing letters of the alphabet; cards showing colours; cards showing parts of the body; cards showing animals; cards showing new vocabulary items; picture cards; cards drawn by the learners with their names and portraits on them.

Ideas for upper primary and secondary levels: photo cards that learners can describe (cut them out of old newspapers); cards showing word stems, prefixes and suffixes; cards illustrating concepts, such as prepositions, tenses or comparatives; cards with test questions.

Fig. C12.4: DIFFERENT TYPES OF FLASHCARDS

How to make flashcards: Flashcards are easy to make. If you have poster card, you can begin by cutting it up into lots of pieces using scissors. You can create a variety of sizes, from 10 × 5 cm to 30 × 20 cm so that they are ready when you need them. If you do not have much poster card, you can also create them from paper (just fold it in half and glue it to make it stronger), or old cardboard boxes.

When you need the flashcards, you can write or draw on these pre-prepared cards using marker pens. If you do not have marker pens, brush and paint are just as good, and if you do not have any paint, you can make traditional ink using the 'recipe' below. If you are creating flashcards to use with a pocketboard, remember that you should make sure they fit in the pockets and do not write or draw on the bottom half of the card, as this will be inside the pocket.

Making traditional ink: You need charcoal, acacia gum and water. First collect some gum from an acacia tree. Most acacias will produce gum if the bark is cut with a knife, although two species *Acacia senegal* and *Acacia seyal* are best. You will need liquid gum. If you collect hard gum, reheat it in a small container over a fire to melt it before you begin. Grind the charcoal down into a very fine powder. Add a little liquid gum to the powder and mix them well. Keep adding more until you have a thick paste. Now add a little water to thin the paste into an ink. If you find that the ink does not stick to the card very well, you can add a small amount of honey or sugar dissolved in water.

Resource 4: A beanbag

Levels: All primary and secondary   **Time to create:** 30 minutes

Materials needed: 100 g of small dried beans, maize or peas, a small piece of fabric 20 cm × 10 cm, needle and thread.

A beanbag is a small bag made of fabric, filled with beans and stitched up. It can be thrown or passed around like a small ball in class, with the advantages that it is very cheap to make, safe to throw around and easy to catch.

Fig. C12.5: HOME-MADE BEANBAG

A beanbag can be used to change the way that learners are **nominated** during the lesson. The traditional way to **nominate** learners is for learners to raise their hands and the teacher to select one of them. This method is fast and sometimes useful, but it often leads to teachers picking the same learners (often the stronger ones), and neglecting the weaker learners, who are less likely to have their hands raised. When a teacher has a beanbag, she can throw or give it to any learner in the class to nominate them. For example, when you are correcting an exercise or doing feedback to an activity, you can throw the beanbag to select a learner to provide the answer. The learners can also nominate other learners by throwing or passing the beanbag. For example, a learner who has answered a question correctly can choose who will answer the next question by throwing the beanbag to them. This is called **peer-nomination** and it is an effective way to give control of a small part of the lesson to the learners. You can specify that boys must always throw to girls and vice versa. Another important advantage to throwing a beanbag around in class is that it stimulates and entertains the learners, especially in lessons with large amounts of writing work. They enjoy the physical activity which stimulates the brain as they prepare to catch the beanbag. It can also be used in games to select learners randomly, and also for singing games and name games.

How to make a beanbag: Take a small piece of fabric approx. 20 cm × 10 cm, fold it in half and sew the edges together to make a square bag. On one side, leave a hole about 3 – 4 cm long to put the beans into. Then take a big handful of dry, uncooked beans, maize or peas and put them into the beanbag through the hole. Sew up the hole to close the bag. Once it is finished it should be easy to throw and catch. You can also make ball-shaped beanbags if you are good at sewing, or even decorate your beanbag with a face and give it a name!

Resource 5: A vocabulary box

Levels: All primary and secondary   **Time to create:** 5 minutes

Materials needed: A small cardboard, plastic or metal box with a lid, lots of small pieces of paper (approx. 5 cm × 2 cm).

One of the most important parts of learning a language is learning vocabulary. In order to learn vocabulary, we need to **revise** it regularly. The vocabulary box is an effective way to do this. It enables us to store all the new words that arise during lessons, and it can be used for revision activities, informal tests and games. Here is how to use it:

Each lesson select one of the learners to be the vocabulary box **monitor**. It is his or her job to write down any new words that come up during the lesson. Each word should be written on a separate piece of paper. If you like (and if all the learners share the same **mother tongue**), you can get them to write a translation on the other side. At the end of the lesson, the monitor comes to the front and reads out all the new words she/he has put into the vocabulary box. The other learners make a note of these words in their notebook, and they can learn them for homework.

At the start of the next lesson, select a new vocabulary box monitor. While you are preparing to begin your lesson, the monitor can test the class using the words in the box, including words from the last lesson and words from previous lessons. The monitor can test the other learners by taking a piece of paper and reading out the word in English. She/He then nominates another learner to either explain the word in English or translate it into the mother tongue.

At the end of the week, the vocabulary box can be used for longer revision games or tests:

Idea 1: The vocabulary box monitor takes 10 pieces of paper from the vocabulary box and writes the 10 words on the chalkboard. Other learners work in teams to write one example sentence with each word in their notebooks.

Idea 2: Five words are shown to the class and they must work in pairs to write a short dialogue or story using these words.

Idea 3: When you have over 50 words in the box (after a few weeks of using it), learners can sit in small groups, each group receiving 5 – 10 words from the box. They must work together to remember the meaning of each word or they could play *Define and Guess* (see *Chapter C4 – Teaching Speaking*). They swap words with other teams every few minutes.

You can probably think of many more activities that can be done with the vocabulary box. It will also be very useful at the end of the term and the year to revise all the vocabulary they have learnt over a longer period of time.

The learners usually enjoy being the vocabulary box monitor and take the job very seriously. Other learners will often help the monitor (they may prefer to do it in pairs) and classes can even borrow the box from you whenever they want to do revision work or if their class is left unattended at any time during the day. At the end of a term or year, it can give the learners a real sense of achievement when they see how many words they have learnt.

How to make a vocabulary box: You need a container large enough to store many pieces of paper in. It could be an old chalk box, a washing powder box or a powdered milk tin from home – anything that can store lots of pieces of paper, ideally with a lid. You will probably need a different box for each class, so if you show the learners an example, one of them can be entrusted with the task of finding a suitable box for their class. To make the pieces of paper, just cut up paper that you already have into small slips and keep them in the box, ready for when new words come up during a lesson.

Resource 6: Reading posters

Levels: Mid-primary to secondary **Time to create:** 30 – 60 minutes per poster

Materials needed: Used rice sacks or poster paper, marker pens or traditional ink.

If you do not have enough copies of the textbook for your learners, you will need to find another way of providing them with texts for reading practice. Traditionally, teachers would copy these texts onto the chalkboard. However, this takes time and is hard work for the teacher. Reading posters are an alternative to this. A reading poster is a textbook text copied out onto a used rice sack (or poster paper if you have it). The poster may also contain comprehension questions above or below the text. While it takes time to create each reading poster, they can be used year after year. If each teacher creates one poster every month, by the end of the year you will have many posters that you can share. In secondary schools, learners can also help with creating reading posters.

Using reading posters is simple. Select the one you need for a particular lesson and take it to class. Conduct a reading lesson as you would normally do (see *Chapter C6 – Teaching Reading*). When you want them to read the text, display the reading poster at the front of the class for learners to read. Reading posters have a few advantages over texts in textbooks. Firstly, you can point out words or sentences easily; useful for analysing things like text structure and grammar at secondary level. Also you can hide the text if you want learners to read a text quickly (to improve their reading speed) or if you want learners to do an activity from memory. If any of your learners are visually-impaired, you should move them to the front of the class so they can read the words on the poster easily. Reading posters can be used in **shared reading sessions** with early **literacy** learners (see *Chapter B7 – Resources and Activities for Developing Literacy*).

How to make a reading poster: The procedure is similar to that of creating a Permanent Visual Resource (see above). Plan the poster first on A4 paper and then write your text on the poster, using either marker pens, paint or traditional ink. Remember to keep your writing large enough so that all the learners in your class will be able to read the text easily. You can also write the comprehension questions on the poster and the answers on the back. Store reading posters carefully together, keeping them flat, rather than rolling them up. Attaching them to coat hangers and hanging them on a rail in a corner of the staff room is a good way to do this.

Resource 7: Sock puppets

Levels: Lower primary   **Time to create:** 30 minutes per puppet

Materials needed: Two old socks (different colours), a small piece of sponge or foam.

Sock puppets are a useful resource for teachers of English working at lower primary level. They are fairly simple and easy to make and really help to make lessons enjoyable for learners as they start to learn English. They are made from old socks with foam balls for eyes, and are worn on the hands. Give each of your sock puppets a name and make sure the two puppets look different; their identity

Fig. C12.6: 2 SOCK PUPPETS

is an important part of their appeal to the learners. You can tell the learners that the puppets only speak English, so if they want to communicate with them they must use English.

Sock puppets can be used in many ways:
- they can greet the learners every day;
- they can demonstrate dialogues or other **pairwork** activities before the learners do the same activity in pairs;
- they can demonstrate and encourage the use of classroom language;
- they can be used to show different concepts (e.g. prepositions of location), to role play stories, and even as a teaching team, asking the learners questions and praising them for their answers;
- they can be used when you are monitoring pairwork or **groupwork** to relax the learners and encourage shy learners to participate more in lessons;
- learners can play with the sock puppets, wearing them and speaking in English when they 'mime' their voices.

A simple alternative to sock puppets is paper bag puppets, made from brown paper bags with the bottom folded and faces drawn on them.

Fig. C12.7: PAPER BAG PUPPETS

How to make sock puppets: Find two old socks of different colours. Get some small pieces of sponge (about 1 cm³), one for each eye (use foam dusters, or the foam found in bed mattresses). Using scissors, trim the pieces of foam into round balls. Using a needle and thread, sew the balls onto the socks to make the eyes. Make sure you put them in the right position. You should attach the eyes onto the top of the sock when worn on your hand. It does not matter if they are not perfectly sewn on; they can look quite funny if the eyes hang loose. Finally, use a marker pen or some paint to draw eyeballs on the sponge eyes.

Resource 8: Classroom display board

Levels: All primary and secondary   **Time to create:** 30 minutes

Materials needed: Plywood boards/Rice sacks/Manila paper, nails or screws, sticky tape, pins or paperclips.

A display board is an essential part of every child-centred classroom. It is a space on the wall of the classroom where the learner's work can be displayed. It provides decoration for the classroom and also serves as an effective way for you to **praise** learners for good work, both individual work and groupwork. It can show labelled pictures, self-portraits, stories, essays, reports, etc. It can also be used to display a **classroom contract** (see *Chapter A6 – Classroom Management and Behaviour Management*) and important information. Other things that can be shown on a display board include:

- the word of the week (each week choose one word that is important for the learners to learn);
- English language newspaper articles (for reading practice during break time);
- new words for the vocabulary box;
- example compositions or text types (written either by the teacher or a learner);
- homework tasks for the week;
- a class duties calendar (describing different monitor roles each week).

Remember that if more than one class is taught in a classroom, each class needs its own display board.

How to make a classroom display board: Display boards can be made out of different materials depending on your classroom and what resources are available. Ask your head teacher if it is possible to buy some thin wooden board, such as plywood to make a strong permanent display board. Get it cut to sizes of at least 1.5 m × 1 m for each class, and put the boards up using screws or nails. Drawing pins or sticky tape can be used to attach work to them.

If you cannot make wooden display boards, there are a number of cheaper options that all work well:

- use rice sacks or poster card, fixed to the walls with nails, and use sticky tape or pins to attach work to it;
- use banana leaves woven together and dried to create a display board, and use paper clips or sticky tape to attach work to it;

- use an old cardboard box opened and flattened, and use drawing pins to attach work to it.

Even if you cannot make a display board, it may be possible to designate a certain area of the wall as the display board, and put work up there. Do not forget to put the class name at the top of the display board.

Resource 9: Mini-boards

Levels: All primary and secondary **Time to create:** 30 minutes to paint a set

Materials needed: 8 – 12 wooden boards, each about A4 size, chalkboard paint, brush.

Mini-boards are small, hand-held chalkboards that are used in classrooms by the learners for groupwork activities. One or two sets can be made for the whole school and borrowed by teachers whenever they need them. You will need one mini-board and a piece of chalk per group of 4 – 6 learners.

The key advantage to mini-boards is that each group can write on their mini-board and display their ideas or answers for the whole class and the teacher to see. They are fast and easy to use, and make feedback exciting, allowing all groups to contribute and allowing you to assess how well the whole class has achieved an objective or learnt a new concept. They also encourage good groupwork practice.

Fig. C12.8: MINI-BOARDS

Here are three basic ideas for using mini-boards:
- The teacher writes an exercise on the chalkboard. Groups receive mini-boards and chalk, and write their answers on their mini-board before bringing them to the front where the boards are displayed and compared. The answers are checked, and a member from each group corrects their own work.
- The teacher asks an important question to check understanding of a new piece of grammar or vocabulary. Instead of learners raising their hands to respond, the teacher encourages them to discuss the question first in groups, then write their answer on their mini-board. The mini-boards are all shown at the same time and the teacher can assess understanding quickly and accurately before confirming the correct answer.
- The teacher writes a quiz for the class. In the lesson the learners work in groups using the mini-boards to answer the questions. After each question, the groups have two minutes to discuss and write down their answer, before displaying them simultaneously. The teacher gives the correct answer, awards marks and moves on to the next question.

Mini-boards can be used in many more ways. Once you start using them you will think of more ideas.

How to make a set of mini-boards: Each mini-board should be about A4 size. Your head teacher will need to buy enough wood to make a class set. If your classes usually have 50 learners, you should make at least 10 mini-boards for a class set. They can be made out of light, thin wood, such as plywood or hardboard. Each board is painted with chalkboard paint. You can paint both sides if you have enough paint, which doubles the writing space on the board. Once dry, each set should be stored with a box of chalk and rags for use as dusters (1 piece of chalk and one rag per board). Try making one set first. If lots of teachers start using them, make more sets. If you have whiteboard pens, you can make very simple mini-whiteboards by putting sheets of white A4 card into transparent plastic A4 document display pockets and writing on the outside of the display pocket; the ink should come off with a piece of tissue paper.

Resource 10: Personalised name tents

Levels: All primary and secondary   **Time to create:** 15 minutes during a lesson

Materials needed: A sheet of paper or card for every learner (the learners can provide this themselves), coloured pens, pencils or paints for decoration.

Name tents are triangular paper stands that each learner has on his/her desk. They display the learner's name. In large classes they help teachers to learn the name of every learner and they provide an important opportunity for the learners to express themselves. At lower primary level, name tents can help with **literacy** learning (see *Chapter B7 – Resources and Activities for Developing Literacy*). Many learners like to draw pictures, decorative patterns and badges (such as the name of their favourite football team or pop star) on their name tent. It is the learners' responsibility to create their own name tent, bring it to each lesson and display it on their desk so that the teacher and other learners can see it. It is also the learners' responsibility to replace it if they lose or damage it.

How to make a name tent: It is a good idea to get the learners to create their name tents at the start of the academic year, and you should dedicate about 15 minutes of a lesson to this task. If you want the learners to bring their own card/paper, inform them a day in advance. Take along a few examples to give them some ideas, and some coloured pens, pencils or paint. If you can provide card, this will last longer, but if you cannot, paper is fine. Each learner needs a piece of paper about A4 size. They should fold it four times, first in half, then in quarters, as shown in Fig. C12.9. Then learners should write their name in big letters on one of the three outer sides of the tent, ideally using a marker pen or paint. They can also decorate their name tent at this stage if they want. With very young learners, you may need to write their name for them. Next they should stand up the tent by folding one side under the other as in Fig. C12.9. It may be necessary to use a staple or a little sticky tape to stop thin paper from slipping.

Fig. C12.9: HOW TO MAKE NAME TENTS

Bibliography

The following bibliography includes titles and papers referenced in the text as well as a number of recommendations for further reading:

Anderson, Lorin W., David R. Krathwohl, and Benjamin Samuel Bloom. **A taxonomy for learning, teaching, and assessing: A revision of Bloom's taxonomy of educational objectives.** Allyn & Bacon, 2001.

Baker, Joanna, and Heather Westrup. **The English Language Teacher's Handbook: How to Teach Large Classes with Few Resources.** New York: VSO/Continuum, 2000.

Barcroft, Joe, and Wynne Wong. **"Input, Input Processing and Focus on Form."** In The Cambridge Handbook of Second Language Acquisition, edited by Julia Herschensohn and Martha Young-Scholten. Cambridge: Cambridge University Press, 2013.

Britto, Pia Rebello, and Maria Cristina Limlingan. **"School Readiness and Transitions."** New York: UNICEF, 2012.

Brown, H. Douglas. **Principles of Language Learning and Teaching 4th Edition.** White Plains, NY: Pearson Education, 2000.

Brown, James D. **Testing in Language Programs: A Comprehensive Guide to English Language Assessment.** New Jersey: Prentice Hall Regents, 1996.

Butzkamm, Wolfgang, and John AW Caldwell. **The Bilingual Reform: A Paradigm Shift in Foreign Language Teaching.** Tübingen: Narr, 2009.

Clemens, Michael. **"The Long Walk to School: International Education Goals in Historical Perspective."** Center for Global Development Working Paper 37 (2004).

Cook, Guy. **Translation in Language Teaching: An Argument for Reassessment.** Oxford: Oxford University Press, 2010.

Cook, Vivian. **"Going beyond the native speaker in language teaching."** TESOL Quarterly 33, no. 2 (1999): 185 – 209.

Coyle, Do, Philip Hood, and David Marsh. **CLIL: Content and Language Integrated Learning.** Cambridge: Cambridge University Press, 2010.

Deller, Sheelagh, and Mario Rinvolucri. **Using the Mother Tongue: Making the Most of the Learner's Language.** London: First Pearson Publishing/English Teaching Professional/DELTA Publishing, 2002.

Dörnyei, Zoltán. **Motivation Strategies in the Language Classroom.** Cambridge: Cambridge University Press, 2001.

Ehri, Linnea C., Simone R. Nunes, Steven A. Stahl, and Dale M. Willows. **"Systematic phonics instruction helps students learn to read: Evidence from the National Reading Panel's meta-analysis."** Review of Educational Research 71, no. 3 (2001): 393 – 447.

Ellis, Rod. **"Principles of Instructed Second Language Acquisition."** In CAL Digest. Washington, DC: Center for Applied Linguistics. 2008.

Ferguson, Gibson. **"The language of instruction issue: Reality, aspiration and the wider context."** In Multilingual Education in Africa: Lessons from the Juba Language-in-Education Conference (2013): 17 – 22.

Gardner, Howard. **Frames of mind: The Theory of Multiple Intelligences.** New York: Basic books, 1983.

Gardner, Howard. **Intelligence Reframed: Multiple Intelligences for the 21st Century.** New York: Basic Books, 1999.

Harmer, Jeremy. **The Practice of English Language Teaching 4th Edition.** Harlow: Pearson/Longman, 2007.

Haznedar, Belma, and Elena Gavruseva. **"Childhood Second Language Acquisition."** In The Cambridge Handbook of Second Language Acquisition, edited by Julia Herschensohn and Martha Young-Scholten. Cambridge: Cambridge University Press, 2013.

Head, Katie and Pauline Taylor. **Readings in Teacher Development.** Oxford: Heinemann, 1997.

Hedge, Tricia. **Teaching and Learning in the Language Classroom.** Oxford: Oxford University Press, 2001.

Holliday, Adrian. **"The house of TESEP and the communicative approach: The special needs of state English language education."** ELT Journal 48.1 (1994): 3 – 11.

Kerr, Philip. **Translation and Own-language Activities.** Cambridge: Cambridge University Press, 2014.

Lewis, Maureen and Sue Ellis. **Phonics: Practice, Research and Policy.** London: Sage, 2006.

Long, Michael H. **"The Role of the Linguistic Environment in Second Language Acquisition."** In Handbook of Second Language Acquisition, edited by William C. Ritchie and Tej K. Bhatia, 413–68. San Diego, CA: Academic Press, 1996.

Mehrotra, Santosh. **"Education for All: Policy Lessons from High-Achieving Countries."** International Review of Education 44, no. 5-6 (1998): 461–84.

Milton, James, and Giovanna Donzelli. **"The Lexicon."** In The Cambridge Handbook of Second Language Acquisition, edited by Julia Herschensohn and Martha Young-Scholten. Cambridge: Cambridge University Press, 2013.

Montessori, Maria. **The Absorbent Mind.** Macmillan, 1995.

Okumu, Ibrahim M., Alex Nakajjo, and Doreen Isoke. "Socioeconomic Determinants of Primary School Dropout: The Logistic Model Analysis." Economic Policy Research Centre (EPRC) Uganda, 2008.

Parrott, Martin. **Tasks for Language Teachers: A Resource Book for Training and Development.** Cambridge: Cambridge University Press, 1993.

Prodromou, Luke "The role of the mother tongue in the classroom." International Association of Teachers of English as a Foreign Language Issues. (2002): 6 – 8.

Richter, Linda. "**The Importance of Caregiver-child Interactions for the Survival and Healthy Development of Young Children. A Review.**" World Health Organization, 2004.

Riley, Jeni, and David Reedy "**Communication, language and literacy: Learning through speaking and listening, reading and writing**" In Learning in the Early Years 3 – 7, edited by Jeni Riley, 65 – 100. London: Sage, 2007.

Scrivener, Jim. **Learning Teaching, 3rd Edition.** Oxford: Macmillan, 2005.

Turnbull, Miles, and Jennifer Dailey-O'Cain, eds. **First Language Use in Second and Foreign Language Learning.** Bristol: Multilingual matters, 2009.

Underhill, Adrian. **Sound foundations: learning and teaching pronunciation.** London: Macmillan, 2005.

UNICEF. "**Child Friendly Schools Manual.**" UNICEF (2009).

United Nations "**United Nations Millennium Declaration.**" United Nations (2000).

United Nations "**United Nations Convention on the Rights of the Child (UNCRC).**" United Nations (1989).

Ur, Penny. **A Course in English Language Teaching.** Cambridge: Cambridge University Press, 2012.

Widdowson, Henry G. **Defining Issues in English Language Teaching.** Oxford: Oxford University Press, 2003.

Wyse, Dominic and Russell Jones. **Teaching English, Language and Literacy**, 2nd Edition. Oxon: Routledge, 2008.

Young, Richard. "**The Negotiation of Meaning in Children's Foreign Language Acquisition.**" ELT Journal 37, no. 3 (1983): 197 – 206.

Useful Websites and Online Materials

This section includes a number of useful websites and links to downloadable resources that you may find useful both for your teaching and for your **continuing professional development**.

Methodology and teacher development

UNICEF Child-friendly Schools Manual:

The UNICEF Child-friendly schools manual includes some new and interesting ideas on how to make your school more child-friendly:

http://www.unicef.org/publications/files/Child_Friendly_Schools_Manual_EN_040809.pdf

Multilingual Education in Africa: Lessons from the Juba Language-in-Education Conference:

A downloadable document that includes a number of interesting papers on languages and education in Africa from the Juba Conference in 2012, including Ferguson's paper on the *Language of Instruction* issue, cited in *Part B* of this book.

http://mlenetwork.org/sites/default/files/C413%20Juba%20Publication_FINAL_WEB%20ONLY%20v3.pdf

Child-centred Learning – A 5-Day Workshop

Two downloadable documents designed for a 5-day teacher training workshop on child-centred learning produced for UNICEF Malawi and MOEST:

http://ibis.atwebpages.com/jason_anderson/downloads/participants_handbook.doc

http://ibis.atwebpages.com/jason_anderson/downloads/facilitators_handbook.doc

Teaching English

The British Council's websites for teachers of English all over the world. Lots of resources here, both to use in your class and to help your professional development as a teacher, including discussions which you can contribute to, lesson plans and articles to read:

www.teachingenglish.org.uk

Three other websites by the British Council for learning English at various ages: children, teenagers and adults, in order:

http://learnenglishkids.britishcouncil.org/en/

http://learnenglishteens.britishcouncil.org/

http://learnenglish.britishcouncil.org/en/

Resource creation

UNICEF Kenya Teaching and Learning Resources Manual

This manual provides details on how to make a pocketboard, how to use it in class to teach a number of subjects, including English, maths and sciences. It also includes a number of other ideas for making learning stimulating:

http://pocketboard.byethost12.com/unicef_kenya_learning_resources.pdf

TALULAR – A User's Guide

A downloadable booklet on TALULAR (Teaching and Learning Using Locally Available Resources) produced by the Domasi Institute of Education in Malawi:

http://www.equip123.net/equip1/mesa/docs/TALULAR-UsersGuide.pdf

Mango Tree

Mango Tree is a Ugandan website that shares a number of interesting ideas for resource development and TALULAR learning, particularly how to use old rice sacks effectively for creating classroom posters:

http://www.mangotreeuganda.org/

Phonic resources

Sounds of the English Phonic Code -Synthetic Phonics

Tami Reis-Frankfort explains and models the sounds of the phonic alphabet accurately. Watch this video to help you to learn the sounds yourself:

https://www.youtube.com/watch?v=IwJx1NSineE

Phonics Song – Preschool Prep Company

A fun phonics song that you can learn and teach to your learners to help them to remember both letter names and sounds:

https://www.youtube.com/watch?v=EjOd6uPj_6c

Jolly Learning

The website for the very successful **Jolly Phonics** course that introduces each new sound with a memorable story. Lots of free resources here, as well as examples of some of the reading materials in the Jolly Phonics series:

http://jollylearning.co.uk/

Kiz Phonics

Lots of printable resources, including phonics flashcards, worksheets and wall charts that can be printed and copied for the classroom:

http://www.kizphonics.com/

Storytelling resources

World of Tales

An interesting website containing a range of stories, both from Africa and other parts of the world that can be either printed for reading activities or remembered and retold for listening practice lessons with intermediate learners and above. Many include dialogue and morals which can be predicted or discussed with learners afterwards.

http://www.worldoftales.com/

African Fables & Myths – Africa Safari Campfire Short Stories

A website containing a number of short fables and myths from southern Africa, which can be used for reading and creative projects:

http://www.gateway-africa.com/stories/

Song resources

School Radio – Audio Resources for Primary Schools

This useful website from the BBC has a large number of traditional nursery rhymes and songs, which you can learn and then teach to your learners. Includes *Old Macdonald* and *The Wheels on the Bus*.

http://www.bbc.co.uk/learning/schoolradio/subjects/earlylearning/nurserysongs

150 Nursery Rhymes and Children Songs – Muffin Songs

A YouTube playlist with all common songs and rhymes for teachers and children to learn. Songs have animations and the words are also displayed on the screen to aid learning. Includes *Heads, Shoulders, Knees and Toes*; *The Hokey Pokey* (similar to *The Hokey Cokey*); *Old Macdonald*; *The Wheels on the Bus* and many more:

https://www.youtube.com/playlist?list=PL9FDA79DC8AB4A032

Resources for listening

British Council Learn English Professionals – Listening Downloads Archive

The following British Council website contains a large number of downloadable **podcasts** that you can download and listen to in your own time or play in class for learners (mainly secondary level). There are also links to the script (a written version of the podcast). In order to save the podcasts, right click the link and choose 'Save Target As …', 'Save File' or similar:

http://www.britishcouncil.org/professionals-podcast-english-listening-downloads-archive.htm

BBC Learning English Downloads

Similar to the British Council website, there are lots of podcasts here to download and documents containing the script. Updated regularly. If you want to download, right click the link and choose 'Save Target As …', 'Save File' or similar:

http://www.bbc.co.uk/worldservice/learningenglish/081222_download.shtml

Glossary

This glossary lists the technical and specialist terms from language and **literacy** teaching used in this book. These words are shown in **bold** in the text the first time they appear in a chapter. All the terms are explained here using simple English.

accent – The distinctive way that a person pronounces the words of a language. An accent may show someone's nationality, region or class, e.g. *"She spoke with an American accent."*

activity cycle – The activity cycle describes three important stages to a child-centred activity; prepare the learners, monitor the activity; get feedback to the activity. See page 46.

alphabet phase – The second of three phases in learning to read and write. See Chapter – B3.

assessment for learning – The regular checking of learning that we do on a daily or weekly basis to help us to decide what to teach next. It is the same as formative assessment.

assessment of learning – When we assess in order to decide how much our learners have learnt in total from a curriculum/syllabus, usually at the end of a course. It is the same as summative assessment.

authentic text – A text from the outside world that we use in class (e.g. a newspaper or magazine article, a novel or a website). Listening texts can also be authentic (e.g. a radio programme).

authentic writing – When we ask our learners to write texts that can be found in the outside world (e.g. a letter, a story or a book review).

behaviour management – Control and organisation of our learners to ensure they all participate in the lesson and behave appropriately.

big book – A very large book (usually stories) that we show to the learners as we tell the story.

blending – A reading skill. Learners say the sounds of the letters and put them together to make a word.

Bloom's taxonomy – A 'map' of different thinking skills first developed by Benjamin Bloom. See page 14.

caregiver – A parent, grandparent or other person who looks after a child.

CHILD – An acronym that helps us to remember five important aspects of child-centred learning. See page 19.

child-centred learning/approach – A method of teaching based on the learner's needs. See *Chapter – A3*.

choral drilling – When we get all the learners to repeat a word or phrase together. See: *drilling*.

chunk – A combination of smaller parts that is recognised and processed as a whole.

class monitor – see: *monitor*.

class reader – Class readers are simple, short storybooks designed for English language learners.

class storybook – A book of stories written by the learners in a class.

classroom contract – An informal agreement between the learners and the teacher that describes everyone's responsibilities. See page 49.

classroom management – The organisation and control of the activities in the lesson. Compare with: *behaviour management*.

CLIL – see: *Content and Language Integrated Learning*

collaborative learning – When learners communicate and work together on an activity (e.g. during pairwork and groupwork).

collocation – A common partnership between two or more words (e.g. 'make friends', 'safe journey').

community language – A language used in a community that may not be the native language of all its speakers (e.g. Kiswahili in East Africa).

comprehensible input – Language that we can understand as learners when we read or listen.

Content and Language Integrated Learning (CLIL) – A method for teaching 'content subjects' (maths, science, etc.) in a foreign language. See *Chapter – C9*.

content teacher – A teacher of any subject apart from languages (e.g. maths, social studies, etc.).

continuing professional development (CPD) – The progress and learning of a teacher through her career.

control level – The degree of freedom that learners have during a speaking or writing activity. See *Chapter – C4*.

controlled practice – An activity or exercise that lets learners practice a specific part of language use (e.g. a gap-fill or sentence completion exercise). Contrasts with: *free practice*.

controlled speaking activity – A speaking activity in which learners have little choice about what they say (e.g. reading out a dialogue). Contrasts with: *free speaking activity*.

co-text – The words around a word that help us to guess its meaning.

curriculum – A document produced by the MOE that tells us what we should teach. See page 37.

demonstration lesson – An example lesson taught by a teacher to other teachers during a workshop.

detention – An extra punishment class at the end of the school day.

dictionary monitor – see: *monitor (noun)*.

differentiation – A way to ensure that learners with different needs are all able to learn effectively in a class. It is often used to describe how we can keep both the faster and the slower learners engaged in a lesson by giving them different tasks or responsibilities.

digraph – A two letter combination with a specific pronunciation (e.g. 'sh', 'th' or 'ai'). See page 86.

double shifting – When a school has different learners in the morning and the afternoon to enable more children to study. It often involves the teachers teaching long hours.

drilling/pronunciation drill – When a teacher says a word or phrase and gets the learners to repeat after him to practise pronunciation. The two main types are individual drilling and choral drilling.

EMI education – English as the Medium of Instruction. See page 213.

endurance punishment – An inappropriate sanction where a child has to sit, kneel, stand or squat in a painful or uncomfortable position for a long time. Endurance punishment violates the United Nations Convention on the Rights of the Child.

engage (verb) – Get the learners interested in an activity or topic.

English club – A club organised at the school for extra English practice and enjoyable activities.

English monitor – A learner who walks around the class during an English speaking practice activity to make sure her classmates are all speaking English.

evaluation of lesson – Assessment of achievement of lesson objectives. See page 207.

exaggerated pronunciation – When a teacher makes a sound or a word clearer to the learners by moving his lips and mouth muscles more than usual.

explicit knowledge – Conscious knowledge that we have 'about' language (e.g. grammar rules). Similar to declarative knowledge. Contrasts with implicit knowledge.

facilitator – A person who helps something to happen.

feedback – A stage in a lesson after a child-centred activity when the learners report back to the teacher (e.g. when answers to an exercise are checked). See page 48.

fine motor skills – The ability to control and move small muscles accurately. Especially important in learning to write at a young age.

first language acquisition – The natural process in which children learn their first language (or languages) at home.

fixed expression – A combination of words that has a specific meaning and rarely changes (e.g. 'on the other hand', 'would you mind if …', etc.).

flashcard – A piece of card or paper with a word, letter or image on it. Large enough for the whole class to see.

follow-up activity – An activity that comes after a different activity to build on or use the learning from the first activity.

free practice – An opportunity for learners to use language naturally to communicate. Contrasts with: *controlled practice*.

free speaking activity – An activity in which learners are able to choose what they say and use language meaningfully (e.g. discussion). Contrasts with: *controlled speaking activity*.

gap-fill – An exercise in which learners write words or phrases in underlined spaces in sentences to complete them. A type of controlled practice.

global context – The location of a word, sentence or text that helps us to understand its meaning.

grammar words – Words like 'the', 'his', 'although' or 'even' that have a functional role in sentences. Contrasts with 'lexical words', such as verbs, nouns and adjectives.

groupwork – A type of collaborative learning where learners work together in teams of 4 – 6 (occasionally larger) to do an activity.

guest speaker – A person invited to visit a lesson to talk about something.

individual drilling – When we get one learner to repeat a word or phrase to check she is able to pronounce it. See: *drilling*.

integrated skills – When learners practise using two or more of the four skills (reading, writing, speaking and listening) in one activity.

Jolly Phonics – A popular phonics programme with books for learners and resources for teachers.

language assistant – A person who helps a teacher who does not speak the mother tongue of his learners. The language assistant is an adult, older learner or colleague who speaks both languages and can help by translating and explaining important concepts in early lessons.

language policemen – Similar to English monitors. Language policemen are learners who check that their classmates are all speaking English during a speaking practice activity.

language proficiency – Level of ability in a language (e.g. elementary, intermediate, advanced).

learning intelligence – A way of learning (e.g. interpersonal, logical, etc.). See page 12.

learning outcome – An objective of a lesson that describes what the learners will have learnt or be able to do by the end of the lesson.

learning resource – Something that helps our learners to learn (e.g. chalkboard, textbook, ball, etc.).

lesson phase – One of several main stages in a lesson. See *Chapter – A4*.

Lifeplayer – A strong MP3 player, recorder and radio with solar and manual power.

literacy – The ability to read and write. 'Early literacy' is when children learn to read and write for the first time.

literate – Able to read and write. Opposite of 'illiterate'.

look, cover, write, check – A 4 stage technique for learning to spell. See page 99.

mind-map – Another name for word 'spidergram'. See page 141.

minimal pairs – Two words with similar pronunciation. See page 155.

monitor (noun: learner role) – A learner who has a special responsibility in the class (e.g. coursebook monitor, board monitor, English monitor).

monitor (verb: teacher activity) – When the teacher observes and guides learners during a child-centred learning activity.

mother tongue – The first language or languages of a child. Also used in this book to refer to shared languages in a community.

national curriculum – The government document that describes what learners should learn for each subject each year.

negotiate meaning (verb) – Interact in conversation with someone to make sure you understand their message.

new language lesson – A lesson in which the main aim is for the learners to learn new vocabulary or grammar. Contrasts with: *skills practice lesson*.

new language lesson phase – The phase in a new language lesson when learners meet the new language. See *Chapter – A4*.

newsbox – A box kept by a teacher, class or school that contains interesting local newspaper articles for reading practice.

nominate (verb) – Choose a learner to answer a question or do an activity. See also: *peer nomination*.

on task (be **on task**) – When the learners are doing the right activity and doing it correctly.

Online Distance Learning Programme (ODLP) – A type of part-time further education for teachers. Uses the internet for communication.

open book exam – An exam or practice exam in which learners are allowed to refer to their notebooks.

out loud (read **out loud**) – When somebody reads words and says them so that others can hear. Contrasts with: *silent reading*.

overcorrection – When a teacher corrects too many of a learner's written errors so that the learner loses motivation.

pairwork – When two (or three) learners work together to do a learning activity. A type of collaborative learning.

paraphrase (verb) – When you say something in a different way. For example, if you cannot remember a word, you can describe what it means instead.

parent-teacher association (PTA) – The organisation that brings the teachers and the parents of the learners together for meetings and other events.

pass the pen – When learners are working in groups, each learner writes one word or sentence, then gives the pen to the next group member, all taking turns to write.

peer observation – When a teacher observes the lesson of a different teacher (and sometimes gives feedback).

peer-correction – When a learner corrects a classmate's mistake.

peer-nomination – When a learner chooses which learner will go next, rather than the teacher.

peer-praise – When learners clap their hands or cheer to celebrate each other's success. See: *praise*.

personalise/personalisation – When the lesson or activity gets the learner to think, talk or write about their own interests and world.

phonics – A method for teaching children to read and write in English. See *Chapter – B3*.

podcast – A radio programme that you can download from the internet.

practical task – One of two tasks in this book, where the readers apply what they have learnt in a chapter to solve a specific problem.

praise – When the teacher congratulates a learner for their success (e.g. "*Well done!*"; "*Good work!*").

pre-alphabet phase – The first of three phases in learning to read and write. See *Chapter – B2*.

pre-teach (vocabulary) – Explain vocabulary that learners will need for an activity before they do the activity.

privilege – A way of rewarding learners for good behaviour or achievement (e.g. letting the learners play a game at the end of a lesson).

proceduralise (verb) – Make language knowledge automatic, so that we can use it fluently.

productive skills – Writing and speaking. Contrast with: *receptive skills*.

puppet – A toy person or animal that is often worn on the hand.

reading assistant – A strong learner in a class who helps other learners to read.

reading fluency – The ability to read quickly.

read for detailed understanding – When learners read a text in order to understand everything.

read for gist – When learners read a text to get the main ideas only.

reading pal – Two learners who sometimes read together; one is usually stronger at reading and helps the other.

realia – Real objects that we take to class to use as learning resources.

receptive skills – Reading and listening. Contrast with: *productive skills*.

recycle (verb) – Use something again (e.g. using vocabulary again to ensure we do not forget it).

reflective task - One of two tasks in this book, where the readers think about what they do as teachers.

review week – A week in the middle of a term when a class revises everything they have learnt so far that term.

revise/revision – When learners refresh their memories on something they have already learnt, often before an exam.

revisiting – When learners study a topic or area of grammar they have studied before to make the learning stronger and/or to add to it.

reward (verb or noun) – Something we give learners to say thank you for good behaviour or success (e.g. prizes or privileges).

rhyme – Noun: A poem for children (e.g. Old MacDonald). Verb: have the same sounds at the end of a word (e.g. 'you' and 'true' rhyme).

role play – When we pretend to be someone else in a different situation (e.g. a seller and a buyer at a market).

sanction – Sanctions can be negative or positive, but the term is usually used to mean 'negative sanctions', which are punishments or other responses to bad behaviour by learners.

scheme of work – The document that 'maps' the national curriculum onto the calendar to create a plan for the whole year.

school cluster – A group of schools that are close together and share resources or meet for workshops.

school readiness – UNICEF term to describe a situation when a learner is able to study without disadvantages caused by family situation, personal obligations or problems at the school itself. [24]

self-correction – When a learner corrects his own mistake.

segmenting – A writing skill. A learner thinks of a word, says it and then breaks up the sounds to 'discover' the letters.

semi-controlled speaking activity – An activity in which learners have some freedom to choose what they say.

senior observation – When a head teacher, head of department or an inspector observes a teacher's lesson.

shared reading – When a teacher leads a reading activity. See page 118.

---

24 Britto and Limlingan, "School Readiness and Transitions."

sight word phase – The third of three stages in learning to read and write. See Chapter – B4.

sight word – A word that is not read as a phonic/phonetic word, but is learnt as a whole. Sight words are exceptions to the rules learnt in phonics.

silent letter – A letter that is not pronounced in a word (e.g. 'w' in 'write').

silent reading – When somebody reads without saying the words. Contrasts with reading: *out loud*.

skills practice lesson – A lesson where the main aim for the learners is to practise one or more of the four skills (reading, writing, speaking or listening). Contrasts with: *new language lesson*.

skim (verb) – A reading skill. When we look quickly at a text to see what it is about. Similar to: *reading for gist*.

sounding (out) – When learners say the phonic sounds of letters in order to: *blend* and then read them.

summative assessment – Another term for: *assessment of learning*.

syllabus – Similar to curriculum. The syllabus describes what topics are studied in a curriculum and sometimes in what order.

TALULAR – acronym; stands for Teaching and Learning Using Locally Available Resources. See page 240.

target language – a specific piece of grammar or vocabulary topic group that a teacher is trying to teach in a specific lesson (e.g. *"My target language today was the future perfect tense."*)

teacher-centred approach – An approach to teaching often used in the past that viewed education from the teacher's point of view. Contrasts with: *child-centred approach* (or 'learner/student-centred learning').

TESEP – acronym; stands for Tertiary, Secondary and Primary and describes an important context for language learning in schools all over the world [25].

textbook – The main book used with a class of learners. Often called Pupil's book or Student's book.

thinking skill – One of several different ways of thinking within either Bloom's taxonomy or other models. See page 14.

threes – An alternative team size to pairs or groups. Practical in classes where three learners sit together at a desk.

time frame – A flexible estimate of the time a lesson stage or activity will take. We usually share time frames with our learners when we give an instruction.

today chart – A display chart in the classroom. It includes information that changes every day (e.g. date, weather, etc.).

---

25 Holliday, "The House of TESEP and the Communicative Approach."

topic group – A set of words or expressions that are all linked in a topic (e.g. food, hobbies, work). It is often a good idea to teach the items in a topic group together.

tripod grip – The correct way to hold a pen or pencil when writing. See page 90.

United Nations Convention on the Rights of the Child – An official document that describes the rights of children and our responsibilities as guardians. [26]

wall board – Parts of the classroom wall painted with chalkboard paint for learners to write or draw on. See page 231.

wall frieze – A set of small posters displayed in a series around the classroom (e.g. alphabet or numerals).

warm up – Prepare learners' minds for learning or a specific type of activity.

washing line – A piece of string displayed across, above or below the board on which we can hang flashcards.

weekly plan – A plan of the basic lesson content for a week.

word stress – In some languages (like English), one syllable of a word is pronounced louder, longer and at a different pitch to other syllables (e.g. the third syllable of 'edu*ca*tion' is stressed).

writing assistant – a learner who helps the teacher in a school where there are very few copies of the textbook. See page 184.

---

26   United Nations, "United Nations Convention on the Rights of the Child (UNCRC)."

Index

A

accent (teaching) 147, 170, 258
activity cycle 46-8, 176, 258
advice for literate parents 109
African fables & myths 257
alphabet frieze 23, 114-5, 241, 266
alphabet game 142
alphabet hopscotch 118
alphabet letter flashcards 66, 78, 82, 112-3
alphabet phase 66, 79-93, 112, 114-5, 119, 258
alphabet run-around 116
anagrams 117, 144
analysing (Bloom's taxonomy) 14
Angry Goat (story) 100-1
animal comparatives 133
applying (Bloom's taxonomy) 14
appraisals 6
assessing achievement of objectives 207
assessing for learning 205-6, 208, 258
assessing reading and writing skills 105
assessment 104-6, 116, 191, 194, 200, 205-11, 224, 258
assessment of learning 205-6, 209, 258
audio material 170-171, 232
authentic texts 184, 236, 258
authentic writing tasks 195, 258
autonomy (learner) – *see* 'independence'

B

back to the board 144
beanbag 235, 245-6
Beatrice from Awai (case study) 67-8
Beep! (game) 144
behaviour management 46, 48, 53, 258
bibliography 252
big books 97, 114-5, 183, 258
blending 86, 94, 113, 115, 118, 258
blind marking 208
Bloom's taxonomy of learning 14-5, 258
board football 145
boards (different types) 23, 231-2, 249-51
bodily-kinaesthetic intelligence 13-4
book reviews 119, 191
break time exclusion 51

C

Call my bluff (game) 225
capital letters 90
caregiver 55, 258
chain stories 203
chalkboard 5, 22-3, 27, 31, 77-8, 84-6, 90, 98-9, 103-6, 112, 117, 125-6, 129-30, 139, 141-5, 148, 150-1, 153-55, 161-4, 166-7, 176-8, 180-2, 184, 189-90, 201-3, 208, 216-8, 224-5, 228-33, 238, 242, 246-7, 250-1
checking for understanding 62
checking understanding of reading texts 188-9
CHILD (acronym) 19-20, 26, 258
child-centred learning/approach 1-2, 18-28, 161, 196, 206, 208, 210, 249, 255, 258
children's literature 115, 119
children's songs 13, 85, 136, 149, 170-1, 180, 220-2, 225-9
choral drilling 126, 139, 149-50, 259, 260
chunks 94, 259
class CDs 169-71
class monitors 5, 49, 62, 104, 160, 234, 246-7, 249, 259, 262
class readers 97, 114-5, 118-9, 183, 191, 231, 233, 239, 259
class storybook 196, 201, 259
classroom contract 49, 249, 259
classroom display board 23, 119, 183, 191, 202, 235, 249-50
classroom management 1, 6, 46, 53, 259
clear routines 5, 48-9
clear rules 48-9, 160
CLIL – *see* Content and Language Integrated Learning
collaborative learning 4, 20, 259
collaborative writing 196
collocation 119, 136, 141, 143-4, 259
community 2, 8, 55, 65, 71, 73, 96, 108-111, 133, 147-9, 170, 202, 214-5, 230, 236, 238-9
community languages 55, 80, 259
completing words 86, 106

comprehensible input 9-11, 259
concept check questions 32
connected speech 148-149, 151
Content and Language Integrated Learning (CLIL) xii, 212-9, 259
content teachers (in CLIL) 212-4, 217
context (importance of) xiii-v, 23, 30-1, 42, 48, 62-3, 67, 96-7, 125, 128, 138, 141, 163, 183, 189, 230, 234, 236, 261
continuing professional development xii, xiv, 2, 6, 255, 259
continuous assessment 191, 206, 209
control level 162-3, 259
controlled grammar practice 127
controlled practice 32-3, 126-7, 129, 139, 143, 163, 259
controlled speaking activity 162-4, 259
corporal punishment 52
correction 5-6, 16, 47-8, 99, 130-1, 150, 161, 188, 196-201, 208, 210-1, 224, 262-4
co-text 96-7, 259
countdown 117
created resources 231, 234-6
creating (Bloom's taxonomy) 14
curriculum xv, 3-5, 18-20, 27, 37-9, 66, 82, 89, 161, 205-6, 209-11, 259

D
daily report 51
debates 12, 16, 42, 140-1, 167
define and guess 164
demonstration lesson 7, 259
describe and draw 143, 172
detail (reading for) 189
detention 51, 260
developing literacy (activities) 112-9, 183, 222
development of your school 8
dialogues 31, 35, 125, 150, 157, 161-4, 238, 246, 248, 257
dictionary monitor 234, 260
differentiation 48, 210, 260
digraphs 73, 86-9, 94, 260
disappearing song 229
discussion 10, 12, 16, 30, 42, 47, 61-2, 101, 130, 140-1, 143, 149, 166-7, 170, 185, 196, 215, 217-8, 221, 224, 228-9, 233, 237, 261
disturbance 172
double shifting xiii, 260

drawing 14, 66, 90, 98, 100, 106, 125, 143, 189, 191, 231, 235
drawing and labelling tasks 98
drilling/drills 124, 126, 137, 139, 148-151, 155, 173, 185, 216, 259-61

E
early literacy xiv, 65, 80, 247, 262
electrical and electronic resources 169, 231-2, 236
EMI education xii, 213, 260
endurance punishment 52, 260
engage 176-7, 179, 220, 260
English as the first language of literacy 80-1
English club 105, 110, 114-5, 167, 184, 260
English language films 111
English monitor 159-60, 260-262
English radio 111
evaluating (Bloom's taxonomy) 14
exaggerated pronunciation 149, 155, 260
explicit knowledge 213, 260

F
facilitator 2-3, 18, 260
feedback 6-7, 21, 25-6, 28, 32-3, 35-6, 43, 46-48, 124, 137, 159, 176-7, 186, 188, 191, 196-9, 208, 215, 231, 245, 250, 260
feedback columns 208, 224
fine motor skills 90, 260
first language acquisition 9, 260
first letter awareness 85, 115
fixed expression 135, 138, 260
flashcards 8, 44, 78, 84-7, 90, 92, 112-4, 116-7, 131, 222-3, 231, 235, 242-4, 256, 261
form (teaching) 30-2, 35-6, 72, 75, 125-7, 132, 138-9, 242
form table 126
formative assessment 116, 206, 258
four areas of literacy awareness 72-4, 79, 110
free practice 32, 34, 126-7, 139, 261
free speaking activities 162-4, 166-7, 261

G
gallery reading 196, 199
games 4, 6, 10, 12, 41, 97, 98-100, 113, 115-9, 136, 140-2, 171, 213, 218, 220-9, 235, 242, 245-6
games for grammar practice 223

games for skills practice 223
games for vocabulary learning 222
gap-fill 32, 34, 47, 124, 126-7, 140, 181, 228, 261
gap-fill dictation 181
get feedback to the activity (activity cycle) 47-8, 176, 258
Girls and boys (game) 179
gist (reading for) 184, 188, 189, 263
giving an opinion 166-7, 189
global context 96, 261
glossary xiv, 184, 258
grammar (teaching) 2, 122-34
grammar dictation 129, 181
grammar practice 127, 223
grammar words 97, 261
Grasshopper and the Frog (The) (story) 172-6
Greedy pig (story) 192
greetings cards 203-4
group reading 97, 104, 115, 119
groupwork 20-3, 25, 27-8, 34, 43, 49-50, 52, 99, 112, 130, 160, 170, 207, 209, 235, 241, 248-50, 261
Guess the word (game) 145
guest speaker 110, 177, 261

H

handwriting 85, 90, 195, 233
Heads, Shoulders, Knees and Toes (song) 221, 225-6, 257
higher qualifications 6-7
Hokey Cokey (song) 227, 257
homework book 232
human sentences 131-2
humiliation 52-3

I

I spy… (Game) 115
images 95-96, 101, 105, 115, 125, 139, 242
independence (learner) 15
individual assessment of reading 106
individual drilling 126, 139, 149-50, 261
individual reading 119, 183
integrated skills 224-5, 261
interpersonal intelligence 12-14, 261
intrapersonal intelligence 12-13
introducing and inventing games and songs 222
introducing new grammar 125, 234
introducing new vocabulary 138, 213

J

jigsaw reading 190-1
Jolly Phonics 83, 85, 256, 261

K

keyword search 63

L

language assistants 73, 109-10, 261
language policeman 49, 59
language proficiency 206, 261
large classes xiii, 59, 66, 156, 160, 194, 251, 252
learning intelligences 12-13, 261
learning outcomes 4, 44, 216, 261
learning resources xiii, 19, 44, 66, 110, 230-9, 256, 264
learning style 12-13
lesson evaluation 44, 207
lesson phases 29-36, 125, 138, 262
lesson plan 1, 3-4, 6, 37-8, 42-5, 100, 232, 255
lesson plan (example) 24, 123, 136, 157, 172, 185, 197, 214
lesson structure 1, 29
letter ordering 86, 113
letters (learning individual) 79-93
library 16, 67, 110, 115, 183-4, 191, 196, 201-2
library books 183-4, 191
Lifeplayer 171-2, 236, 262
linguistic intelligence 12-14
listening (teaching) 169-81
literacy xiv, 8, 65-119, 183, 222, 254, 262
literate 108-9, 262
live listening 177
logical-mathematical intelligence 13
Let's talk about teeth! 184-7
look, cover, write, check 87, 99-100, 262
lower case letters 90, 113-4

M

magic 'e' rule 86, 88-9
making animal sounds 101, 151
matching cards to pictures 114
matching letters to pictures 105
memory games 142, 164
mentor 6
mind-maps 13, 141-2 262
mini-boards 231-2, 250-1
minimal pairs 148, 155, 262

modelling of writing 98, 140, 196-7
monitor (learner role) 5, 49, 62, 104, 160, 234, 246-7, 249, 259, 262
monitor the activity (activity cycle) 47, 176, 258
monitoring (teacher activity) 20-1, 26, 46, 53, 248
mother tongue 24, 27, 31, 47, 52-3, 55-63, 65, 67-8, 70, 73-6, 80-1, 90, 101, 104-5, 109-11, 116, 136, 148-50, 159-60, 207, 212, 246, 262
musical intelligence 13
My favourite animal 101
My favourite things 166
My Pet dinosaur (poem) 151-3

N
name tents 112, 235, 251
names of learners 73, 160
national curriculum xv, 3-5, 18-20, 27, 37-9, 66, 82, 89, 128 161, 205-6, 209-11, 262
naturalist intelligence 13
negotiating meaning 170
new language lessons 29-30, 33-4, 40, 42, 125, 138, 262
new language phase 33, 125, 138
news articles 138, 184, 191, 196, 202, 249, 258, 262
newsbox 184, 191, 202, 262
noise 4, 27, 78, 161, 172-3, 175
nominate 116, 245-6, 262
noting down mistakes 200
nursery rhymes 151, 221, 257, 264

O
Obi from Ibadan (case study) 67-8, 71, 80, 96-8
objectives (of lesson) 3-4, 6, 16, 24, 30-6, 44, 46-7, 56, 61, 100, 123, 136, 157, 172, 184, 197, 207-8, 214, 216, 232, 250, 261
observation (of lesson) 6-7, 263-4
Odd one out (game) 143, 150-1
Old Macdonald (rhyme) 151-2, 257, 264
on task 47, 53, 262
One Laptop Per Child 236
Online Distance Learning Programmes (ODLP) xii, 7, 262
online materials 255
open book exam 210, 262
order of lesson phases 29, 34-36

our first story 91-2
overcorrection 200, 262

P
pairwork 20-2, 26-8, 49, 52, 115, 140, 158, 160, 170, 196-7, 201, 217, 248, 262
paraphrasing 170, 263
parent-teacher association (PTA) xii, 8, 263
pass the pen 100, 263
past tense pelmanism 133
peer marking 208, 211
peer observation 6, 263
peer-correction 5, 16, 43, 188, 196-8, 200, 208, 263
peer-nomination 245, 263
peer-praise 50, 263
pen pals 195, 203
people as resources 231, 234
permanent visual aids 241
personalise/personalisation 12, 23, 140-1, 158, 161, 166-7, 170, 224, 263
phonemes 82-3, 86-7
phonetic symbols 82-3, 86-7
phonic alphabet 82-4, 86, 88, 91, 94, 97, 105, 112, 115, 256
phonics 65-6, 79-93, 256, 263
planning 1, 37-45, 55, 100, 128, 206, 214, 217
pocketboard 8, 112, 116, 231, 235, 242-4, 256
podcasts 257, 263
Point at... (game) 116
posters 8, 23, 66-7, 71, 74, 76, 81, 85, 114-5, 118-9, 140-1, 151, 184, 195, 206, 216-7, 225, 229-31, 234-5, 238, 241-4, 247-9, 256
practical tasks xiv
practising new vocabulary 139
praise 25, 28, 30, 33-4, 36, 43, 48, 50, 53, 60, 73, 86, 91, 98-9, 104, 109, 124, 158-60, 174, 186, 190, 196, 199-200, 249, 263
pre-alphabet phase 66, 70-8, 95, 99, 112, 263
prepare the learners (activity cycle) 30, 33, 47, 176, 258
preparing for listening lessons 172
preparing learners for exams 209
pre-teach(ing) vocabulary 173, 176-9, 185, 188, 263

printed resources 66, 231-2
privilege 50, 263
proceduralise 161, 263
productive skills 128, 188, 194, 263
progressive deletion 157, 164
pronunciation (teaching) 147-55
    pronunciation chase 153-4
publishing 196-7
pupil's book 183, 232, 265
puppets 231, 235, 248-9, 263

Q
quizzes and quiz games 41-2, 210, 224, 238, 242, 250

R
reading (teaching) 182-93
reading assistants 104-5, 263
reading fluency 96-7, 119, 263
reading in the sight word phase 95-7
reading out loud 150, 183, 262
reading pals 104, 264
reading posters 8, 74, 76, 114-5, 118-9, 184, 234-5, 247-8
reading simple sentences 90
reading words 85-9, 106
realia 44, 139, 231, 236, 238-9, 264
receptive skills 128, 188, 264
recording vocabulary 136, 217-8
recycling vocabulary 40, 141, 183, 264
reflective tasks xiv
remember, rewrite and check 201
remembering (Bloom's taxonomy) 14
resources for developing literacy 112-5
review week 128, 264
reviews and reports (writing activity) 202
revising 41, 116, 128, 136, 141, 150, 213
revisiting 29, 31, 128, 264
rewards 12, 46, 48-50, 264
rhymes and poems 151-3
rhyming words 116
Right or wrong grammar? (activity) 130
role of the teacher 2, 196
role play 25-6, 53, 127, 140-1, 157-8, 161, 164-5, 170, 179-80, 209, 236-8, 248, 264
running dictation 225

S
sanctions 48-53, 264
say and draw 113-4
scheme of work 18, 37-9, 44, 210-11, 217, 264
school clusters 7, 264
school or class community service 51
school readiness xiii, 264
seating arrangement 21-2
second language (use of): see 'mother tongue'
segmenting 86, 94, 99-100, 113, 115, 118, 264
self-correction 5, 200, 264
semi-controlled speaking activities 162-4, 166, 264
senior observation 6-7, 264
sentence dictation 106
sentence jumble 129
shared reading 97, 105-6, 115, 118-9, 183, 247, 264
showing and explaining (pronunciation activity) 150
sight word phase 66, 94-101, 113-5, 119, 265
sight words 86-92, 94-101, 113-19, 265
silent letters 73, 265
Simon says … (game) 171, 178-9
skills practice 29, 33, 40, 121, 223, 265
skimming 189
sock puppets 235, 248-9
song discussion 229
song gap-fill 228
songs 10-13, 85, 136, 149, 151, 170-1, 180-1, 220-9, 238, 257
songs for older learners 228
songs for younger learners 225
sound group 84, 88-90, 92
sounding (phonic activity) 77, 86, 105, 118, 183, 265
sounds of English (phonemes) 82-3, 86-7, 148
sounds to letters (writing assessment) 105
spatial-visual intelligence 13-4
speaking (teaching) 156-67, 170
spelling 31, 79, 97-101, 109, 113-4, 116, 139, 195, 242
Spellman (game) 117, 222
stimulating classroom 21, 23, 241
story prediction 190
story writing 201
storycards 114
storytelling 178, 257

student's book 183, 232, 265
suggested sequence for phonics teaching 88, 91
summative assessment 200, 206, 258, 265
suspension 52
syllables 88, 139, 148, 150-1, 154, 266
syllabus (*see also* 'curriculum') 38, 265

T
target language 161-2, 265
teacher performance appraisals 6-7
teacher's guide 90, 232-3
teacher's resource pack 232
teacher's voice (for listening) 169-70
teacher-centred approach 2, 19, 27, 265
teaching and learning using locally available resources (TALULAR) xii, 236, 240, 256, 265
Tertiary, Secondary and Primary (TESEP) xii, xv, 265
textbook xiii, xv, 16, 27, 31, 34, 37, 44, 49-50, 55, 61, 66-7, 77, 95, 97, 105, 109, 119, 139, 163, 169-70, 181, 182-4, 190-1, 199, 210, 213, 217, 224, 230-33, 242, 247, 265
theatre in English 111
thinking skills 14-5, 18, 189, 220, 258
three phases of literacy 66, 74
threes 16, 21, 163-4, 166, 196, 198, 265
time frame 47, 52, 185, 189, 198, 265
today chart 23, 265
topic groups 12, 30, 135-6, 141-4, 266
topic-based lesson (planning) 100
total physical response (TPR) xii, 171
Toto and the Hen (story) 91-2
traditional ink 235, 241, 243-5, 247-8
translation challenge 62
tripod grip 90-1, 266
truth or lie games 224

U
understanding (Bloom's taxonomy) 14
UNICEF Child-friendly Schools Manual 255
United Nations Convention on the Rights of the Child (UNCRC) xii, 52, 254, 266
upper case (capital) letters 90

V
verbal reprimand 51
vocabulary (teaching) 122-46, 151, 244
vocabulary box 30, 62, 141, 144, 164, 201, 213, 218, 235, 246-7, 249
vocabulary list (for CLIL) 217-8

W
wall boards 23, 231-2
wall frieze 23, 114-5, 241, 266
washing line 112, 116, 244, 266
websites 38, 171, 174, 196, 202, 225, 255-7
weekly plan 37-8, 40, 266
What am I doing? (game) 133
What did you do at the weekend? (game) 224
Wheels on the Bus (song) 171, 226, 257
Who am I? (game) 132
word and morpheme shape (phonics) 95
word dictation (writing assessment) 106
word flashcards 87, 113, 160
word spidergrams 141-2, 262
word stress 148, 150-1, 154, 266
words within words (phonics) 95
workbook 232
working together (CLIL teachers) 213
workshops 6-8, 73, 105, 108-9, 255, 264
writing (teaching) 194-204
writing assistant 184, 266
writing in the sight word phase (phonics) 97
writing sentences 195
writing whole texts 195

Y
yearly planning 37

www.ingramcontent.com/pod-product-compliance
Lightning Source LLC
Chambersburg PA
CBHW061707300426
44115CB00014B/2594